DIVERSIONARY WAR

DIVERSIONARY WAR

Domestic Unrest and
International Conflict

Amy Oakes

Stanford Security Studies
An Imprint of Stanford University Press
Stanford, California

Stanford University Press
Stanford, California

Library of Congress Cataloging-in-Publication Data

Oakes, Amy, author.
    Diversionary war : domestic unrest and international conflict / Amy Oakes.
        Pages cm
    Includes bibliographical references and index.
    ISBN 978-0-8047-8245-6 (cloth : alk. paper) —
    ISBN 978-0-8047-8246-3 (pbk. : alk. paper)
    1. Politics and war.   2. War—Causes.   3. Political stability.   4. War—Decision making.   5. International relations—Decision making.   I. Title.
    JZ6385.O35 2012
    355.02′72—dc23

                                                                    2011052156

Special discounts for bulk quantities of Stanford Security Studies are available to corporations, professional associations, and other organizations. For details and discount information, contact the special sales department of Stanford University Press. Tel: (650) 736-1782. Fax: (650) 736-1784.

Typeset by Newgen in 10/14 Minion

To my parents, Jack Stanley and Ginger

Contents

Tables and Figures

Tables

Figures

Acknowledgments

I T GIVES ME GREAT PLEASURE TO THANK THE MANY COLLEAGUES and friends who helped me complete this project. While I was a graduate student at the Ohio State University, Janet Box-Steffensmeier, Yoav Gortzak, Yoram Haftel, Richard Herrmann, Elizabeth Kloss, Richard Ned Lebow, John Mueller, David Rowe, Goldie Shabad, Kevin Sweeney, Donald Sylvan, Sean Williams, and, especially, the chair of my dissertation committee, Brian Pollins, each made integral contributions to this research. Thomas Christensen and Jack Snyder offered valuable guidance in the early stages of the project.

I am fortunate to work with an outstanding group of scholars at the College of William and Mary. Paul Manna, Christine Nemacheck, Susan Peterson, Simon Stow, and Michael Tierney provided wise council and encouragement as I navigated the perils of writing a book.

Dennis Smith deserves special thanks for the many excellent suggestions that advanced the manuscript. Michael Horowitz also offered incisive comments that substantially sharpened the theoretical argument. Dangers abound when political scientists engage in historical analysis, and William MacKinnon and Roger Ransom provided expert critiques of the chapter on the U.S. expedition to Utah. Matt Golder, Robert Hicks, Ross Iaci, Stephen Shellman, and Alicia Uribe helped to unravel particularly knotty challenges with the statistical analysis. My gratitude also goes to the wonderful William and Mary students—David Newbrander, Hannah Thornton, and Alena

Stern—who tidied up the footnotes and bibliography. Churchill and Nimbus also left their footprints throughout the manuscript.

The book was completed during my sabbatical leave, which was generously funded by the College of William and Mary and a grant from the John D. and Catherine T. MacArthur Foundation. I also benefited greatly from my years as a pre-doctoral fellow at the Mershon Center for International Security Studies and as a research fellow at the Belfer Center for Science and International Affairs.

For his early interest in the book and for shepherding it through the publication process, I am grateful to Geoffrey Burn at Stanford University Press. And I would like to thank *Security Studies* for granting permission to reprint parts of my article "Diversionary War and Argentina's Invasion of the Falkland Islands" (*Security Studies* 15, no. 3 [July–September 2006], copyright Taylor & Francis Group, LLC; reprinted by permission of Taylor & Francis, http://www.tandfonline.com).

I would also like to thank my mentors and teachers at Davidson College, who shared with me their time, wisdom, and love of politics: Peter Ahrensdorf, Kenneth Menkhaus, Louis Ortmayer, Brian Shaw, and Mary Thornberry.

I am deeply indebted to Dominic Tierney. His superb ideas and ready wit were necessary conditions for the completion of this book.

For their love and unflagging support, I dedicate this book to my parents.

DIVERSIONARY WAR

1 Introduction

Be it thy course to busy giddy minds
With foreign quarrels; that action, hence borne out,
May waste the memory of the former days.
—*William Shakespeare, Henry IV, Part 2*[1]

IN THE LATE SUMMER OF 1998, AT THE HEIGHT OF THE MONICA Lewinsky scandal, U.S. President Bill Clinton authorized air strikes against alleged terrorist targets in Sudan and Afghanistan. Several Clinton critics asserted that the bombings were intended to shift focus from the president's admission that he had lied about having an improper relationship with White House intern Lewinsky. In a *Salon* editorial, for example, Christopher Hitchens wondered why the president hurried to attack: "There is really only one possible answer to that question. Clinton needed to look 'presidential' for a day."[2] And every major media outlet, from the *New York Times* and the *Washington Post* to ABC, CBS, CNN, Fox, and NBC, ran stories on the speculations that the bombings were an attempt to divert attention from the scandal.[3]

Indeed, on several occasions the administration's top national security aides were compelled to deny publicly that the attacks were linked to the president's personal and legal troubles. For example, Secretary of Defense William Cohen was asked during a press conference whether he had seen the movie *Wag the Dog,* in which a Washington spin doctor fabricates a war to distract the public from the president's liaison with a teenage girl. Cohen declined to answer directly, saying that "The only motivation driving this action today was our absolute obligation to protect the American people from terrorist activities."[4] Meanwhile, video rentals of *Wag the Dog* soared.[5]

Despite the administration's emphatic denials, the event exhibited many hallmarks of a classic diversionary use of force, which is to say an international conflict provoked to whip up nationalist sentiment and rally the populace behind the regime or simply to distract the public from the government's failings. First, the timing was felicitous. Clinton gave the mission a green light on the same day he was asked to provide federal investigators with a DNA sample, which signaled that the Starr Commission had potentially damning forensic evidence of intimate contact with Lewinsky. The White House also announced the strikes just three days after Clinton's prime-time television appearance, in which he confessed to "a critical lapse in judgment, a personal failure" in having an affair with Lewinsky.[6] And the attacks themselves coincided with Lewinsky's second and final grand jury appearance, in which she was questioned about the veracity of Clinton's testimony.

Second, the operation was generally popular. The target, Osama bin Laden's terrorist network, was believed to be responsible for the deadly bombing of American embassies in Kenya and Tanzania. As a result, even the Republican leadership praised Clinton's decision to use force. House Speaker Newt Gingrich's reaction was typical when he remarked that "if you saw the TV coverage of the two embassy bombings and the caskets come home to America, you know that this is real. . . . I think, based on what I know, that it was the right thing to do at the right time."[7] The public's response was also favorable. In a poll conducted immediately after the raids, 68 percent of respondents approved of Clinton's foreign policy—a high point in his presidency. Most people believed he had acted to protect U.S. national security, not to distract them from the scandal.[8] The American public may have distrusted their president, but they also believed that he was a capable commander-in-chief. Whatever Clinton's actual motivation, the attacks changed the national conversation from sordid assignations in the Oval Office to combating global terrorism.

This is a book about diversionary war. Do leaders use foreign adventure to improve their domestic political fortunes? If so, under what conditions are unpopular governments most likely to deploy this strategy? Are diversionary uses of force successful in reducing domestic discontent? Is diversionary war a more-effective response to internal unrest than, say, making political concessions to opposition groups or suppressing dissent?

Conventional wisdom among the political class maintains that leaders in trouble routinely initiate diversionary conflicts. Since World War II, for example, most U.S. presidents have been suspected, at one point or another, of provoking or escalating a foreign conflict to rally support for the government or divert attention from the administration's blunders.

In 1948 Harry Truman's political opponents accused him of aggravating the conflict with the Soviet Union, particularly during the Berlin blockade, in order to win votes in a tough election.[9] If Truman had excited tensions with Moscow to increase his popularity with voters, he would have been following the advice of his campaign strategists. Truman's advisors crafted a memo predicting that he would benefit politically if the "battle with the Kremlin" intensified because the "worse matters get, up to a fairly certain point—real danger of imminent war—the more is there a sense of crisis. In times of crisis the American citizen tends to back up his President."[10]

John F. Kennedy also was thought to have engaged in "aggressive posturing in international affairs . . . to improve his domestic image," in particular in his handling of the 1962 Cuban missile crisis.[11] Republicans argued that the president manufactured the conflict, which became public less than one month before midterm elections, to help Democrats keep their majority in both houses of Congress. For example, Representative Thomas Curtis of Missouri told his constituents that the crisis was "phony and contrived for election purposes."[12] Even the president's allies questioned his motives. Robert Hilsman, a Kennedy appointee to the Department of State, commented that "behind the policy choices loomed domestic politics. . . . The United States might not [have been] in mortal danger but the administration certainly was."[13]

In May 1975, Gerald Ford sent a Marine task force to rescue the 39-person crew of the U.S. freighter *Mayaguez*, which had been seized by Cambodian Khmer Rouge forces in international waters—a mission described by the *Wall Street Journal* as having "all the elements of an Errol Flynn swash-buckler."[14] When the prisoners were freed, the president's approval ratings surged by 11 points—even though more U.S. troops died in the operation than there were hostages to be rescued.[15] Five years later, while under fire for not using force in the Iranian hostage crisis, Jimmy Carter implied in an interview that Ford had acted in a self-serving manner: "I have a very real political awareness that at least on a transient basis the more drastic the action taken by the President, the more popular he is. When President Ford expended 40 American lives on the *Mayaguez* . . . it was looked upon as a heroic action, and his status as a bold and wise leader rose greatly. This is always a temptation."[16]

Following the U.S. invasion of Grenada on October 25, 1983, Ronald Reagan faced scrutiny from members of Congress and the media, who hinted that the president might have sought to distract the public from the deadly suicide bombing of American and French barracks in Beirut two days earlier.[17] For example, Democratic Representative Peter Kostmayer of Pennsylvania declared that "I haven't seen a single shred of evidence that American lives were in danger in Grenada."[18] Francis Clines of the *New York Times* went further, baldly asserting that Reagan had used a "rallying 'round the flag" strategy.[19]

In 1989 George H. W. Bush dispatched more than 24,000 troops to depose the government of Manuel Noriega and restore democracy to Panama. Observers wondered whether the administration was simply "trying to cure its political image problems at home," as the president had "long been accused of being a 'wimp'" in matters of foreign policy.[20] But when the administration's press secretary, Marlin Fitzwater, was asked whether the invasion of Panama "was the test of fire that will cause [the president] to be more respected at home and abroad," Fitzwater responded simply: "We see him . . . as the same bold, visionary, outstanding, strong, macho, strong, whatever, leader he's always been."[21]

Critics of George W. Bush maintained that the president escalated the crisis over Iraqi weapons of mass destruction in the summer and fall of 2002 in order to guarantee Republican control of Congress in the upcoming midterm elections. For example, columnist Frank Rich wrote that Bush's political strategists knew that "an untelevised and largely underground war [on terror] . . . might not nail election victories without a jolt of shock and awe. It was a propitious moment to wag the dog" in Iraq.[22] Vice President Dick Cheney, in an interview on *Meet the Press,* described such allegations as "reprehensible."[23]

Presidents have often been accused of using force to distract attention from domestic ills. But do governments actually provoke diversionary wars? And do they work?

Investigating the existence of a diversionary motivation for war is a critically important task for several reasons. First, there is little consensus regarding the accuracy of the diversionary theory of war. Some media and political elites see diversionary war as pervasive, but many scholars deny the existence of a diversionary motivation for interstate conflict, describing it as a "myth."[24] By clarifying when leaders use diversionary tactics, this book contributes to an important research program in the field of international relations.

Second, interstate wars have enormous consequences in international politics. War can bankrupt treasuries, trigger revolutions, and reshape cultures. And conflict is one of the chief mechanisms by which wealth and power are redistributed in the international system. If there is a relationship between domestic unrest and foreign adventurism, exploring that link may help policy makers anticipate and head off these wars. For example, following the death of North Korea's leader, Kim Jong Il, analysts have conjectured that his son and successor, Kim Jong-un, might be tempted to provoke a diversionary war with South Korea to consolidate his rule and promote domestic cohesion.[25] Insight into the plausibility of this scenario, as well as strategies to dissuade Pyongyang from using diversionary tactics, would be valuable given the potential for such a conflict to destabilize the region.

Third, if governments put their troops in harm's way for domestic political gain rather than to promote the national interest, this is a major issue for legitimate rule. Diversionary war is widely considered immoral, if not criminal. In a democracy the public demands a voice in policy making, but for leaders to use force to win their favor may amount to an impeachable offense.

To some degree, a relationship between domestic politics and the use of force abroad is uncontroversial. The effect of public opinion on foreign policy decision making can be thought of as concentric rings, like those on a shooting target. In the outermost ring are cases in which the willingness of the public to tolerate a leader's decision, say, to commit ground troops is a necessary condition for the use of force. Here, the public has a veto on the government's behavior: if the leader perceives a significant domestic political downside from a bellicose foreign policy, a different course of action will be taken. In 1994 the Clinton administration declined to intervene militarily in the Rwandan genocide, in part because it concluded that the conflict was not a sufficient threat to U.S. interests to expend the political capital required to overcome widespread domestic opposition to action.[26] Almost all uses of force in a democracy such as the United States fall at least within this circle, where domestic opinion provides an acceptability constraint.

In the middle band of the target, we find instances in which domestic political gains are seen as a side benefit of the use of force. Here, generating a rally effect does not contribute to the final policy choice, but the government takes advantage of any domestic dividends from using force. Several of the examples discussed above may fall into this category. For example, Reagan would have invaded Grenada regardless of events in Beirut—the plan to send

troops was set before the bombing. And when he was warned that his opponents might accuse him of using diversionary tactics by intervening in Grenada, Reagan reportedly said that "if this [invasion] was right yesterday, it's
right today and we shouldn't let the act of a couple terrorists dissuade us from
going ahead."[27] Nevertheless, his administration skillfully used the successful
mission in Grenada to shelter the president from criticism over his policy in
Lebanon.[28]

In the center of the target are international conflicts that are provoked primarily to reduce the public's opposition to the government, that is, where domestic discontent is a necessary condition for a leader's decision to use force
abroad. It is these cases—true diversionary wars—that are most contested by
scholars.

In *Diversionary War* I argue that the key to understanding the relationship between domestic and international conflict can be found through a new
model of government decision making based on the concept of policy substitutability drawn from the literature on foreign policy analysis.[29] The central
insight is that governments choose their responses to a given problem from
a menu of alternatives that can be substituted for one another. Thinking in
terms of policy substitutability puts us in a decision maker's shoes so that we
view diversionary war as one option among many for managing civil unrest.
The challenge for the scholar is then to explain why embattled governments
initiate diversionary wars instead of attempting a rival solution to their domestic problems, such as buying off opponents—in other words, providing
butter instead of using guns.

The book develops the idea of policy substitutability and creates an innovative theoretical framework that can explain when and why leaders select a
particular option from the policy menu—in this case, when unpopular leaders use diversionary force. The new policy substitutability approach proposes
that government decisions are a product of leader preferences and environmental factors. *Leader preferences* refers to how the decision maker assesses
the desirability of each option on the policy menu and then ranks these options from most to least attractive. *Environmental factors* are those conditions
that enable or constrain a leader's ability to pursue these options. Decision
makers will choose their preferred response if it is practicable. Alternatively,
environmental factors may rule out the top-ranked policy, and the government may select an alternative, and less-palatable, response—the next-highest
option on the leader's policy ranking. Thus, by studying the interaction

between preferences and environmental factors, we can explain the policy choices made by leaders in individual cases.

Therefore, whether and why a government provokes a diversionary war is determined by where this option falls on a decision maker's policy ranking, as well as by whether it is feasible. If the use of diversionary force is a leader's preferred policy response and it is possible, then the state will initiate a diversionary war. However, if another strategy for managing domestic unrest is ranked higher but environmental factors eliminate it from the menu of available responses, then the government again may be pushed toward fighting a diversionary war. The substitutability approach suggests then that some (or perhaps even most) diversionary wars could occur not because they are an intrinsically attractive response to unrest but rather because environmental factors have eliminated higher-ranked options. It also suggests that diversionary war might occur only rarely because most leaders place it low on their policy ranking and at least one of the more-appealing policies will generally be practicable.

Another advantage of this decision-making framework is that it enables scholars to discover new causal variables that may be both crucially important and otherwise overlooked, namely, those factors in the environment that alter the practicability of various menu options. It is easy to neglect the effect of environmental factors on decision making because they may only indirectly contribute to a government's final policy choice, by eliminating preferred alternatives and compelling leaders to select riskier policies. To detect the effect of these environmental factors, scholars have to ask the following: what are the main options on a menu for addressing a given policy challenge, and which conditions are likely to eliminate one or more of these options? Without using the substitutability approach, one is unlikely to systematically consider these questions, and the critical role played by environmental factors will remain hidden.

Applying the substitutability approach to the question of whether governments wage diversionary wars reveals the importance of one critical environmental factor, extractive capacity, or a state's ability to efficiently mobilize societal resources, generally through taxation. Along with launching a full-scale diversionary war, the menu of common responses to domestic unrest includes low-level diversionary conflicts against targets that are unlikely to fight back (which I term "diversionary spectacles"), political reform, economic reform, repression, inviting foreign military intervention, and "muddling through," or delaying action. Extractive capacity shapes whether governments can adopt these policies because several of the menu options (e.g., diversionary war, economic reform, and repression) are likely to be more expensive than others (e.g., diversionary spectacles, political reform, requesting foreign intervention, and muddling through). Crucially, governments with a high extractive capacity, which I label *princely* states, can afford a wide range of responses to unrest, while those with a low extractive capacity, or *pauper* states, choose from a more-limited policy menu.

Extractive capacity has been neglected in prior studies of diversionary war because it functions as a permissive condition in princely states and often indirectly shapes decision making in pauper states. However, if a high extractive capacity enables the leader of a princely state to adopt the preferred response to unrest from the menu of options (for example, expensive economic reforms), it is a necessary condition for this policy choice. Similarly, if the leader of a pauper state stages a diversionary spectacle because enacting economic reforms (a response that he or she prefers) is deemed too costly, then a necessary cause of the decision to provoke a spectacle lies in the state's limited ability to extract resources.

Using the substitutability approach, I deduce hypotheses regarding how leader preferences and extractive capacity together influence whether and when unstable governments use diversionary force. The core prediction is a counterintuitive one: pauper states are more likely than princely states to fight diversionary wars.

Why would impoverished regimes wield the sword? The basic logic is that a full-scale diversionary war is often seen by decision makers as an especially treacherous response to internal instability and will be placed low on their policy rankings. If leaders are drawn to using diversionary tactics, they will prefer a diversionary spectacle to a war—although the potential rally effect is smaller, because it does not entail major combat operations, the danger of having the conflict result in a battlefield defeat or foreign occupation is also smaller. Leaders of princely states will rarely provoke diversionary wars because they can generally afford to adopt more-palatable alternatives. Leaders of pauper states would also rather avoid fighting diversionary wars, not only because this policy option is unattractive, but also because it is too costly.

But pauper states may occasionally be pulled into fighting unwanted and expensive diversionary wars, precisely because of their limited resources. The reason is that diversionary spectacles staged by pauper states are more likely to escalate. All else being equal, governments targeted by resource-poor governments will tend to fight back, viewing their adversary as vulnerable. Further, pauper states are more likely to provoke diversionary spectacles because preferred policies are too costly, meaning that they are often acting out of desperation. And when leaders are faced with few alternative courses of action, they are inclined to succumb to psychological bias and exaggerate the likelihood that the policy they select will succeed. This may mean downplaying the likelihood that the crisis will escalate into full-scale war.

Thus, the substitutability approach can explain why scholars are inclined to question the existence of full-scale diversionary wars—they are infrequent and rarely intended.

Diversionary War also takes on an additional, seldom studied question: do diversionary wars work? There are reasons to suspect that a diversionary war is not a sound strategy for managing domestic instability, namely high-profile debacles such as Argentina's diversionary war with Britain over the Falkland Islands in 1982, which resulted in the junta's ouster. However, there is little empirical research on whether war generally fuels or dampens unrest. And no studies have examined whether a diversion is more or less effective than the other options on the policy menu. Yet to accurately assess the wisdom of using diversionary force, we must weigh its utility compared to alternative responses to unrest. The book demonstrates that prudent leaders should avoid fighting diversionary wars; at best, they have no effect on internal stability. Instead, unpopular leaders will likely have greater success by addressing the public's pocketbook concerns and enacting economic reform measures.

In summary, *Diversionary War* makes important contributions to both our understanding of diversionary war and the wider scholarship on government decision making. It illuminates when and why unstable governments fight diversionary wars: the most likely scenario is that embattled pauper states provoke crises against high-risk targets that spiral uncontrollably into major military campaigns. This research also assesses the consequences of diversionary war, revealing that this policy is an ill-advised response to domestic disaffection.

The book advances the literature on policy substitutability more generally, by introducing a new decision-making framework that can better explain why governments select particular options from a given policy menu. This framework has wide applicability beyond diversionary war—it can be used to analyze how leaders respond to any policy challenge where they could pursue many alternative courses of action.

The book also has significant implications for policy makers who want to prevent diversionary wars. By shedding light on the conditions that precipitate diversionary war, leaders can identify which unstable regimes are most likely to employ diversionary tactics—particularly pauper states that are inclined to initiate spectacles against high-risk targets—and channel them toward a substitute strategy for managing their domestic troubles. Indeed, the book identifies several new avenues that could prompt embattled governments to select a different option from the menu of responses to domestic unrest, such as political or economic reform.

• • •

The remainder of the book is divided into six chapters. Chapter 2 presents the new policy substitutability approach for explaining government decision making and articulates how this framework can reveal the conditions under which unstable states fight diversionary wars. This chapter also reviews the state of knowledge regarding the efficacy of diversionary war and argues that we must study the utility of war as a tactic for reducing domestic unrest relative to the alternative strategies on the policy menu.

Chapter 3 is the first of four empirical chapters examining the causes and consequences of diversionary war. This chapter includes a cross-national statistical analysis, which examines whether the propensity of unstable states to fight interstate wars depends on extractive capacity. It finds, for example, that pauper states are indeed more likely than princely states to fight full-scale diversionary wars.

Beginning with a quantitative analysis has at least two advantages. First, nearly all of the prior research on the diversionary theory of war is quantitative. Using a statistical approach makes it possible to directly compare the argument presented here with claims in the extant literature. Second, examining a large number of cases increases our confidence that any findings are generalizable.

Chapter 3 also describes a quantitative study of how interstate war affects domestic unrest compared to alternative options on the policy menu. This analysis, the first of its kind, demonstrates that interstate war is a misguided strategy for managing civil strife and that leaders are better served adopting alternative policies.

Chapters 4 through 6 present five in-depth studies of responses by pauper states to domestic unrest. Building on the quantitative finding that extractive capacity is generally related to interstate war, here I examine the mechanism by which extractive capacity shapes government decision making. I focus on pauper states because resource-poor governments are most likely to fight diversionary wars. Chapter 4 examines a case of diversionary war: Argentina's invasion of the British Falkland Islands in 1982. Chapter 5 investigates a diversionary spectacle that did not escalate into a full-scale diversionary war: the U.S. government's expedition to replace Brigham Young as territorial governor of Utah in 1857. And Chapter 6 presents three cases in which unstable pauper states chose not to use diversionary tactics: French King Louis XVI's political reform measures to address growing elite discontent in 1788, the Habsburg monarchy's appeal for Russian military intervention to suppress the Hungarian revolution in 1849, and the Peruvian government's attempt to muddle through with a failing policy of repression against the communist movement Sendero Luminoso in 1988.

The purpose of the case studies is fourfold. First, they permit a close analysis of the manner by which extractive capacity shapes government decision making. In each case, for example, I find that a low extractive capacity consistently caused leaders of pauper states to avoid preferred, but costly, strategies for managing unrest, such as widespread repression, full-scale diversionary war, and economic reform. Second, these cases are similarly organized, enabling a structured, focused comparison of the conditions that lead some pauper states to use diversionary tactics while others avoid them altogether. The comparative analysis also points to the factors that cause some diversionary spectacles to escalate into full-scale wars, while others do not. Third, the case studies are used to search for new environmental factors, in addition to extractive capacity, that might influence government decision making during periods of internal instability. That is, they aid with theory building. Fourth, having found in Chapter 3 that diversionary wars are generally ineffectual, the cases generate new insights into why this strategy is not particularly successful in managing unrest.

Chapter 7 reviews the main findings of the book, including when and why unstable governments use diversionary tactics, the conditions that cause some diversionary spectacles to escalate into wars, and a new explanation for why diversionary uses of force fail to busy giddy minds with foreign quarrels, and waste memories of former ills. It concludes with the implications of the book for policy making.

2 The Causes and Consequences of Diversionary War

O N THE EVE OF THE CIVIL WAR, U.S. SECRETARY OF STATE
    William H. Seward counseled Abraham Lincoln to provoke
a war with the European great powers in order to create a common cause
around which the country could rally, thereby preventing disunion: "We
must change the question before the public from one upon slavery, or about
slavery . . . to one of patriotism or union."[1] Doing battle with Britain, Russia,
Spain, and France, Seward reasoned, would "wrap the world in flames" and
"rouse a vigorous continental spirit of independence."[2]

Although Lincoln dismissed Seward's advice, it is remarkable to note how
many wars are preceded by domestic turmoil in one or both of the warring
countries. A causal link between civil unrest and international conflict is sometimes thought to be so commonplace that wars often represent little more than
a cynical crusade to unite a badly divided nation. For example, Quincy Wright
casually asserts that the use of "foreign war as a remedy for internal tension,
revolution, or insurrections has been an accepted principle of government."[3]

However, scholarship is divided about whether leaders initiate diversionary wars—that is, provoke crises abroad to distract the public from problems
at home. There is a lack of consensus regarding the strength, or even the existence, of a relationship between domestic and international conflict. This has
prompted some to liken the study of the relationship between internal and
external conflict to the quest for the Holy Grail: "[M]any have searched for it;
the search has taken place over long periods of time and in diverse research

areas; its location has been the subject of many theories; and its existence has been the source of continual debate."[4]

This dissensus has been attributed, at least in part, to the fact that research on the link between domestic unrest and war has not fully specified the conditions under which diversionary wars are most and least likely. A cursory survey of the past reveals that social strife does not always or even usually herald war. Therefore, because any relationship between domestic unrest and foreign conflict is likely to be contingent, the question we should ask is this: *when* are governments prone to see foreign adventure as an attractive solution to escalating internal unrest? Recent studies have made progress in identifying scope conditions for the diversionary theory of war. Even so, many question these findings, asserting that there are no conditions under which states provoke interstate conflicts to ease their domestic woes. Like the Holy Grail, diversionary wars are popular fiction.

Another tack is needed. In this chapter I argue that the key to understanding the relationship between domestic and international conflict may be found through the concept of policy substitutability. The idea of substitutability suggests that we should consider diversionary war as being merely one option on a menu of potential responses for leaders facing civil unrest. The correlation between internal conflict and external conflict does not always hold because sometimes leaders choose diversionary war from the menu, and sometimes they select another policy path.

A substitutability model of decision making has the great advantage of prompting the researcher to search for the conditions that lead to policy substitution. In other words, particular variables may consistently drive a government toward diversionary war rather than the alternatives. Locating the sources of variation for state responses to domestic unrest will enable a more-accurate theory of how leaders act when confronted by internal turmoil and, more specifically, predict whether states are likely to initiate diversionary wars or attempt a rival solution to their domestic problems.

One such variable is a state's *extractive capacity*. The government's ability to extract resources from society heightens or lessens the feasibility of various menu options because some policy responses are more expensive than others. High-extractive-capacity governments—which I term *princely* states—can often afford to wage diversionary wars. But in general, they will avoid this potentially risky remedy because their wealth also gives them the latitude to adopt other more-attractive policies.

Instead, it is governments with low extractive capacity—or *pauper* states—that are more likely to fight diversionary wars. Their lack of ready access to revenues limits their ability to select resource-intensive policies, such as economic reform and widespread repression, pushing them toward cheaper policies, such as low-level diversionary conflicts. These low-level conflicts, initiated out of desperation, then spiral out of control into full-scale wars.

In summary, the policies that a government chooses from the menu of alternatives will be shaped by what it can afford. Although extractive capacity alone does not determine how a state responds to unrest, an inability to efficiently mobilize societal resources narrows the range of options for managing unrest, alters the probability of certain responses, and therefore is an important and previously overlooked cause of diversionary war.

This chapter also addresses the question of whether diversionary wars work by reducing public opposition to the government. In comparison to the causes of diversionary war, the efficacy of diversionary tactics is largely unmapped terrain. Most scholars believe that it is a misguided response to unrest. However, to accurately evaluate diversion as a strategy for reducing social strife, we must view it alongside the other options on the policy menu; that is, we must assess its relative utility.

The chapter has four sections. First, I distinguish diversionary wars from other types of international conflict. Second, I present a general model of policy substitutability and explain how it illuminates the conditions under which states initiate diversionary wars. Third, I discuss how extractive capacity influences the feasibility of using force to divert attention in predictable and logical ways. Finally, I review the little that is known about whether diversionary war is a useful strategy for managing domestic unrest.

What Is a Diversionary War?

Diversionary wars are interstate wars initiated in large part to bolster the government against growing domestic opposition, rather than simply to promote the national interest.[5] In a diversionary war, domestic unrest is a necessary condition for the government's decision to use force. Such unrest must be significant enough to represent a fundamental threat to the continued legitimacy, capacity, or existence of a regime—it may even endanger the political system itself. In the face of such a challenge, leaders instigate an armed international conflict in order to (1) distract the public from its woes, (2) whip up nationalist sentiment and rally the populace behind the government, (3) shift blame for internal troubles to an external scapegoat, and/or (4) demonstrate the government's competence in foreign policy to improve its image. The unstable regime selects a target that promises to unify the public, such as reclaiming territory that has cultural, historical, or symbolic significance, or defending the country against a generally recognized threat.

Therefore, diversionary wars are defined by a leader's motivation, not by whether they do in fact successfully divert public attention from domestic travails.[6] As we will see, like the debtor who heads to the casino, diversionary conflicts are a risky wager that could make a leader's problems worse.

The logic of diversionary war is straightforward: when the domestic situation becomes unstable, governments have less to lose from choosing a risky military policy. In such a situation, doing nothing looks certain to produce losses for the regime, while gambling through war offers the hope of turning things around. While defeat in war may signal the end of the regime, at least the government will go down fighting, rather than passively waiting while the guillotine blade is sharpened. For example, Arno Mayer contends that beleaguered governments are "particularly inclined to advocate external war for the purpose of domestic crisis management even if the chances for victory are very doubtful."[7]

Although widespread unrest may heighten an embattled ruler's propensity to accept policy risks, one cannot rely solely on the magnitude of domestic instability to make accurate predictions about when states will initiate a diversionary war. Internal upheaval may be necessary for diversionary war, but it is clearly not sufficient because it does not invariably result in war. As Richard Rosecrance notes, there "tends to be a correlation between international instability and the domestic insecurity of elites. This correlation does not hold in all instances. War may occur in the absence of internal instability; internal friction may occur in the absence of war."[8] The question then is this: *when* do embattled governments choose to initiate diversionary conflicts?

Traditional Approaches to Explaining Diversionary War

The first studies of the diversionary war hypothesis looked for a correlation between social unrest and war, and "made no attempt to incorporate the effects of other variables that might affect the relationship between domestic and foreign conflict."[9] Given the fact that any link between these variables is, at best, contingent, these early studies found little or no support for the diversionary theory of war.

Recent research—almost exclusively statistical analyses—has made some progress toward specifying the scope conditions for the diversionary war hypothesis by identifying the role played by domestic-level variables, such as degree of elite opposition to the state, public opinion, the health of the domestic economy, and the extent of violent social unrest.[10] Others have explored the effect of international factors, such as the availability of an external target against which to use diversionary force.[11] However, little consensus has emerged regarding the effect of these variables on a government's propensity to respond to unrest by initiating a diversionary war.[12]

The greatest concentration of research has been on whether democratic or autocratic states are more likely to provoke a war to allay internal tensions. And here the lack of agreement is especially stark, leading Giacomo Chiozza and Hein Goemans to remark that "almost every possible regime type has been suggested as particularly prone to engage in diversionary war."[13] Christopher Gelpi, for instance, sees diversionary war as a peculiarly democratic pathology. Elected leaders are more likely to turn to diversion when facing unrest than authoritarian leaders because they may be voted out of office if they use repressive tactics.[14] In this vein, Edward Mansfield and Jack Snyder contend that diversionary wars are most likely in young democracies.[15] During the early stages of democratization, they argue, political elites struggle to rally support from a newly expanded electorate and are tempted to invoke "threats from rival nations" in order to "shore up their legitimacy."[16] In contrast, Ross Miller concludes that autocratic leaders are most likely to use diversionary tactics.[17] This is because democratic leaders face higher domestic political costs from fighting and especially losing wars, raising the risks of attempting a diversion. Finally, some scholars have found no evidence that regime type affects whether leaders use force to solve their domestic problems.[18]

Thus, to a large extent, the question of when diversionary wars are most likely to occur remains unanswered.

Diversionary War and the Concept of Policy Substitutability

The conflicting findings within the extant literature may result from the traditional approach to investigating diversionary war (see Figure 2.1). First,

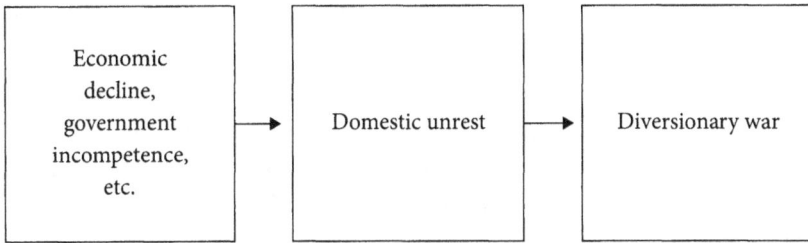

FIGURE 2.1 The traditional approach to studying diversionary war

scholars determine whether there is a correlation between domestic unrest and the use of force; second, they treat a government's response to unrest as being the product of a chain of direct causal variables. According to this view, domestic problems and government failure produce social strife, and the leadership responds to this instability by engaging in foreign adventure.

The traditional approach to understanding diversionary war is perfectly reasonable. But it is also overly narrow. As an alternative, we can consider the problem from the decision maker's perspective. Leaders may react to domestic unrest in a variety of ways, which is to say they select policies from a menu of substitutable options.

The literature on state responses to unrest has identified several additional strategies that leaders use to cope with social strife (see Table 2.1). First, instead of initiating a full-scale diversionary war, governments may provoke a low-cost diversionary conflict by using or threatening to use force against a symbolic target that is unwilling or unable to resist, which I term a "diversionary spectacle." Second, leaders may repress dissent by restricting the freedom of its citizens (e.g., banning political parties, halting elections, withdrawing the right to freely assemble, imprisoning dissidents) and/or using violence against them (e.g., forcefully dispersing demonstrations, torturing

TABLE 2.1 Menu of common policy
responses to domestic unrest

Diversionary war
Diversionary spectacle
Repression
Political reform
Economic reform
Foreign intervention
Muddling through

regime opponents, committing genocide).[19] Third, leaders can enact political reforms—that is, alter the country's political institutions or public policies in accordance with the demands of opposition groups, for example, by permitting competitive elections, allowing greater freedom of the press, and legalizing civil society organizations.[20] Fourth, governments can address unrest through economic reform, which is the use of financial tools to jump-start the national economy, reduce poverty and inequality, or buy off opponents. Common measures include tax reform, deregulation, tariff adjustments, social welfare spending, and land redistribution. Fifth, unstable governments may invite foreign intervention. Leaders may request troops from a friendly country to aid in suppressing a domestic uprising. Finally, a regime may choose to muddle through. Muddling through is the tactic of delay. A leader tries to deny victory to opposition groups long enough for some unforeseen turn of events to stabilize the state or for the passage of time to enervate the opposition. It often entails simply doing nothing. But muddling through also includes attempts at reform or repression that amount to little more than tokenism—that is, repressive measures, economic reforms, or vague promises of future political concessions that buy the government time but are not expected to end the unrest.

Thus, the question "Does domestic unrest precipitate international conflict?" should be reconsidered as "Under what conditions do leaders choose diversionary war from the menu of at least theoretically available policy alternatives?" As Gordon Craig succinctly states, "The duty of the historian is to restore to the past the options it once had."[21]

The main virtue of thinking in terms of policy substitutability is that it prompts us to search for the hidden causes of a government's decision (see Figure 2.2). There may be many cases in which leaders would have chosen a particular option from the policy menu but some set of conditions prevented them from doing so, forcing the adoption of a substitute strategy. That is, a policy was selected because *indirect* causal variables rendered the more-desirable option impracticable and *changed* the state's response. What can appear at first glance to be an irrational decision may turn out, when examined through the lens of policy alternatives, to be an instance of a leader being forced to select an unpalatable policy because a more-attractive path was obstructed. At a restaurant, a patron may choose the red-hot curry not because he is trying to impress his date or because he likes the taste, but because he cannot afford any of the other menu options.

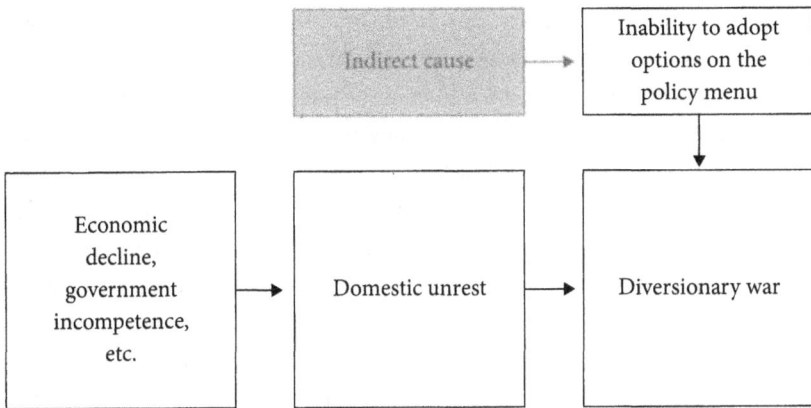

FIGURE 2.2 Policy substitutability and diversionary war

Therefore, leaders may initiate a diversionary war if the use of force is more practicable than the other responses, not necessarily because they believe that diversionary war is a generally useful strategy for managing unrest or even that such a strategy is likely to work in a particular situation. For example, repression of dissent may be a more-appealing option for a leader than initiating a risky diversionary war, but for a variety of reasons this strategy may not be feasible. So the causes of diversionary war may lie as much in a state's inability to repress as they do in the perceived utility of military adventure as a solution for domestic strife.

Thus, to improve our ability to predict when leaders initiate diversionary wars, we must search for factors that push leaders away from alternative options on the policy menu, thereby making a diversion more likely. Because they indirectly shape decision making, these causes are easily missed, but they may, in fact, be necessary and/or sufficient for policy decisions.

Policy Substitutability in the Research on Diversionary War

In the literature on the diversionary war hypothesis, a growing number of scholars have implicitly or explicitly employed the idea of policy alternatives to predict when diversionary wars might occur. However, this research suffers from several shortfalls: discussions of how substitutability might shape decision making are often underdeveloped, direct evidence of policy substitution is generally lacking, and because it is dominated by quantitative methods, any proposed causal mechanisms for how policy substitution occurs are unexamined.

Several articles examining the relationship between domestic institutions and diversionary war make policy substitution arguments. For example, Gelpi hypothesizes that leaders in autocracies repress domestic strife, whereas leaders in democracies may lose office if they repress and are forced instead to initiate diversionary conflicts. But he does not directly test whether and how regime type changes government responses to domestic unrest. Instead, Gelpi asserts that because the evidence suggests that autocratic states are less likely than democracies to use force abroad when faced with increasing domestic turmoil, there is "strong support" for the argument that autocracies are choosing to repress rather than distract their opponents.[22] To fully assess this claim, however, Gelpi would need to demonstrate not only that democratically elected leaders are less likely to engage in repressive internal policing but also that the fear of losing office is the reason they choose to use force abroad. He is not alone: no study suggesting that domestic institutions alter the probability of diversionary war by rendering alternative options on the policy menu more (or less) practicable provides direct evidence of policy substitution.[23]

Research on whether diversionary war requires the availability of a suitable international target also tends to employ a policy substitutability logic. For instance, Benjamin Fordham argues that governments facing a dissatisfied public may be blocked from initiating a diversionary conflict and compelled to choose another policy response because likely targets will steer clear of a dispute—a tactic known as "strategic conflict avoidance."[24] He contends that governments are more conciliatory toward a rival when the latter's economy is in a downswing, precisely because the rival may be tempted to divert attention with force. However, Fordham does not identify which alternative policy is likely when a diversionary use of force is impracticable, and why. Indeed, none of the studies focusing on international-level causes of diversionary war include such a discussion.[25]

A few scholars explicitly incorporate policy choice in their empirics—for example, assessing the correlates of diversionary war and at least one alternative policy. But these arguments fall short of providing a general model of how policy substitutability influences government decision making during periods of internal instability. Commonly, they test for whether policies such as repression and diversionary war are substitute responses to domestic unrest, but these studies do not fully explore why leaders might choose one option over another. Alternatively, they offer more-fleshed-out arguments intended to apply only to a small subset of cases, such as U.S.-style presidential democracies.[26]

Kurt Dassel offers perhaps the most developed argument about the conditions that lead governments to wage diversionary wars instead of repressing regime opponents, which he illustrates with a series of short examples.[27] The military, he argues, always desires to restore domestic order with repression. But if both the military and society are riven by, for example, deep ethnic, religious, or class cleavages, the suppression of popular dissent will create dangerous tensions within the military organization—violence against any societal group will alienate some faction within the military. Under these conditions, where repression is closed off as an option, military leaders are especially likely to be pushed toward provoking a diversionary war. And if the state is experiencing extreme levels of domestic unrest, such that the public is challenging the country's basic political institutions, then the military may have free reign over the government's foreign policy. Dassel does not conduct in-depth case studies of government decision making (his aim is to make a theoretical contribution rather than an empirical one), but the anecdotal evidence he offers does suggest a rough correlation between changes in his variables of interest, such as the emergence of ideological cleavages within the military and society, and a change in the government's response to domestic unrest.

Although Dassel furthers our understanding of diversionary war, his argument applies only under a narrow set of conditions. First, he assumes that leaders choose from a highly circumscribed policy menu: in response to unrest, governments either repress or initiate a diversionary war. Second, his approach does not allow for the possibility that some decision makers, even military elites, might not view repression as the best response to social strife. Third, his predictions apply only to countries in which there is no civilian oversight of the military.

In short, we need a theoretical framework that allows us to explain why any leader chooses diversionary war from a broad menu of policy alternatives. Here we might ask this question: does the larger research program on policy substitutability provide guidance for how we might build such a framework?

Borrowing from the Research Program
on Policy Substitutability?

The recognition that leaders have alternative options for dealing with any single problem has prompted considerable interest among students of foreign policy decision making in the concept of policy substitutability. This scholarship has argued that statistical analyses attempting to explain when specific foreign policies are adopted "have produced surprisingly weak results," precisely because "a decision maker can address any specific foreign policy problem with any of several instruments."[28] Given this complex reality, "we are unlikely to find significant, simple relationships explaining the variation in the use of any foreign policy tool."[29] Thus, analyses of government decision making must incorporate the insight that leaders choose policies from a set of alternatives and select the one that is most likely to achieve their aims.[30]

To date, nearly all studies in this research program have searched for empirical evidence of substitution. In other words, if policies are bona fide alternative options on a menu, they ought to be inversely related. For example, we should find that leaders who crush dissent are less likely to also implement economic reforms. Consequently, the balance of research on substitutability has been quantitative analyses that examine whether the adoption of one option on the policy menu is negatively correlated with the likelihood that another strategy is chosen. More specifically, these studies search for variables, such as democratic institutions, that are positively associated with one policy while being negatively associated with another.[31]

However, more-recent scholarship has argued that there need not always be "an inverse relationship between any two behaviors that are substitutable."[32] In A Theory of Foreign Policy, for example, T. Clifton Morgan and Glenn Palmer claim that "[a negative] relationship can hold, but only under certain circumstances."[33] Leaders sometimes select one option over the alternatives. But the adoption of one strategy can also make the selection of another option more likely. The challenge is to identify why policies are substituted in some cases but combined in others (or are at least positively correlated).[34]

Although this line of inquiry is an important step forward, the research program has yet to produce a theoretical model of policy substitutability. Namely, we need a framework that not only informs our quantitative analyses—that is, produces more accurately specified models of decision making—but is also useful for explaining policy outcomes in particular cases. As noted above, some progress has been made toward developing statistical models of policy substitution. But the literature currently provides no guidance for how we might identify and explain instances of policy substitution in individual cases. Crucially, there are no case studies that explicitly use the concept of policy alternatives to explain why a government substituted one option for another.[35]

In the section below I present a general model of policy substitutability that can be used in quantitative and qualitative analyses of government decisions. I then demonstrate how this framework produces a theory of diversionary war with broad applicability that highlights previously overlooked causes of diversion.

A Model of Policy Substitutability: The Interaction Between Leader Preferences and Environmental Factors

How do we move from the basic insight that leaders choose policies from a menu of alternatives toward a general model of policy substitution that predicts when and why leaders choose one option over another? We can create an improved model of substitution by employing two concepts from the literature on foreign policy decision making: opportunity and willingness. Opportunity refers to whether a course of action is "physically, technologically, or intellectually possible."[36] Willingness is the extent to which decision makers desire to pursue a given policy.[37]

Opportunity and willingness are useful concepts with which to construct a general model of substitutability because the policy a leader chooses from the menu of alternatives will invariably be influenced by whether specific options are practicable and desirable.[38] Thinking about policy selection in terms of opportunity and willingness requires the scholar to identify two broad categories of variables that affect decision making: first, variables that shape the desire of leaders to adopt a given policy, and second, variables that enhance or diminish the ability of leaders to adopt that policy. Systematically considering how *both* opportunity and willingness contribute to policy choice ensures that we do not overlook the effect of either on government decisions.[39]

However, the concepts of opportunity and willingness in the foreign policy decision-making literature provide only the rough building blocks of a theoretical model of substitution. In practice, analyses of how opportunity shapes government decision making usually examine how a single variable influences the feasibility of a course of action. When scholars study how opportunity affects the likelihood of interstate war, for example, they often focus on whether countries are contiguous and/or can easily project military power.[40] But this is a limited understanding of opportunity. Decision makers actually encounter a range of domestic and international variables that determine the practicability of a policy—for example, the structure of their political institutions, domestic lobbies, treaty commitments, and so on. To underscore this fact, I use the term *environmental factors* instead of *opportunity* when describing the set of conditions that widen or narrow the range of available options on the policy menu. And, in both the statistical analysis and case studies, I examine how a number of environmental factors together shape government decision making.

Further, the concept of willingness is inadequate for explaining decisions in individual cases or identifying specific instances of policy substitution. Willingness usually refers to the leader's attraction to the policy response that was ultimately chosen. But, as with opportunity, we need to broaden the concept. In the case of willingness, we must understand how decision makers weigh the merits of *all* options on a policy menu, which I term *leader preferences*. In other words, we consider the appeal of the path that is ultimately followed, as well as the allure of the roads that were untraveled. With this information, we can construct a decision maker's ranking of policies, from the ideal response to the least-desirable response to a given problem. Ascertaining a leader's policy ranking then makes it possible to determine whether a policy substitution has occurred. For example, if a leader adopted policy A in a given case, willingness would tell us only how the leader assessed that course of action. However, a leader's policy ranking might reveal that policy A was not the decision maker's favored response. All else equal, the decision maker would have chosen policy B—but this option was rendered impractical by external constraints. In this manner we can discover evidence of a policy substitution.

Thinking in terms of leader preferences rather than willingness has two further advantages. First, knowing a leader's policy ranking clarifies whether and how environmental factors shape decision making in a given case. Indeed, as I will demonstrate below, whether an environmental factor contributes to a policy outcome is entirely contingent on a leader's preferences. Second, if a decision maker's preferred response has been eliminated by constraints in the environment, a leader's policy ranking allows us to identify which strategy the decision maker will choose as a substitute, namely the next-most-preferred option on the list.

Modeling Policy Substitutability

Once a government has determined a goal, such as reducing political unrest while remaining in power and preserving the political system, its policy choice is the product of two main elements: *leader preferences* and *environmental factors*. Again, leader preferences are how a decision maker evaluates the desirability of every option on the policy menu. Environmental factors are conditions that aid or constrain a decision maker's ability to pursue options on the policy menu. At least analytically, we can separate leader preferences from environmental factors. (I will discuss the challenges of doing so in practice below.) Preferences are solely the product of the decision maker's personality, beliefs, values, past experiences, and so on—that is, generally individual-level variables. Environmental factors are domestic and international-level variables, such as bureaucratic structure, public opinion, regime type, international law, and alliance obligations. Therefore, government decisions will result from the interaction between preferences (what the leader would do in a perfect world) and environmental factors (what the leader can do).

This new model of substitutability proposes that when governments consider, say, how to respond to rising social unrest, they weigh the main options on the policy menu—such as diversionary war, diversionary spectacle, repression, economic reform, political reform, foreign intervention and muddling through—and form a ranking of most- to least-preferred strategies. The particular rankings may vary considerably across cases. In 1832, for example, the British government faced internal unrest, and its preferred response was to buy off opponents with political reform: the "Great Reform Act." By contrast, sixteen years later, the Habsburg monarchy faced a potential revolution in its Hungarian territory, and the preferred response was to suppress the uprising with violence.

After evaluating the alternatives, the government will then enact its favored option—assuming of course that environmental factors make this policy practicable (see Figure 2.3). When the top-ranked option is viable, the set of conditions in the environment that make it possible are permissive conditions for the government's policy choice.

In reality, environmental factors often eliminate several options on the menu. There are two scenarios in which such constraints are critically important for explaining a government's decision. The first situation is when an environmental factor rules out a strategy that a leader would have preferred to the final selection. In other words, variable X removes policy A, and so the leader pursues substitute policy B. Here, the constraint may be a necessary condition for the decision. In a counterfactual, if that variable had been absent, the leader would have had a broader menu of available policies and

```
                                    ┌─────────────────┐   ┌──────────────────┐
                                    │ Constraint in the│──▶│ Inability to adopt│
                                    │  environment     │   │   preferred       │
                                    └─────────────────┘   │ response to unrest│
                                                          └──────────────────┘
                                                                    │
                                                                    ▼
┌──────────────┐   ┌──────────────┐   ┌ ─ ─ ─ ─ ─ ─ ─┐   ┌──────────────────┐
│ Economic     │   │              │   │              │   │                  │
│ decline,     │   │              │   │ Opportunity in│   │                  │
│ government   │──▶│Domestic unrest│──▶│ the environment│─▶│ Diversionary war │
│ incompetence,│   │              │   │              │   │                  │
│ etc.         │   │              │   │              │   │                  │
└──────────────┘   └──────────────┘   └ ─ ─ ─ ─ ─ ─ ─┘   └──────────────────┘
```

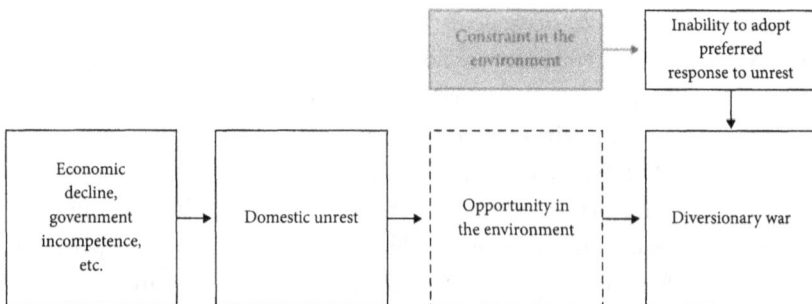

FIGURE 2.3 Leader preferences, environmental factors, and policy substitutability

would have chosen differently. Constraints in the environment are also important in a second scenario, when a leader has no preference among policy alternatives. Here, the environmental factor narrows the range of options from which the leader may choose and may therefore also be a necessary condition for the final policy selection.

An environmental factor is not a necessary condition for a government's decision if it rules out a course of action to which the leader is already averse. Variable X may remove policy B from the menu, but the leader would have preferred policy A even if B were also available. In other words, a leader's preferences determine whether particular environmental factors assume causal importance in a given case. Some variables—such as whether an ally is willing and able to repress a regime's domestic opponents—will be critically important in some cases and irrelevant in others, depending on the government's preferences. If a government prefers an alternative policy to requesting military assistance from an ally, whether external variables allow for foreign intervention may be inconsequential.

To explain government decision making, we must perform a thought experiment. First, we consider the leader's ranking of the policy alternatives in a "perfect world," ignoring environmental factors. Second, we reintroduce the environmental factors and determine whether they enable or eliminate certain alternatives.

Such an approach is obviously difficult. But the challenges arise because this model of decision making makes the inner workings of the causal analysis explicit rather than implicit. We pull a decision apart into its constituent elements, separating preferences from environmental factors. And in the cold light of day, the problems in locating the necessary evidence become obvious. For this reason, most case studies avoid identifying how preferences and environmental factors interact to produce a final policy choice, instead hiding the logic behind narrative, allusion, and turns of phrase.

Particularly demanding is the task of identifying leader preferences. For each option on the menu, we must ask this: all else being equal, would the leader have preferred a given policy to the alternatives? Leaders will rarely offer an explicit ranking, so we have to reconstruct preferences from the available evidence. In practice, this means a careful reading of historical sources, in particular letters, memoranda, minutes from meetings, journals, and memoirs. And, of course, if environmental factors rule out a particular option on the policy menu, leaders may never discuss that policy at all. Nevertheless, it should appear in our "perfect world" ranking, and it could even be in first position: a decision maker would have pursued this avenue if the constraints had not existed. Thus, we may have to rely on counterfactuals and circumstantial evidence to build a case for what a leader's preferred policies would have been.

Importantly, however, one is not trying to establish the precise attraction of a particular option on the policy menu but simply the ordering. In other words, one does not necessarily need to find direct evidence of how a leader viewed policy A or whether he or she was, say, 65 percent or 85 percent in favor of it. We just need evidence that the leader preferred policy A to policy B. For example, the Argentine junta might never have spoken about the advantages of a diversionary conflict in the buildup to the Falklands War, but we can still make a strong case that the junta favored a diversion to enacting political reforms.

Scholars have options here to simplify the substitutability approach. First, we could assume that leaders have no preferences regarding policies—that is, no preexisting attitudes about the relative merits of the options on the policy menu. Second, we could construct a theory of preferences, based on a deductively derived logic for how most leaders will rank the policy alternatives. I will discuss each method for handling preferences and its limitations in turn.

By assuming that an actor has no predilection for any given strategy, the first tack eliminates altogether the need to establish a leader's policy ranking. Theories of decision making that adopt this approach—most commonly, expected-utility models—instead assume that decision makers have preferences only in regard to the possible outcomes of a given situation (e.g., whether a crisis will result in peace or war).[41] Policy makers weigh all of the alternative strategies for achieving the preferred outcome and select the option that is most likely to produce the desired result, given the constraints and opportunities in the environment—which is to say that they maximize their utility.[42]

Although it places fewer demands on the scholar, this approach may produce inaccurate explanations for government decisions. In expected-utility models, leaders consider the practicability of each option on a policy menu before making their selection. Thus, the entire set of constraints and opportunities in the external environment shapes their final decision. However, the substitutability model maintains that leaders do view some policies for achieving an outcome as inherently more attractive than others because of their values, past experiences, personalities, and so on. In other words, they favor particular ends—and particular means. As a result, whether an environmental factor matters in a given case depends on the leader's policy ranking. A factor will not influence a government's decision if it rules out (or enables) a policy that the decision maker already perceives as unpalatable. Therefore, using the substitutability approach means that we can identify more precisely the set of factors in the environment that contributes to a leader's decision.

Further, recognizing the potential for significant variation in policy rankings can explain why leaders choose different policies to achieve the same outcome in nearly identical environmental conditions. For example, one leader may select the option with the highest utility, while another avoids this choice because he or she believes it to be unethical and pursues an alternative policy path.[43]

The second method for dealing with preferences is to construct a theory of how leaders weigh the options on a given policy menu. For example, we could posit that governments order the alternative strategies for managing domestic unrest in the following manner: (1) repression, (2) economic reform, (3) diversionary spectacle, (4) diversionary war, (5) political reform, and (6) foreign intervention. Then we could locate the environmental factors that are required for each option to be practicable. With this information we could identify the precise combination of factors that cause leaders to adopt each policy—and, more importantly, make pinpoint predictions about when and why one option is substituted for another. For instance, if repression is feasible only in nondemocracies and economic reform requires support from the business elite, then we can generate a hypothesis regarding the conditions under which embattled leaders enact economic reforms: when the government is democratic and the reform plan is championed by the corporate community.

However, history does not generally provide simple rules like "leaders prefer repression to political reform." Indeed, there is probably an example of every conceivable ranking of the alternative responses to domestic instability. And because leader preferences are often idiosyncratic, any policy ranking will not apply to many (or perhaps even most) governments. Therefore, the substitutability approach accepts the reality that a universal theory of preferences is almost certainly out of reach.

That said, there may be several patterns in how leaders judge the relative merits of some of the options on a policy menu. For instance, a wealth of evidence suggests that repression is less common in democracies than in nondemocracies. Many scholars attribute these findings to differences in the preferences of the leaders who rise to power in democratic and nondemocratic states. Autocrats have "*preferred* repression to other mechanisms of influence, even if alternatives were available," because they are, for example, paternalists convinced that their subjects ought to follow orders.[44] In contrast, democratically elected leaders prefer political reform to repression because they "accept specific values regarding passivity, toleration, communication, and deliberation—values that are challenged and undermined by the use of repression."[45] It is also likely that foreign military intervention is low down on most rankings as a strategy for dealing with unrest, perhaps because leaders view trading some measure of national sovereignty for regime survival as traitorous. Although the International Military Intervention data set does not record unfulfilled requests for outside assistance, foreign interventions to shore up unstable governments are relatively uncommon.[46] The rarity of pro-government international intervention is no doubt due in large part to the fact that this response to unrest is usually a last resort for embattled leaders.

When these tendencies exist, we can produce hypotheses about the conditions under which those policies will be chosen and why. Importantly, there are good reasons to expect that such patterns exist regarding how leaders assess the relative advantages of diversionary wars and spectacles, allowing us to predict when these responses to internal instability are most likely to be selected.

The new policy substitutability approach promises to advance the research on diversionary war in at least two ways. It can be used to explain why leaders use diversionary tactics in individual cases. In suspected instances of diversionary war, the researcher first identifies where this policy fell on the leader's preference ranking and then determines how environmental factors contributed to its selection. The two most common scenarios are that the leader provoked a diversionary war either because (1) it was the preferred response to internal unrest and environmental factors rendered it practicable or (2) environmental factors eliminated higher-ranked options from the menu of alternatives but enabled a diversion—that is, a diversionary war occurred because the leader was forced to make a policy substitution.

This model of policy substitutability also has considerable promise for producing a more-accurate general theory of diversionary war. It prompts the researcher to think about government decisions as the result of both leader preferences and environmental factors. And this exercise brings to light new variables that influence when diversionary force is selected from the policy menu.

In the following section I discuss an environmental factor—extractive capacity—that can significantly affect the range of available options for managing internal unrest. I then present hypotheses regarding how leader preferences and extractive capacity together alter the likelihood that regimes will provoke diversionary wars and spectacles.

The Prince and the Pauper: Extractive Capacity and Government Decision Making

A factor that has been neglected in studies of diversionary war but that will act as an important determinant of how governments respond to domestic unrest is the state's extractive capacity, or its ability to efficiently mobilize societal resources, especially through the collection of tax revenues.[47] The limited attention paid to the relationship between extractive capacity and diversionary war is surprising because this variable has been used to explain many phenomena in international relations—for example, in studies of foreign policy, the causes of war, grand strategy, civil wars, and foreign expansion.[48]

Extractive capacity represents the efficiency with which a government acquires societal resources, primarily through taxation. A high extractive capacity means that at any given moment, leaders will possess more readily available resources to finance new projects. Importantly, it also means that when leaders do not have enough slack in the budget and cannot divert sufficient money from existing programs, the government can more easily extract additional revenues from the public to pay for new initiatives. Thus, as Theda Skocpol contends, a "state's means of raising and deploying financial resources tells us more than could any other single factor about its existing (and immediately potential) capacities to create or strengthen state organizations, to employ personnel, to co-opt political support, to subsidize economic enterprises, and to fund social programs."[49]

Rarely will the alternatives on a policy menu require the same resources to implement. Therefore, a state's extractive capacity will influence the range of available options from which leaders select their response to a given policy problem. Leaders of governments with a high extractive capacity—what I term *princely* states—have a broader menu of viable policy options from which to choose, including strategies that require substantial resources to enact.[50] In contrast, a government with low extractive capacity—or a *pauper* state—confronts a more-limited policy menu. And in some cases, a state may be so weak that, by a process of elimination, it is forced to embrace a risky policy that it otherwise would not have considered.[51] It is the poor, after all, who buy lottery tickets.

The efficiency with which a government can extract revenues from society is a better predictor of which options on a policy menu are practicable than the country's aggregate wealth or even total tax revenues. First, as Thomas Christensen and Fareed Zakaria have documented, countries that are peers in terms of national capabilities may act very differently in similar circumstances because the leaders diverge in their ability to convert societal riches into government revenues.[52] A state with a large national economy and a barren treasury will avoid policies that require considerable resources to implement. At the same time, the leaders of a poorer country might adopt costly policies because they can easily mobilize additional funds. Even if the pie is smaller, princely states can consume most of the slices.

Second, a state's current tax revenues will give us some insight into what policy paths a government might pursue—all considered, leaders with full treasuries will have more choice in how they respond to unrest. But we also must evaluate how much flexibility leaders have in mobilizing additional revenues to pay for big-ticket policies. This is important because when weighing the practicability of, say, full-scale interstate war, leaders will consider not only how full the treasury is now but also how easily it can be replenished in the future.[53]

How does extractive capacity influence government responses to domestic unrest?[54] In the next section, I make general predictions regarding the relative propensity of pauper and princely states to wage diversionary wars and then identify the main causal pathways linking extractive capacity to the use of diversionary tactics.

Hypotheses on Extractive Capacity and Diversionary War

Extractive capacity influences whether leaders can implement options on the policy menu in predictable ways. Some strategies are likely to be within the means of most pauper states, such as political reform, requesting foreign military intervention, and muddling through. For example, allowing political parties to compete in free elections entails a loss of control over the reins of state, but such concessions are not necessarily costly in terms of material resources. Similarly, inviting a third party to send ground troops to quell the unrest may diminish national sovereignty and international prestige, but as long as the intervener is a white knight that does not expect lavish compensation for its assistance, this policy is also affordable. Finally, muddling through, especially if it means doing nothing, demands limited or even no resources.

Other options on the policy menu may be impracticable for pauper states. Under the best of circumstances, paying the agents of repression can be a heavy financial burden.[55] For example, an estimated 667,000 Iraqis were employed by the Ba'athist regime in suppressing internal unrest in 1980.[56] And as the magnitude of unrest increases, pauper states will face greater constraints on their ability to subdue domestic threats. Similarly, many economic policies, such as raising wages and improving working conditions for state employees, creating or expanding social welfare programs, and funding large public works projects, will be out of reach for resource-poor governments.

How will extractive capacity affect the likelihood that states use diversionary tactics—either low-level spectacles or full-scale interstate wars?

A diversionary spectacle refers to noisy saber rattling or the use of force against a symbolic target, where significant resistance is deemed unlikely and the expense manageable. Based purely on cost, princely and pauper states should be similarly likely to stage a spectacle.

On the one hand, princely states have more resources and therefore more capacity to initiate spectacles. Princely states can almost always afford to engage in saber rattling or other symbolic uses of force. Given the low cost, pauper states can usually afford a spectacle, but not always. Diversionary spectacles are cheap, but they are not free. On the other hand, a second dynamic reduces the number of spectacles orchestrated by princely states and increases the number by pauper states. For princely states, spectacles may be more affordable and therefore more plausible. But the alternatives to a diversion are also more feasible, and economic reform or repression may be selected instead. For pauper states, alternatives on the policy menu could be prohibitively expensive. And if a low-cost diversion is one of the few policies that is practicable, then it is more likely to be selected. The net effect, then, is for spectacles to be equally likely among princely and pauper states.

However, this discussion sidesteps the question of leader preferences—the other determinant of policy choice in the substitutability approach. If diversionary spectacles are an inherently appealing response to unrest, then this option will be more common among princely states. Leaders of both princely and pauper states will be drawn to this policy response, but more princely states will have the capacity to stage a diversionary spectacle. However, if diversionary spectacles are generally unattractive, then we would expect this policy to be more prevalent among pauper states. Princely states will use their considerable resources to implement more palatable, but perhaps also more expensive, responses to unrest. And because pauper states cannot afford these more-attractive but costlier options, they will be pushed toward engineering a diversionary spectacle. Finally, if preferences are highly variable, then they will not alter our prediction regarding the relative likelihood that princely and pauper states will stage a diversion: princely states and pauper states should exhibit roughly the same propensity to adopt this policy option.

Is a spectacle likely to be a leader's preferred policy response to unrest? The short answer is that there is no a priori reason to expect a symbolic show of force to be ranked either high or low. The use of spectacles is a problematic strategy for dealing with unrest because, unlike repression or reform, it fails to tackle the root cause of a disgruntled population. Any amelioration in unrest depends on the continuing diversion of the public, a condition that could end at any time. The problem with offering circuses without bread is that the population is still hungry after the performance ends. Decision makers may see spectacles as an essentially palliative measure rather than as a reliable remedy for domestic problems.

But leaders may still judge diversionary spectacles to be a prudent strategy for managing unrest. First, unstable regimes may wager that even if the rally effect produced by a spectacle is brief, a few months of calm may buy enough time for new economic or social policies to come into effect or for resistance movements to lose momentum and collapse. Second, the alternatives on the policy menu, while affordable, may be less appealing than a diversionary spectacle. For example, governments might prefer initiating a spectacle to acceding to the public's demands for political and economic change. Leaders may worry that reforms—especially those that could strengthen and embolden dissident elites—are little more than death by installments. States might also prefer a spectacle to widespread repression. Although provoking an international crisis to distract the public might seem riskier than clearing the streets with a whiff of grapeshot, the violent suppression of unrest can backfire. Particularly in democracies, repression can delegitimize an already unpopular regime and bolster opposition groups.[57]

Given that a diversionary spectacle is a fairly low-risk policy, carrying both advantages and disadvantages, there is no reason to assume that leaders will consistently rank this option above or below the alternatives on the menu. Consequently, when considering both preferences and constraints, the propensity of princely and pauper states to engineer a diversion should be similar.

Hypothesis 1: Princely states and pauper states are equally likely to stage diversionary spectacles.

Based purely on cost, princely states should be much more likely than pauper states to initiate diversionary wars. Indeed, several scholars have argued that princely states can and will pursue expansionist foreign policies. Geoffrey Blainey claims that it "would be surprising if most wars broke out when or where economic pressures and needs were most compelling, for these are times and places which are less capable of financing a war."[58] Neoclassical realists echo this assertion by arguing that states are more aggressive when a government's ability to mobilize societal resources improves.[59] As Zakaria puts it, "[N]ations try to expand their political interests abroad when central decision-makers perceive a relative increase in state power."[60] Extending this logic to diversionary war, princely states should be more likely to respond to domestic unrest by launching a major military campaign than states with limited access to revenues. Simply put, for pauper states, a protracted and expensive interstate war is off the menu.

But if we reintroduce the concept of preferences, the prediction actually reverses: pauper states are more likely to initiate diversionary wars. Leaders will not usually place diversionary war high on their policy ranking for managing unrest.[61] Going to war is a gamble under any conditions. As Winston Churchill once cautioned, "The statesman who yields to war fever must realize that once the signal is given, he is no longer the master of policy but the slave of unforeseeable and uncontrollable events."[62] A diversionary war is no exception. For instance, the Italian government entered World War I in part to reduce internal divisions, but the longer-than-anticipated war inflamed opposition to the state.[63] And Italy was on the winning side. If a diversionary campaign ends in defeat, this often signals the end for the regime. In 1982, when the embattled Argentine junta attempted to reverse its fortunes by invading the British Falkland Islands and subsequently lost, the architects of the war were thrown out of office and put on trial.

Given that princely states have the freedom to select alternative, less-risky responses to unrest, they will be unlikely to launch diversionary wars.[64] (Of course, princely states could be forced to initiate a diversionary war if their preferred policy responses were eliminated by other environmental factors.) Paradoxically, however, pauper states, by virtue of their limited resources, will find themselves drawn into costly diversionary wars. Why?

There is always the potential for a diversionary spectacle to turn into a full-scale war. But there are at least two reasons why crises initiated by pauper states are especially likely to escalate. The first is that the target of a diversionary spectacle is more likely to put up a fight if the initiator is a pauper state rather than a princely state. Targets of any diversionary spectacle will be aware of the potential for escalation should they choose to resist because their adversary is likely to be sensitive to the domestic political costs of backing down. Targets could capitulate for this reason, as the literature on strategic conflict avoidance suggests.[65] All else equal, however, targets are more likely to fight back against pauper states because the chances of military success are much greater against a government lacking the resources for a fight.

This prompts us to ask this question: why do pauper states fail to recognize in advance that their target will resist and avoid the use of force in the first place? The answer may lie with psychological bias. The diversionary spectacles engineered by princely states will generally be policies of choice rather than necessity—after all, they can afford to select alternative responses. In comparison, more of the diversionary spectacles staged by pauper states will be the product of desperation: a lack of resources closes off costlier alternatives, such as repression and economic reform. When the preferred strategies for confronting a grave challenge to one's interests or values are impracticable, there is a tendency to overrate the likelihood that the remaining riskier option(s) will succeed. In Richard Ned Lebow's words, policy makers display overconfidence in their decisions when they "believe that they will not find a better alternative for coping with . . . [a crisis] than their present defective policy."[66] Or, as Jack Snyder puts it, when leaders are "cornered by circumstances," they begin to see "the 'necessary' as possible."[67] In the context of staging a diversionary spectacle, this bias might lead pauper states to underestimate the likelihood that a target will fight back. Thus, diversionary spectacles staged by pauper states escalate because these governments are more likely to choose high-risk targets.

These dynamics are mutually reinforcing. Driven by desperation, pauper states are overconfident about spectacles and downplay the odds of enemy resistance—which may be significant.

Why are pauper states prone to have positive illusions about a diversionary spectacle, rather than, say, reform or repression? One simple reason is that there is more room for bias with strategies that are rarely employed. Governments have more experience implementing economic reforms and engaging in repression—they will have a good sense of how much increasing wages for state employees or imposing a curfew will cost. But because international crises are uncommon, leaders find it more difficult to predict whether a dispute with their neighbor will escalate, making it easier to exaggerate their chances of keeping the costs of the conflict low. Fewer data points allow for more wishful thinking.

Of course, some countries do have an extensive history of violent conflict or war with an adversary, and they are more likely to accurately gauge the potential for escalation should they provoke a new crisis. This suggests that the effect of wishful thinking on decision making is bounded. If the objective odds of a spectacle spiraling into a full-scale war are considerable, they may trump the tendency of desperate leaders toward overconfidence.

When we consider likely preferences regarding diversionary war, therefore, our prediction regarding which kind of states will select this policy option is reversed. Instead of expecting wealthy states to choose the more-expensive strategy for managing unrest, we predict that pauper states are more likely to be drawn into risky interstate wars. But again, when pauper states do end up fighting diversionary wars, this will not have been the original aim. By engaging in foreign adventure, pauper states are tempting fate: if they pick enough quarrels, one will eventually come to blows.

Hypothesis 2: Pauper states are more likely than princely states to fight diversionary wars.

In Figure 2.4 we see this logic displayed in terms of causal pathways. Causal pathways (a) and (c) concern princely and pauper states that prefer to stage a diversionary spectacle in response to rising internal instability. Here, extractive capacity functions as a permissive condition, enabling this policy option. Looking only at these causal pathways, spectacles should be more common among princely states. Causal pathway (a) will be more frequently

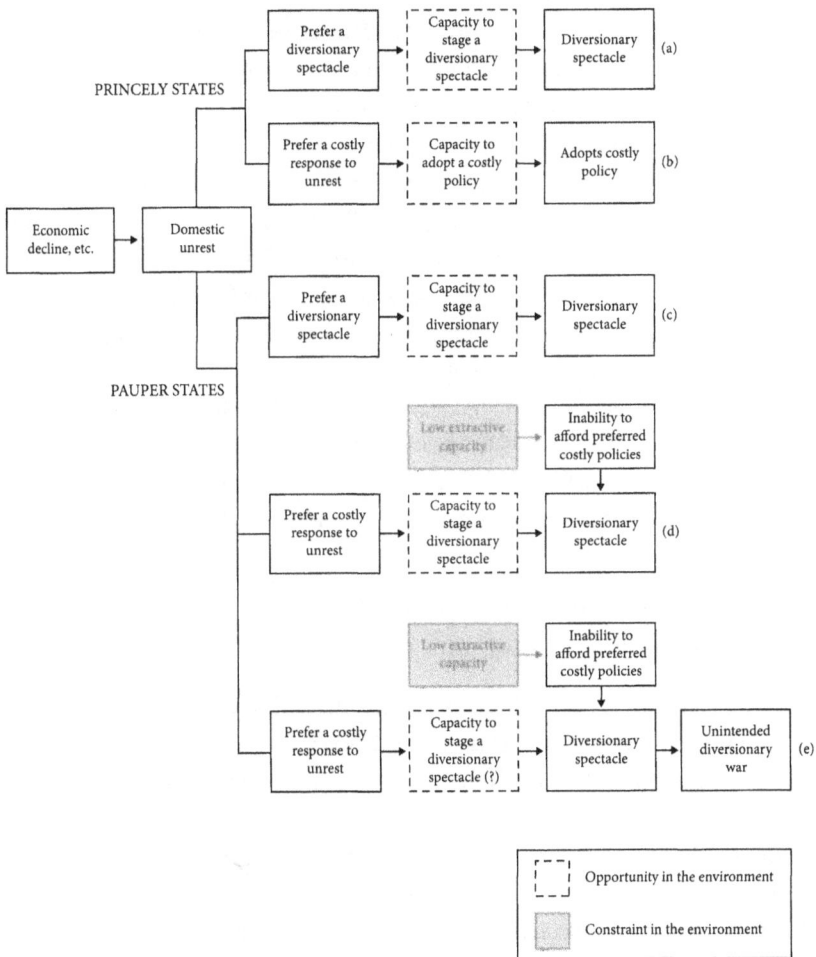

FIGURE 2.4 Extractive capacity and the use of diversionary tactics

observed than (c) because we can expect more princely states to be able to afford a spectacle than pauper states.

But causal pathways (a) and (c) are offset by pathways (b) and (d). In causal pathway (b), the princely state prefers a costly strategy for managing unrest to staging a diversionary spectacle and uses its considerable resources to implement it. And in causal pathway (d), pauper states that would prefer to adopt a resource-intensive response to internal instability are prevented from doing so by their limited extractive capacity, pushing them toward selecting a less-palatable but cheaper option, in this case a diversionary spectacle. Here, extractive capacity is operating as an indirect cause of a diversionary spectacle because it serves to eliminate more-attractive but also more-expensive policies. On balance, then, we should expect diversionary spectacles to be as common among princely states as pauper states.

Causal pathway (e) depicts the sequence of events that is most likely to produce a diversionary war. Any spectacle initiated by a pauper state has the potential to escalate because the target believes it has a chance to win. But when a low extractive capacity closes off preferred alternatives, war is particularly likely—the narrowing of available options increases the probability that desperate pauper states will miscalculate and initiate spectacles against targets that are prepared to retaliate.

In the end, explaining why leaders might use diversionary tactics is only one side of the coin. On the other side is the question of whether diversionary wars succeed in reducing public opposition to the government. Are leaders who use diversionary force simply making a bad situation worse?

Out of the Frying Pan and into the Fire: Do Diversionary Wars Work?

Political leaders have often been cautioned that initiating a diversionary war in response to domestic unrest is a foolhardy strategy that is, in the long term, doomed to failure. Adding foreign enemies to domestic opponents simply multiplies a leader's adversaries. Arthur Stein warns in *Nations at War*, for example, that "political leaders who count on foreign adventures to unify their countries and cement their positions should think again."[68] And I argued above that leaders rarely place diversionary war at the top of their policy ranking because it is perceived as an especially risky strategy for managing internal instability.

However, little is known about the actual effect of foreign adventure on domestic unrest. The belief that diversionary wars are a particularly dangerous response to social strife could be an example of what psychologists have termed a "negativity bias"—the well-documented tendency for decision makers to pay greater attention to and draw lessons from negative events rather than positive ones.[69] High-profile failures such as Argentina's Falklands War—or indeed any incident in which a bellicose foreign policy triggered a public backlash—may serve as powerful, but perhaps ultimately unrepresentative, cautionary tales about the perils of diversion.

Even less is known about whether provoking a diversionary war or spectacle is generally a more (or less) successful strategy for combating civil strife than the alternative options on the policy menu—from political reform to foreign intervention. After a brief overview of the extant research on the domestic political consequences of diversion, I examine the *relative* efficacy of this policy response versus the alternatives and generate hypotheses about whether and when each option on the menu is likely to restore societal order.

International Conflict and War

The influence of international crises and war on public opinion in the United States, particularly on presidential approval ratings, has been studied extensively.[70] These analyses have generally found that the "rally-around-the-flag" effect is real: the public often unites behind the president after high-profile and dramatic uses of force.[71] However, even when a military victory is swiftly achieved, the rally effect is often small and short-lived.[72] And as battlefield casualties mount, or the public perceives the mission as a failure, support for the government rapidly declines.[73] A number of studies have also looked for a relationship between the outcomes of international crises or wars (i.e., whether they result in a win, loss, or draw) and how long leaders remain in power. Winning wars lengthens a leader's tenure in office, although a victory on the battlefield may benefit democratic leaders more than nondemocratic ones.[74]

Compared to the effect of interstate war on public opinion and the tenure of office holders, however, the relationship between foreign adventurism and domestic unrest is uncharted territory. This is an important oversight because while public opinion and leader tenure correlate with the level of unrest within society, they are not identical. For example, an interstate war might

only temporarily boost public opinion while having a lasting ameliorative effect on levels of internal violence. Further, interstate war could simultaneously
shorten a leader's tenure and reduce domestic unrest: as an unpopular foreign
policy makes the removal of a leader all but certain, the opposition's appetite
for protest could dissipate.

Emizet Kisangani and Jeffrey Pickering have conducted the only research
directly addressing whether a bellicose foreign policy reduces internal instability. In a cross-national quantitative analysis, they found that military interventions reduce unrest in mature democracies but lead to wider discord in
nondemocracies. The logic is that because democratic leaders are punished
on election day for military defeats, they use force only when it promises to
be effective. By extension, they are also careful to "select themselves into diversionary military missions that will result in military success and will help
them achieve their domestic goals."[75] In contrast, autocrats are less judicious
when choosing targets and are consequently less likely to win on the battlefield and increase support for the regime.[76] Hypothesis 3 summarizes the current thinking about whether diversionary wars work.

Hypothesis 3: Interstate war reduces domestic unrest in democracies while
    increasing domestic unrest in nondemocracies.

Kisangani and Pickering's study betters our understanding of whether interstate war reduces domestic unrest. Yet, without considering diversionary
tactics alongside the other options on the policy menu, it is difficult to judge
their efficacy. As David Baldwin argues, "Even if the expected utility of using
a technique of statecraft is low, the expected utility of alternative techniques
may be even lower. . . . No matter how much one detests swimming, it may
seem quite appealing if the only alternative is sinking."[77] Indeed, relative to
available alternatives, using force abroad may prove to be the optimal strategy
for reducing opposition at home—even for some nondemocratic states. And
it is also possible that a statistical model that controls for the full range of
responses to unrest may reveal that interstate war either has no effect on the
internal stability of democratic states or that it actually backfires.

If determining whether the use of diversionary tactics is a prudent response to domestic unrest requires that we weigh it against the other options
on the policy menu, what do we already know about the utility of repression, political reform, economic reform, foreign intervention, and muddling
through?

Repression

Scholars are divided about the relationship between repression and social strife. Many have argued that repression is not typically an effective response to unrest because attempts by the state to coerce loyalty from society intensify opposition to the regime. In particular, indiscriminate repression radicalizes the public and causes it to form or join violent resistance movements.[78] The more repressive the regime, the greater the public backlash.

However, others maintain that there is a nonlinear relationship between repression and domestic discontent in the shape of an inverted U.[79] Citizens are unlikely to take to the streets if the government allows them alternative means by which to voice their discontent. And a highly repressive regime can effectively stifle opposition. But a moderate degree of repression is neither too cold to reduce the public temperature nor too hot to stifle dissent—it's just right to stir opposition. Dipak Gupta, Harinder Singh, and Tom Sprague qualify this argument, contending that the inverted-U hypothesis applies only to nondemocracies. In democracies, any infringement of the citizenry's rights provokes wider unrest.[80]

Hypothesis 4: Repression increases domestic unrest.

Hypothesis 5: Moderate repression increases domestic unrest.

Hypothesis 6: In nondemocracies, moderate repression reduces domestic unrest. In democracies, repression increases domestic unrest.

Political Reform

Much of the research on political reform and domestic instability examines whether institutional change (i.e., autocratization and/or democratization) increases the probability of civil war. The consensus is that any recent regime transition makes internal violence more likely.[81] A few studies look more narrowly at whether appeasing the demands of opposition groups aggravates social strife—and they also suggest that political reforms may be a dangerous strategy for unstable regimes. For example, Karen Rasler concludes that conciliatory policies adopted by the Shah before the Iranian Revolution to diffuse the rising unrest, such as selecting a prime minister with ties to the Islamic clergy and closing casinos, only fomented greater unrest.[82] Making political concessions signaled the regime's vulnerability and whetted the appetite of opponents for further gains. Similarly, in their study of twenty-one African governments between 1989 and 1991, Michael Bratton and Nicolas van de Walle find that regimes that responded to unrest with token concessions provoked wider unrest and were forced to adopt more-extensive political reforms than they had anticipated.[83]

Hypothesis 7: Political reforms increase domestic unrest.

Economic Reform

Leaders may adopt a wide range of economic policies to address social strife, from imposing fiscal austerity measures to jump-start a sluggish economy to increasing government spending to reduce poverty. Scholars have examined mainly whether a turn toward greater global economic integration reduces the likelihood of civil war. Nearly all find that globalization (e.g., dependence on trade and openness to foreign direct investment) has a pacifying effect on society, at least in the long term.[84] In the short run, the process of opening the economy to international trade might precipitate greater civil unrest as it redistributes societal wealth and creates new economic winners and losers.[85]

A handful of studies examine the effect of other economic measures on intrastate violence, namely government expenditures on social programs. These provide some evidence that social spending may reduce internal conflict.[86] For example, Clayton Thyne argues that to reduce public grievances against the regime, a state "can signal that it cares about the population" and promote economic growth—for example, by increasing funding for education, health care, and clean water.[87] And in a statistical analysis of civil war onset, he finds that investing in the educational system and providing for the public's basic health needs significantly stabilizes society.

Hypothesis 8: Economic liberalization reduces domestic unrest in the long term.

Hypothesis 9: Government social spending reduces domestic unrest.

Foreign Intervention

Whether foreign military interventions aimed at propping up unstable governments reduce civil strife is unclear. Some scholars have found that progovernment interventions may increase the duration and deadliness of civil wars. For example, Dylan Balch-Lindsay and Andrew Enterline conclude that the length of a civil war increases by more than 300 percent when a third party sides with the government.[88] And Patrick Regan finds that when compared to conflicts in which there is no outside meddling, pro-government foreign military interventions lead to bloodier civil wars.[89]

At the same time, third-party military interventions may improve a government's chances of prevailing over rebel groups in a civil war. Balch-Lindsay, Enterline, and Kyle Joyce find that pro-government interventions increase the likelihood of a victory by the state, although, as the conflict persists, the odds of success decline.[90] Stephen Gent also argues that foreign military assistance generally bolsters unstable regimes but that it may be insufficient to produce a victory in many cases. This is because third parties tend to aid embattled governments only when they face stiff opposition and look likely to lose.[91]

Because this research focuses on whether foreign intervention influences the length and outcomes of civil wars, it is difficult to deduce specific predictions regarding foreign intervention's likely effect on levels of domestic unrest in the target state over time. For example, two scenarios are equally consistent with the finding that third-party assistance enables the state to defeat its opposition: (1) foreign intervention causes unrest to first rise and then decline, or (2) foreign intervention causes unrest to steadily decline.

Hypothesis 10: Pro-government foreign military interventions increase domestic unrest in the short run and reduce unrest in the long run.

Hypothesis 11: Pro-government foreign military interventions reduce domestic unrest.

Muddling Through

Scholars have recognized that the menu of government responses to domestic unrest includes muddling through. For example, in his classic work on democratization, *The Third Wave,* Samuel Huntington writes that embattled authoritarian leaders may "simply refuse to acknowledge their increasing weakness with the hope or the conviction that they . . . [will] somehow survive in power."[92] However, there is no systematic research on the utility of, for example, simply ignoring one's unpopularity.

Does muddling through work? Both outcomes are plausible. By failing to act, the government could deny opposition groups new grounds to protest, causing the unrest to subside over time. Or, by failing to act, the government could feed the perception that it is indifferent to the demands of opposition groups, causing the unrest to intensify.

Hypothesis 12: Muddling through reduces domestic unrest.

Hypothesis 13: Muddling through increases domestic unrest.

• • •

TABLE 2.2 Summary of hypotheses

Hypothesis 1: Princely states and pauper states are equally likely to stage diversionary spectacles.

Hypothesis 2: Pauper states are more likely than princely states to fight diversionary wars.

Hypothesis 3: Interstate war reduces domestic unrest in democracies while increasing domestic unrest in nondemocracies.

Hypothesis 4: Repression increases domestic unrest.

Hypothesis 5: Moderate repression increases domestic unrest.

Hypothesis 6: In nondemocracies, moderate repression reduces domestic unrest. In democracies, repression increases domestic unrest.

Hypothesis 7: Political reforms increase domestic unrest.

Hypothesis 8: Economic liberalization reduces domestic unrest in the long term.

Hypothesis 9: Government social spending reduces domestic unrest.

Hypothesis 10: Pro-government foreign military interventions increase domestic unrest in the short run and reduce unrest in the long run.

Hypothesis 11: Pro-government foreign military interventions reduce domestic unrest.

Hypothesis 12: Muddling through reduces domestic unrest.

Hypothesis 13: Muddling through increases domestic unrest.

In the next chapter I review the results of two large-N quantitative studies. The first examines the relative propensity of princely and pauper states to use force abroad in response to domestic unrest (for a summary of the hypotheses presented in this chapter, see Table 2.2). With a statistical approach, we can assess whether extractive capacity affects the conflict behavior of unstable states as predicted, while controlling for the influence of other factors, and increase our confidence that any findings are generalizable by examining a large number of cases. The quantitative analysis also lays the groundwork for the historical cases discussed in chapters 4 through 6. Having demonstrated that the proposed relationship between extractive capacity and the outbreak of interstate war and low-level conflict generally holds, I then investigate in a series of in-depth case studies whether the manner by which extractive capacity shapes government decision making matches the causal pathways mapped out above.

The second study examines whether diversionary wars are better at restoring social order than the other options on the policy menu. Here, using quantitative methods allows us to simultaneously assess the effect of adopting each policy on domestic unrest and then draw general lessons about their relative utility.

3   Quantitative Results

THIS CHAPTER USES STATISTICAL TECHNIQUES TO EXPLORE THE conditions under which unstable governments fight diversionary wars and to evaluate whether foreign adventure is more effective at reducing domestic unrest than other responses. The results suggest that diversionary war is most often undertaken by pauper states—and here, full-scale war may not have been the original intent. Furthermore, distracting the public with the threat or use of force abroad is typically an ineffectual strategy.

The first part of the chapter examines the causes of diversionary war and the second its consequences. The chapter concludes with a discussion of the empirical strategy employed in the remainder of the book.

The Frequency of Diversionary Wars and Spectacles Among Princely and Pauper States

The model of policy substitutability presented in Chapter 2 views government decisions as the product of (1) a leader's preferences, or the policies that he or she would adopt in a perfect world, and (2) a set of environmental factors, or the external constraints and opportunities that determine whether those policies are practicable. This section explores how a particular environmental factor—extractive capacity, or a state's ability to efficiently mobilize societal resources—influences whether governments provoke diversionary wars and spectacles. In the preceding chapter I argue that when demonstrators take to the streets, princely and pauper states are equally likely to stage low-cost diversionary spectacles (Hypothesis 1), but pauper states are more likely to be drawn into full-scale diversionary wars (Hypothesis 2). Desperate regimes may be prone to overconfidence and stage spectacles against targets that are likely to resist.

I evaluate these claims by examining the conflict behavior of 117 countries over a 22-year period. This statistical analysis finds support for both hypotheses. Whether governments provoke low-level spectacles is not contingent on their extractive capacity. And pauper states are more likely than princely states to fight interstate wars during periods of domestic unrest.

Below I describe the data used to evaluate the relationship among extractive capacity, domestic unrest, and foreign adventurism and then present the results of the analysis.

Dependent Variables: Interstate War and Low-Level Spectacles

To assess the relative propensity of princely and pauper states to initiate wars and spectacles during periods of unrest, I created two dependent variables using the Militarized Interstate Disputes (MID) data set (Version 3.1), which records four types of state conflict behavior: threats to use force, displays of force (such as fortifying a contested border), uses of force (such as imposing a blockade), and interstate war.[1] The first dependent variable is *low-level spectacle*, which is coded 1 for years when a MID began in which a state threatened to use force, engaged in a show of force, or used force short of war. Years in which no such conflict began are coded 0 (see Appendix 3.1 for descriptive statistics for all variables discussed in this chapter). The second dependent variable is *interstate war*. The war indicator documents whether a state became involved in a dispute categorized as an interstate war in a given year—that is, a militarized dispute resulting in greater than 1,000 battle-related fatalities.[2]

Independent Variables: Extractive Capacity and Domestic Unrest

Extractive capacity$_{t-1}$ is measured using an indicator originated by Jacek Kugler and A. F. K. Organski and later updated by Kugler and Marina Arbetman, which they label "relative political extraction."[3] I define extractive capacity as the ease with which governments mobilize resources from society. Relative political extraction is a good approximation of what I term extractive capacity because Kugler and Arbetman's measure is specifically designed to assess "efficiency" in transferring "resources from the population to the government to allow the government to achieve its policy goals."[4]

In order to evaluate each state's extractive capacity (i.e., relative political extraction) in a given year, Kugler and Arbetman calculate two statistics: one measuring the tax revenues that a government could collect based on the country's total societal economic resources (i.e., "predicted government revenue") and one measuring the amount the government actually extracted (i.e., "actual government revenue"). The predicted state revenue for a given country is obtained using the parameter estimates produced by running an ordinary least squares regression on the following model:

$$\frac{Tax}{GDP} = \beta_0 + \beta_1(Time) + \beta_2\left(\frac{Mining}{GDP}\right) + \beta_3\left(\frac{Agriculture}{GDP}\right) + \beta_4\left(\frac{Exports}{GDP}\right) + \varepsilon$$

Finally, a ratio is calculated using these two statistics to identify governments that collected a larger (or smaller) than expected amount of tax revenues from society in a given year, based on economic factors:

$$Extractive\ Capacity = \frac{Actual\ Government\ Revenue}{Predicted\ Government\ Revenue}$$

If the ratio of actual to predicted revenue is greater than 1, then that government is better than expected at extracting revenue—here termed a princely state. For example, a value of 2 indicates that the state's ability to mobilize resources is twice that of the value predicted for that country. An extractive capacity ratio of less than 1 indicates that the government is worse than expected at extracting tax revenues (either through choice or inability)—here termed a pauper state. For example, an extractive capacity of 0.5 indicates a state whose extractive performance is half that of the predicted value for that government.[5]

When one considers which countries are categorized as princely and pauper states using this measure of extractive capacity, the results generally conform to one's expectations. One anticipates that relatively weak and poorly governed countries will be pauper states, and, for example, Mexico, Turkey, and the Philippines all have a low extractive capacity (see Figure 3.1).

Similarly, we expect that relatively strong and well-governed countries will be princely states, and, for example, Sweden, the United Kingdom, and France all have a high extractive capacity (see Figure 3.2).

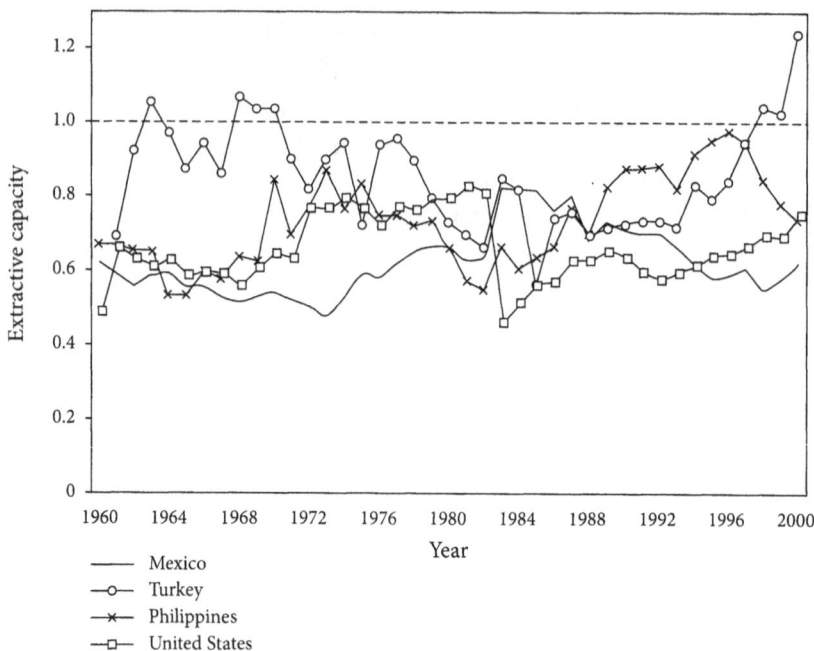

FIGURE 3.1 Examples of pauper states

SOURCE: Data from Kugler and Arbetman, "Relative Political Capacity."

However, this measure of extractive capacity does produce a few anoma-
lies. For example, the United States is coded as a pauper state. Although I
have argued that governments that are unable to easily extract revenues from
society have fewer policy options, it is quite possible that the United States'
limited extractive capacity may not act as a significant constraint on its behavior because of its considerable potential to mobilize a greater percentage of
society's resources in extremis. Thus, there may be a small number of sleeping
giants in the analysis: governments that limit their take from society until crises rouse the nation to act. However, these exceptions are relatively rare. Most
countries do not tie their own hands to the same extent as the United States,
because of its tradition of limited government.

Extractive capacity$_{t-1}$ is lagged by one year. Involvement in an interstate
conflict or war can affect a state's ability to mobilize societal resources. If a
mission is seen as a failure, for example, the government may face additional
obstacles when trying to extract revenues from the public. Lagging *extractive
capacity*$_{t-1}$ assures that we measure the state's access to resources *before* the
outbreak of violence and not after.

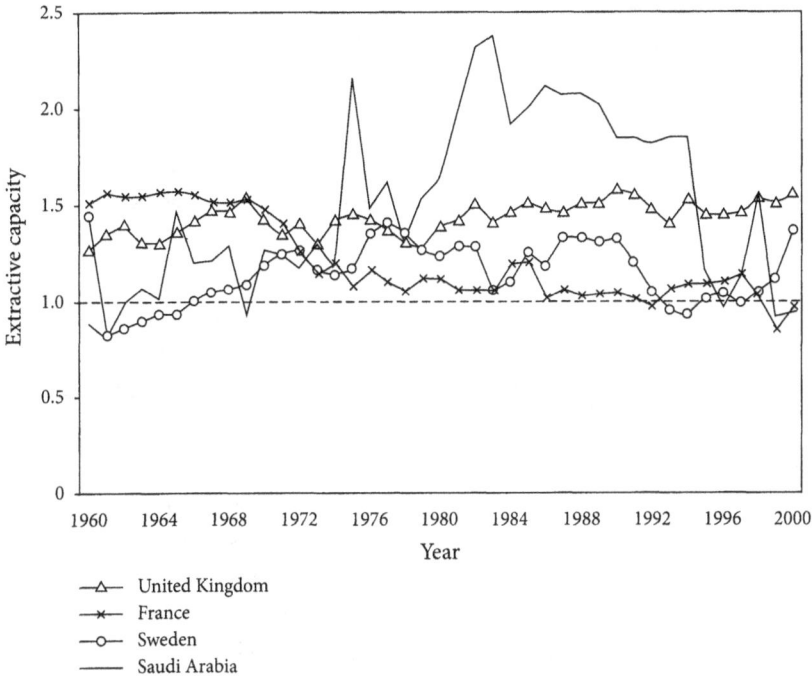

FIGURE 3.2 Examples of princely states
SOURCE: Data from Kugler and Arbetman, "Relative Political Capacity."

Domestic unrest$_{t-1}$ is constructed with a measure of social strife used in several influential statistical analyses of diversionary war: events data from the *World Handbook of Political and Social Indicators,* which tallies antigovernment protests, politically motivated strikes, riots, and armed attacks by insurgents against a government.[6] This variable counts the total number of incidents for each state in a given year.[7] An alternative would be to use a per capita measure of domestic unrest. The advantage of a per capita measure is that it does not assume that, say, 25 incidents of unrest have the same effect on countries of different sizes. That is, a moderate absolute amount of unrest could threaten the survival of the government in a small state while being merely an annoyance for the government in a more populous one. However, the limitation of using a per capita measure of unrest is that it may underestimate the threat posed by a high absolute degree of unrest in a very populous country. For example, Swaziland has a population of 1.4 million people, while China has a population of 1.4 billion people—or 1,000 times greater.

If Swaziland had 1 incident of unrest in a given year and China had 1,000 incidents of unrest in the same year, they would be coded as experiencing equivalent degrees of instability. But the Chinese leadership would be more concerned than the leadership in Swaziland about the amount of unrest their regime faced. The number of incidents necessary to overthrow a regime does not necessarily increase proportionate to population. A single mob can storm the Bastille in Swaziland or in China.

Because there will be cases in which some or even all of the unrest occurred after, or perhaps because of, the initiation of an international crisis, any results would capture both the effect of internal unrest on external conflict *and* the reverse: the impact of conflict on unrest. To address this problem, *domestic unrest$_{t-1}$* is lagged by one year, guaranteeing that the unrest predated the outbreak of international conflict.[8]

Because the hypotheses examine whether the effect of domestic unrest on a government's propensity to use force abroad varies based on its ability to mobilize societal resources, I included a multiplicative term, *domestic unrest$_{t-1}$ × extractive capacity$_{t-1}$*. Interactions are appropriate whenever the relationship between an independent and dependent variable is believed to be conditional on the values of another independent variable.

In the model of low-level spectacles, we should find that the effect of domestic unrest on the propensity of governments to provoke international crises does not depend on their extractive capacity—that is, there is no significant interaction between *domestic unrest$_{t-1}$* and *extractive capacity$_{t-1}$*.[9] And in the model of interstate war, we should find that rising domestic unrest increases the likelihood of war among pauper states but that its effect weakens as the extractive capacity of governments improves.

Control Variables

Several domestic and international-level variables were also included in the analysis to control for explanatory factors that are often found in models of diversionary war and interstate war more generally.[10] With the exception of *regime transition*, which measures changes in a state's political institutions over the preceding five-year period, the control variables were lagged by one year to ensure that they cause the dependent variable and not the reverse.

Given the large literature on the pacifying effect of democratic institutions, a variable measuring regime type was included. *Democracy$_{t-1}$* is a dichotomous measure that is coded 1 if a state is democratic and 0 if it is not.

Using the scale of regime characteristics from the Polity IV data set, which ranges from −10 (hereditary monarchy) to 10 (consolidated democracy), countries with a rating of 7 or higher were classified as democratic.[11]

As discussed in Chapter 2, many scholars have argued that whether governments respond to domestic unrest by provoking interstate wars varies by regime type—though there is no consensus regarding whether democracies or nondemocracies are more likely to use diversionary tactics. Therefore, I also included the product term *domestic unrest*$_{t-1}$ × *democracy*$_{t-1}$.

Because Mansfield and Snyder argue that states are particularly bellicose during periods of institutional change, each model includes *regime transition*. This variable is a country's Polity score at time *t* minus its Polity score at time *t*-5. Thus, if a country's policy score was 6 in 1960 (a mixed regime) and 10 in 1966 (a liberal democracy), *regime transition* would equal +4, indicating that the government democratized during the previous five-year period.

An indicator for aggregate state capabilities was included in both models, given that powerful states are more likely to initiate an interstate conflict or war. *National capabilities*$_{t-1}$, which assesses a country's military strength, was measured with the Correlates of War Composite Index of National Capabilities (Version 3.02).[12]

To assess the ease with which unstable states can find targets against which to use diversionary force, I included a measure of how often a country has been involved in wars and low-level spectacles in the past. Countries that frequently come to blows with other states may more easily find a pretext for staging a diversion. *Disputes*$_{t-1}$, which is a five-year moving average of the annual number of MIDS in which a state is involved, was included in each model.[13] This variable was then interacted with *domestic unrest*$_{t-1}$ to reveal whether internal instability increases the probability of low-level spectacles or war when there are regular opportunities to use force abroad.

An "enduring rivalry," as conceptualized by Paul Diehl and Gary Goertz, exists when there are regular militarized disputes between two states, namely at least six such conflicts within a twenty-year period.[14] Because a history of friction with an adversary increases the probability of future hostilities, *enduring rivalry*$_{t-1}$, a dichotomous variable indicating whether a state is part of an enduring rivalry, was included. Further, an enduring rivalry may increase the likelihood of low-level spectacles and wars for unstable states. Established enemies are seen as ideal targets for a diversion because confronting a hated foe promises to produce an especially large rally effect. Of course, the opposite is also possible. As the literature on strategic conflict avoidance suggests, a long-standing rival may recognize that that states facing severe unrest may find a diversionary use of force attractive and will strategically avoid quarrels until calm is restored.[15] To explore these hypotheses, I included the interaction *domestic unrest*$_{t-1}$ × *enduring rivalry*$_{t-1}$.[16]

Data Analysis

I conducted two probit analyses, one for low-level spectacles and one for interstate war.[17] This estimation technique is appropriate given the dichotomous structure of the dependent variables. However, binary models can underestimate the probability of rare events, and interstate war occurs in fewer than 2 percent of cases in the sample. Consequently, I also estimated the model of interstate war using rare-events logit.[18] For several variables, the coefficients produced by the probit and rare-events models do differ in terms of their statistical significance and signs. Therefore, I focus on the rare-events logit model, noting when and how it deviates from the probit model. Tables 3.1 and 3.2 summarize these findings.

Looking first at the results for low-level spectacles, we see that the coefficient for *domestic unrest*$_{t-1}$ × *extractive capacity*$_{t-1}$ is statistically insignificant. This suggests, as predicted in Hypothesis 1, that the effect of social strife on the likelihood of low-level spectacles is not contingent on extractive capacity—princely and pauper states are equally likely to become involved in small-scale conflicts (see Model II in Table 3.1). This finding is robust to alternative specifications of the model.[19]

In the analysis of interstate war, the coefficient for *domestic unrest*$_{t-1}$ × *extractive capacity*$_{t-1}$ is statistically significant and negative in both the rare-events logit and probit analyses (see Models II and III in Table 3.2). This finding again holds across alternative specifications of the model, such as the inclusion or exclusion of any combination of the control variables. It suggests that, as predicted, the effect of internal instability on a government's propensity for war is conditional on its extractive capacity and that the magnitude of its effect weakens as a government's access to revenues increases.

That said, one cannot infer whether internal instability has a meaningful conditional effect on the likelihood of war solely from the significance of the coefficient on the interaction term. For example, it is possible for the interaction term to be significant and, at the same time, for domestic unrest not to have a statistically significant effect on the likelihood of a major military campaign for some values of extractive capacity.[20]

TABLE 3.1 Probit analyses of low-level spectacles, 1960–1982

	Model I	Model II
Domestic unrest$_{t-1}$	0.0009**	0.0012*
	(0.0005)	(0.0008)
Extractive capacity$_{t-1}$	—	0.012
		(0.072)
Domestic unrest$_{t-1}$ × extractive capacity$_{t-1}$	—	−0.0004
		(0.0007)
Democracy$_{t-1}$	−0.142**	−0.145**
	(0.081)	(0.082)
Domestic unrest$_{t-1}$ × democracy$_{t-1}$	−0.0002	0.00001
	(0.001)	(0.001)
Regime transition	0.005	0.005
	(0.006)	(0.006)
National capabilities$_{t-1}$	6.371***	6.408***
	(1.575)	(1.644)
Enduring rivalry$_{t-1}$	0.607***	0.605***
	(0.083)	(0.083)
Domestic unrest$_{t-1}$ × enduring rivalry$_{t-1}$	−0.0009*	−0.0008
	(0.0006)	(0.0008)
Disputes$_{t-1}$	0.156***	0.157***
	(0.042)	(0.042)
Domestic unrest$_{t-1}$ × disputes$_{t-1}$	−0.00002	−0.0001
	(0.0002)	(0.0003)
Constant	−0.677***	−0.688***
	(0.086)	(0.109)
Wald X^2	556.86***	598.89***
Pseudo-R^2	0.20	0.20

NOTES: N/countries = 2,367/117
Robust standard errors (adjusted for clustering by country)
*** = $p < 0.01$; ** = $p < 0.05$; * = $p < 0.10$ (one-tailed tests)
Numbers in parentheses are standard errors.
Cubic polynomials are included in the models but not displayed.

To interpret the interaction term fully, I calculated the change in the predicted probability of an interstate war associated with an increase in domestic
unrest, along with 95-percent confidence intervals, for a range of extractive
capacities.[21] If zero is included in the confidence interval, then domestic unrest does not have a statistically significant effect on the likelihood of a major
military campaign at that particular value of extractive capacity. For instance,
if the probability of war is 0.01 for stable states with an extractive capacity

TABLE 3.2 Rare-events logit and probit analyses of interstate war, 1960–1982

	Model I	Model II	Model III[a]
Domestic unrest$_{t-1}$	0.032***	0.033***	0.002*
	(0.005)	(0.003)	(0.001)
Extractive capacity$_{t-1}$	—	0.104	0.033
		(0.294)	(0.128)
Domestic unrest$_{t-1}$ × extractive capacity$_{t-1}$	—	−0.005*	−0.003**
		(0.003)	(0.001)
Democracy$_{t-1}$	−0.009	0.005	−0.096
	(0.384)	(0.390)	(0.166)
Domestic unrest$_{t-1}$ × democracy$_{t-1}$	−0.002	−0.001	0.001
	(0.002)	(0.002)	(0.001)
Regime transition	0.026	0.021	0.011
	(0.021)	(0.022)	(0.009)
National capabilities$_{t-1}$	−3.759	−1.140	−0.778
	(4.166)	(4.515)	(2.152)
Enduring rivalry$_{t-1}$	1.900***	1.828***	0.561***
	(0.458)	(0.458)	(0.176)
Domestic unrest$_{t-1}$ × enduring rivalry$_{t-1}$	−0.027***	−0.022***	0.003**
	(0.005)	(0.004)	(0.002)
Disputes$_{t-1}$	0.281***	0.292***	0.162***
	(0.102)	(0.105)	(0.055)
Domestic unrest$_{t-1}$ × disputes$_{t-1}$	−0.0002	−0.0014	−0.0008*
	(0.0002)	(0.0012)	(0.0005)
Constant	−5.600***	−5.684***	−2.665***
	(0.398)	(0.493)	(0.189)
Wald X^2	—	—	185.45***
Pseudo-R^2	—	—	0.16

NOTES: N/countries = 2,367/117
Robust standard errors (adjusted for clustering by country)
*** = $p < 0.01$; ** = $p < 0.05$; * = $p < 0.10$ (one-tailed tests)
Numbers in parentheses are standard errors.
[a]Results from the probit analysis

of 1.5 and the probability of war increases to 0.03 when these states experience a high level of domestic unrest, then the change in probability is +0.02. However, if the confidence interval is −0.01 to 0.06—that is, if it includes zero—then the effect of domestic unrest at this value of extractive capacity is statistically insignificant.

Figure 3.3 plots these results, which were calculated based on the rare-events logit analysis (see Model II in Table 3.2).[22] The solid line indicates how

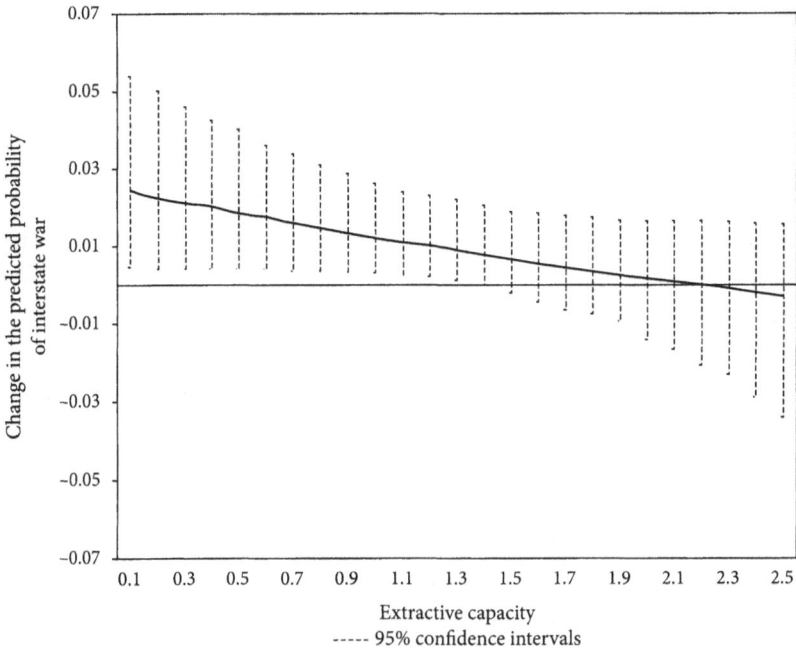

FIGURE 3.3 The effect of an increase in domestic unrest on the predicted probability of interstate war as extractive capacity varies

the effect of domestic unrest on the probability of war changes as extractive capacity increases, and the dotted lines are 95-percent confidence intervals. For states with a low (0.1) to moderate (1.3) extractive capacity, domestic unrest has a positive and statistically significant effect on the probability of an interstate war, but its effect dramatically weakens as the ability to mobilize societal resources improves. For example, the probability that a pauper state with an extractive capacity of 0.1 will fight an interstate war increases by 0.024 when the government faces significant civil strife. In comparison, the probability that a princely state with an extractive capacity of 1.3 will fight an interstate war increases only slightly (+0.009) in response to social turmoil. That is, the increase in the probability of war caused by rising domestic unrest is nearly three times larger for the poorest pauper states than for moderately wealthy princely states. More striking, for princely states with an extractive capacity above 1.3, internal instability does not have a statistically significant effect on the probability of an interstate war, as zero is included in the confidence intervals. The absence of a relationship between social dissent and decisions for war is unsurprising given that these leaders have ample resources to adopt alternative and less-risky responses to instability. Thus, as Hypothesis 2 predicts, regimes with an uncertain political future may fight diversionary wars, but this outcome will be more common among pauper states than princely ones.

The analyses also shed light on the other prominent arguments regarding the conditions under which governments use diversionary tactics. First, *domestic unrest*$_{t-1}$ × *democracy*$_{t-1}$ is not statistically significant in any of the models of low-level spectacles and interstate war. In other words, the effect of domestic unrest on the probability of conflict abroad is not contingent on regime type—both elected leaders and unelected leaders may use a bellicose foreign policy to distract a disgruntled public from problems at home.

Second, the findings do not corroborate Mansfield and Snyder's claim that a recent institutional change increases the likelihood of foreign adventurism. The coefficient for *regime transition* is positive in all of the models, which is consistent with their argument, but it is not statistically significant.

Third, *disputes*$_{t-1}$ × *domestic unrest*$_{t-1}$ is negative in the models of low-level spectacles and interstate war, which suggests that states in dangerous neighborhoods are less likely to engage in conflict abroad while experiencing internal instability. As the number of potential adversaries grows, there may be more targets against which to use diversionary tactics—but it is also more likely that the state will be stabbed in the back by a third party if it becomes embroiled in another conflict. That said, the coefficient is statistically insignificant in the analyses of low-level spectacles and the rare-events logit analysis of interstate war.

Finally, low-level spectacles and interstate wars are more likely among unstable states that are not party to an enduring rivalry. *Domestic unrest*$_{t-1}$ × *enduring rivalry*$_{t-1}$ is negative and just misses statistical significance at the 90-percent confidence level in the model of low-level spectacles. However, when any of the other multiplicative terms, which consistently fail to achieve significance, are omitted from the model, the interaction between *domestic unrest*$_{t-1}$ and *enduring rivalry*$_{t-1}$ is significant. For example, in Model I, which excludes *domestic unrest*$_{t-1}$ × *extractive capacity*$_{t-1}$, this interaction is significant at the 90-percent level of confidence (see Table 3.1).

Calculating the change in the probability of a low-level spectacle because of rising unrest for states in an enduring rivalry, and for those that are not, reveals that internal instability has a significant effect only for countries without an established adversary. The change in the probability of war for states without a rival is 0.025 (with a 90-percent confidence interval of 0.001 to 0.050), and for states with a rival it is 0.001 (with a 90-percent confidence interval of −0.031 to 0.034).[23]

In the analyses of interstate war, *domestic unrest*$_{t-1}$ × *enduring rivalry*$_{t-1}$ is consistently significant. However, in the probit model the coefficient is positive, and in the rare-events logit model it is negative—that is, it switches signs. The results of rare-event logit estimation indicate that rising domestic unrest increases the probability of war for states without long-standing enemies by 0.029, with a 95-percent confidence interval of 0.012 to 0.064. And growing internal instability also increases the probability of a major military campaign for states with rivals, but to a lesser extent—by 0.012, with a 95-percent confidence interval of 0.004 to 0.028.[24]

These findings are consistent with the literature on strategic conflict avoidance, which maintains that the use of diversionary tactics is unlikely when an unstable state is part of an enduring rivalry, because its rival, and likely target, will recognize the heightened potential for escalation and dodge any disputes. And the results are at odds with the claim that shaky regimes are more likely to use force abroad when they have a long-standing enemy because such adversaries are seen as especially attractive targets for diversionary action.

Two additional findings deserve mention. First, *enduring rivalry*$_{t-1}$ and *disputes*$_{t-1}$ are positive and statistically significant in all of the models. The coefficients for these variables represent their effect on the likelihood of an interstate war or low-level spectacle when there are no incidents of unrest in a given year.[25] We see that in the absence of social turmoil, a history of conflict, either with a single rival or many adversaries, makes both small-scale disputes and interstate wars more likely.

Second, the coefficient for *extractive capacity*$_{t-1}$, which is the effect of a government's ability to mobilize societal resources upon the likelihood of external conflict during times of domestic stability, is consistently positive in the models of low-level spectacles and interstate war. This is in line with arguments made by neoclassical realists, such as Fareed Zakaria and Thomas Christensen, that wealthy states are more likely to adopt bellicose foreign policies. But, surprisingly, *extractive capacity*$_{t-1}$ is not significant in either the model of low-level spectacles or the model of interstate war.

In summary, the foregoing analysis provides empirical support for hypotheses 1 and 2. When demonstrators take to the streets, princely and pauper states are equally likely to rattle their sabers, but pauper states are more likely to find themselves in full-scale wars.

Do Diversionary Wars Work? An Empirical Test

As discussed in Chapter 2, existing studies provide at most a partial answer to the question of whether diversionary wars work. Only one study has directly examined whether interstate war reduces domestic unrest—finding that it restores stability in democracies while producing greater instability in nondemocracies—and none explore whether this option is a better remedy for social turmoil than the alternatives on the policy menu.

To evaluate whether interstate war is a more-successful strategy for managing domestic unrest than other options on the policy menu—namely low-level spectacles, economic reform, political reform, repression, foreign intervention, and muddling through—I examine the extent to which each strategy has a dampening effect on domestic unrest in 132 countries over a 34-year period.

Interstate war does not distract the public from problems at home. And it is a less-effective strategy for managing unrest than other options on the policy menu. Similarly, low-level spectacles are also misguided response to internal troubles. Indeed, regardless of regime type, spectacles are destabilizing. Thus, the principal lesson for unpopular governments is that they should avoid foreign adventurism.

In the following sections I describe the data and models used to evaluate the relative utility of the responses to domestic unrest and present the results of the analysis.

Dependent Variable: Domestic Unrest

To measure internal stability, now the dependent variable, I again use data drawn from the *World Handbook of Political and Social Indicators*.[26] *Domestic unrest* is an annual count of antigovernment demonstrations, strikes, riots, and armed attacks targeted against the government.

Independent Variables: Alternative Policy Responses to Domestic Unrest

The independent variables are the five options on the policy menu that governments may adopt in response to domestic unrest. Each variable is lagged one year to ensure that the decision to adopt a particular policy was made before the observed level of domestic unrest. Although this does not allow us to gauge the immediate effect of these policies, it will reveal their medium-term consequences.

As in the models above, *low-level spectacle*$_{t-1}$ was constructed using the MID data set and was coded 1 for years when a dispute began in which a state threatened to use force, made a show of force, or engaged in a limited use of force.[27] Years in which such a dispute did not begin were coded 0. *Interstate war*$_{t-1}$ was also created using MID data and records whether a war, namely a dispute resulting at least 1,000 battle-related deaths, began in a given year.

Repression$_{t-1}$ was constructed from the *World Handbook of Political and Social Indicators* and catalogs instances when a government imposed "negative sanctions" in a given year.[28] A negative sanction includes any attempt by the state to suppress or eliminate a domestic threat to the security of the government—for example, by instructing national or local police units to imprison or execute dissidents, arresting protestors, limiting or intimidating the mass media, and imposing curfews. To test the hypothesis that there is an inverted-U-shaped relationship between repression and unrest—that is, whether moderate oppression stokes antigovernment sentiment—the square of *repression*$_{t-1}$ was also included in the model (see Hypothesis 5).

Political reform$_{t-1}$ records the number of times a state modified or eliminated "negative sanctions" against regime opponents during a given year, for example, by reducing government controls on the popular media, permitting free assembly, allowing political parties to reorganize, granting opposition elites the right to speak publicly against the government, and ending martial law or compulsory military service.[29] This indicator is a better approximation of political reform than, say, a general measure of institutional change constructed from Polity, as it specifically identifies attempts by the government to conciliate opposition groups.

As discussed in Chapter 2, scholars have examined whether social spending and integration into the global economy reduce internal instability. *Government expenditures*$_{t-1}$ is the log of total government spending in a given year.[30] The data for this indicator were drawn from the Arthur Banks *Cross-National Times-Series Data Archive* (CNTS).[31] *Economic liberalization*, as discussed above, measures how the ratio of exports plus imports as a percentage of gross domestic product changes for each country over a five-year period, using data from the Penn World Tables and the International Monetary Fund.[32] Because this variable calculates changes in exposure to the global economy over an extended span of time, it allows us to assess the effect of longer-term trends in openness on internal instability and more accurately test Hypothesis 8 (economic liberalization reduces domestic unrest in the long run).

Foreign intervention$_{t-1}$ was created with data taken from the International Military Intervention (INT) data set, which documents cases in which a state is the target of a unilateral or multilateral military intervention.[33] An international military intervention is the movement of regular troops or forces (naval, air, and/or ground) of one country into the territory or territorial waters of another country, including shelling locations in the target country. This indicator also includes forceful military action by troops already stationed by one country inside the target state. An intervention has not occurred when the activities include only transporting arms or materiel into the target state, or covert subversion in the target state. The INT data set also codes the purpose of the intervention—for example, whether the intervening state intended to aid regime opponents or to support the government. Only foreign military interventions that were intended to assist the government against rebel groups were included in the analysis. Therefore, *foreign intervention*$_{t-1}$ counts the number of times a state was the target of a military intervention in a given year and the intervening actor's goal was to assist the government.

The analysis below also examines the wisdom of selecting none of the options on the policy menu, or "muddling through." Here the government aims to survive long enough for some unforeseen development to strengthen the state and/or weaken the opposition.

In order to determine whether the efficacy of these strategies varies depending on regime type, as is often predicted in the extant literature, I divided the sample into democratic states (a Polity score of 7 or greater), nondemocratic states (a Polity score of –7 or below), and mixed regimes (a Polity score between –6 and 6), and reestimated the models.[34]

Control Variables

The analyses also control for several variables that are thought to affect levels of domestic unrest. The log of a state's population is one of the most widely cited and well-supported correlates of domestic unrest, with the consensus being that countries with larger populations are more likely to experience instability.[35] This finding may be due to the greater ease with which opposition movements can recruit followers—as the pool of potential rebels grows, the probability that rebellious action will be punished declines, making protest more attractive.[36] *Population* is calculated with data from the CNTS.[37]

A number of studies have found that prosperity reduces the probability of severe domestic unrest.[38] Therefore, the model includes *economic growth*$_{t-1}$, which is the percentage change in GDP per capita. These data were also taken from the CNTS.[39]

James Fearon and David Laitin, among others, have hypothesized that ethnically diverse societies are less prone to major violence because "small ethnic groups must join coalitions to have political influence, and there are many possibilities for cross-cutting and shifts in coalition membership."[40] *Ethnic fractionalization* represents the probability that two randomly selected individuals are from different ethno-linguistic groups. Higher levels of ethnic fractionalization are expected to lower the risk of social upheaval, in particular civil war.

Finally, I included a lag of the dependent variable—*domestic unrest*$_{t-1}$. This variable was added because unrest in a previous year is generally thought to be a strong predictor of future unrest, which is to say that there is a contagion effect. Antigovernment violence can trigger further rebellion, as people become confident that they are both not alone in their dissatisfaction with the government and may be successful.[41] Given that the amount of unrest experienced in one year (at time t-1) is expected to influence the amount unrest in the following year (at time t), including *domestic unrest*$_{t-1}$ is an effective way to control for temporal dependence.[42]

Data Analysis

To test the relative effectiveness of interstate war and alternative strategies for managing unrest, I used negative binomial regression, which is appropriate for analyzing dependent variables that are event counts—that is, nonnegative integers.[43] In this case, the dependent variable counts the number of incidents of domestic unrest occurring in each year. Table 3.3 reports the estimates of these models. Column 1 presents the results for the entire sample, while columns 2, 3, and 4 are the estimates for democracies, nondemocracies, and mixed regimes.

The analysis reveals that, regardless of regime type, low-level spectacles trigger wider social instability. The coefficient for *low-level spectacles*$_{t-1}$ is consistently positive and achieves statistical significance in every model. The coefficient for *interstate war*$_{t-1}$ is positive for democracies and mixed regimes and

TABLE 3.3 Negative binomial regression model of domestic unrest, 1948–1982

	All states	Democratic states	Nondemocratic states	Mixed regimes
Interstate war$_{t-1}$	0.121	0.052	−0.146	0.433
	(0.306)	(0.186)	(0.409)	(0.694)
Low-level spectacle$_{t-1}$	0.456***	0.466**	0.182*	0.479**
	0.143	(0.230)	(0.141)	(0.219)
Repression$_{t-1}$	0.038***	0.046***	0.016**	0.032***
	(0.009)	(0.016)	(0.010)	(0.011)
Repression$^2_{t-1}$	−0.0002***	−0.0003***	−0.0002***	−0.0001***
	(0.00004)	0.0001	0.00004	0.00003
Political reform$_{t-1}$	−0.002	−0.006	0.084***	−0.022
	(0.014)	(0.013)	(0.032)	(0.022)
Economic liberalization	0.001	0.018*	−0.018***	0.004
	(0.009)	(0.011)	(0.006)	(0.010)
Government expenditures$_{t-1}$	−0.054	−0.027	−0.100**	0.051
	(0.057)	(0.089)	(0.054)	(0.090)
Foreign intervention$_{t-1}$	0.601**	0.521	0.212	0.665*
	(0.306)	(0.509)	(0.269)	(0.474)
Population	0.368***	0.390***	0.368***	0.184
	(0.108)	(0.159)	(0.090)	(0.159)
Economic growth$_{t-1}$	−0.493	0.955	−0.133	−0.334
	(0.988)	(2.289)	(0.546)	(1.551)
Ethnic fractionalization	−0.775***	−0.345	−0.622**	−0.821*
	(0.331)	(0.562)	(0.334)	(0.548)
Domestic unrest$_{t-1}$	0.010***	0.005***	0.033***	0.010**
	(0.004)	(0.001)	(0.005)	(0.005)
Constant	−0.334	−1.703	−0.167*	−0.124
	(1.030)	(1.873)	(0.905)	(1.352)
	$X^2 = 180.07$***	$X^2 = 265.08$***	$X^2 = 218.85$***	$X^2 = 89.51$***
	$\alpha = 3.059$	$\alpha = 2.591$	$\alpha = 2.977$	$\alpha = 2.194$
	$N = 3{,}152$	$N = 938$	$N = 1{,}464$	$N = 750$

NOTES: Robust standard errors (adjusted for clustering by country)
*** = $p < 0.01$; ** = $p < 0.05$; * = $p < 0.10$ (one-tailed tests)
Numbers in parentheses are standard errors.

negative for nondemocracies; that is, war destabilizes governments in more-open societies while benefiting governments in closed ones. But *interstate war$_{t-1}$* is statistically insignificant in each model, meaning that we cannot with confidence rule out the possibility that a major military campaign simply has no effect on levels of domestic unrest. Why might low-level spectacles, which presumably impose fewer costs on society, produce more opposition than full-scale wars? One possibility is that the public is willing to protest the country's role in limited conflicts, but they see open dissent as unpatriotic during major military campaigns.

The findings regarding regime type and the efficacy of diversionary war are contrary to prior research, which has concluded that initiating an interstate war benefits democratic leaders and erodes public support for autocratic ones (Hypothesis 3). The signs on the coefficients for *interstate war*$_{t-1}$ suggest that the opposite may be the case: if any states profit from a bellicose foreign policy, it is nondemocracies. But because *interstate war*$_{t-1}$ is consistently insignificant, it is more likely that major military campaigns do not produce the desired rally-around-the-flag effect for any governments—war does not significantly aggravate a regime's domestic troubles, but it does not ameliorate them either. While diversionary wars may be, at best, futile, low-level spectacles are hazardous for all regimes. Thus, prudent leaders recognize that foreign adventurism is either an ineffectual or ill-fated response to a disgruntled public and place it low on their ranking of preferred policy options.

Turning to the results for the alternatives on the policy menu, we see that repressing dissent is also a dangerous course of action for embattled regimes. The coefficient for *repression*$_{t-1}$, which represents the overall effect of this variable on domestic unrest, is positive and statistically significant, meaning that public disapproval generally intensifies as a government becomes more oppressive. But *repression*$^2_{t-1}$ is negative and statistically significant, indicating that the effect of adopting this policy on internal stability is nonlinear. Specifically, there is an inverted-U-shaped relationship between repression and incidents of domestic unrest: moderate levels of repression produce the strongest backlash. We also see that this finding holds across regime types—even autocratic leaders do not benefit from repression. This represents support for Hypothesis 5 (repression has an inverted-U-shaped effect on unrest), but not for Hypothesis 4 (repression has a positive, linear effect on unrest) or Hypothesis 6 (whether repression stifles unrest varies by regime type).

Prior research on political reform suggests that governments adopt this policy at their peril: granting political concessions signals weakness to domestic opponents and fans the flames of discontent (see Hypothesis 7). However, this analysis finds that political reforms fuel protest only in nondemocratic states. In the model for nondemocracies, the coefficient for *political reform*$_{t-1}$ is positive and statistically significant. But for democracies and mixed regimes, this variable is insignificant.

This result may be due to the fact that in nondemocracies, political reform gives regime opponents a taste of liberty, prompting them to press for further changes in government policy. In a democracy, or even in many mixed regimes, the public already enjoys many freedoms, and political reform satisfies their appetite for change or at least does not lead to wider unrest.

Nondemocratic governments are buttressed by greater integration in the global economy, even when controlling for economic growth. For these states, *economic liberalization* is negative and statistically significant. In contrast, there is some evidence that unrest intensifies as policy makers in democracies liberalize their national economies. *Economic liberalization* is positive and statistically significant for these states. These findings partially substantiate Hypothesis 8: exposure to the international economy can shore up unstable governments—but only in nondemocratic states. This pattern may be because of the greater ease with which any economic losers from globalization can register their disapproval with government policy in democratic regimes.

In each model the coefficients for *government expenditures$_{t-1}$* are negative, suggesting that increasing government spending bolsters all regimes. But this variable is statistically significant only for nondemocracies. This may be because in authoritarian countries a few strategic groups—such as business, the military, the church, and labor unions—have considerable control over the degree of opposition to the state, and these groups can be bought off. In open societies, there are a multitude of interest groups that can organize against the state, and it will be difficult to distribute sufficient resources to satisfy all of them. Hypothesis 9, which predicts that investing in social programs has an ameliorative effect on internal instability, is then only partly substantiated by these results.

Finally, there is some evidence that foreign military interventions foment civil unrest. *Foreign intervention$_{t-1}$* is statistically significant and positive in the model for the full sample and for mixed regimes. The coefficient also narrowly misses achieving statistical significance in the model for democracies, where it is again positive.[44] As *foreign intervention$_{t-1}$* is lagged by one year, we are testing the medium-term effects of adopting this policy option. And these findings are roughly in line with the first half of Hypothesis 10, which posits that third-party military assistance is initially destabilizing. To explore the longer-range consequences of this policy for social unrest, I then estimated additional models with different lags on the foreign intervention variable (two, five, and ten years). Nearly all of these variables were positive, but few achieved statistical significance. Only *foreign intervention*$_{t-5}$ and *foreign intervention*$_{t-10}$ were significant and only in one model—that for democracies. Both were also positive. Therefore, foreign military intervention does not seem to pay off, even in the longer term. Together, these results run counter to the second half of Hypothesis 10 (intervention quiets unrest in the long run) and Hypothesis 11 (intervention steadily moderates unrest over time).

Regarding the control variables, the results are largely in line with findings in the extant literature. Larger states experience higher rates of social protest. Ethnically diverse societies are less likely to experience civil unrest. Domestic unrest is also contagious: once citizens begin airing their grievances, they tend to challenge the state in the future. The one exception is *economic growth*$_{t-1}$. In the past, scholars have found that economic growth reduces opposition to the state. However, here it is statistically insignificant in each of the models, indicating that an expanding economy has no effect on unrest in any regime type.

To determine the magnitude with which the policy alternatives affect internal stability, I calculated the percentage change in predicted incidents of unrest after a strategy is adopted. The baseline is the amount of turmoil a state experiences if none of the policies are implemented—that is, muddling through—and in the case of muddling through it is the median amount of unrest experienced in the previous year (see Table 3.4).[45] This will reveal (1) whether the extent to which a policy influences domestic unrest varies by regime type and (2) whether a policy is a better (or worse) response to social disorder than selecting another option from the menu.

Examining how the extent to which the policy options shape domestic unrest differs across regime types produces several results of note. First, staging a low-level spectacle has a large adverse effect on the size of the government's opposition. That said, a low-level spectacle is less risky for nondemocracies (a 16.7-percent increase in unrest) than for democracies and mixed regimes (approximately a 60-percent increase for both). It seems that in a more-open political system, any misstep in the government's handling of an international crisis invites additional criticism from an already skeptical public that has access to more official avenues of protest.

Second, the political fallout from repression is greater in democracies (a 253.3-percent increase in unrest) and mixed regimes (a 152.8-percent increase)

TABLE 3.4 Percentage change in incidents of domestic unrest across regime types

	All states	Democratic states	Nondemocratic states	Mixed regimes
Interstate war	+12.2	+5.0	−16.7	+53.9
	(5.5)	(6.3)	(2.0)	(13.7)
Low-level spectacles	+57.1	+58.3	+16.7	+60.7
	(7.7)	(9.5)	(2.8)	(14.3)
Repression	+202.0	+253.3	+29.2	+152.8
	(14.8)	(21.2)	(3.1)	(22.5)
Political reform	−2.0	−5.0	+75.0	−14.6
	(4.8)	(5.7)	(4.2)	(7.6)
Economic liberalization	+2.0	+46.7	−33.3	+9.0
	(5.0)	(8.8)	(1.6)	(9.7)
Government expenditures	−16.3	−6.7	−33.3	+23.6
	(4.1)	(5.6)	(1.6)	(11.0)
Foreign intervention	+81.6	+66.7	+20.8	+93.3
	(8.9)	(10.0)	(2.9)	(17.2)
Muddling through	+145.0	+200.0	+20.0	+345.0
	(4.9)	(6.0)	(2.4)	(8.9)

NOTES: Results in **bold** are statistically significant at the 90-percent confidence level or higher. Predicted counts are in parentheses.

than in nondemocracies (a 29.2-percent increase). This finding is likely because of the fact that the suppression of dissent is viewed as illegitimate in freer societies and will trigger widespread opposition to the government.

Finally, doing nothing—that is, muddling through—is generally a poor response to social turmoil, which is consistent with Hypothesis 13. The predicted counts were calculated assuming two incidents of unrest in the prior year, the median value for *domestic unrest*$_{t-1}$. In each model, internal instability increases if no action is taken. That said, muddling through is more detrimental to democracies and mixed regimes than to nondemocracies. If autocratic leaders adopt none of the policy alternatives, unrest will increase by only 0.4 incidents (a 20-percent increase). However, if leaders of democracies fail to respond, unrest will triple, from 2 to 6 annual incidents (a 200-percent increase). And in mixed regimes, inaction will cause unrest to increase from 2 to 8.9 incidents (a 345-percent increase). In closed societies, therefore, the absence of state action may make it harder to recruit new protesters to join the barricades. But elected leaders are punished for turning a deaf ear to the demands of domestic opponents.

Having evaluated the utility of the options on the policy menu in isolation, how then do they compare? For leaders of ailing democratic regimes, political reform and increased government spending may offer the best hope of easing their domestic woes—though their effect is weak and the coefficients are statistically insignificant. The overall lack of clearly beneficial strategies for reducing unrest in democratic regimes is striking and may stem from the challenge of simultaneously pleasing a wide range of constituencies in free societies, where any disgruntled citizen can take to the streets.

However tempting, repression should be avoided in democracies and mixed regimes. Aside from muddling through, it produces the largest increase in antigovernment protests, demonstrations, and strikes. Externally oriented responses to unrest, from interstate war and low-level spectacles to foreign military intervention, are also ill-advised, being ineffectual if not counterproductive.

In more-open societies, therefore, domestic problems likely have domestic solutions. In particular, governments must address the underlying causes of unrest, whether it is meeting the political demands of regime opponents or improving their economic lot.

Autocratic leaders hoping to restore internal order are best served by adopting economic reform measures, either liberalizing the economy or increasing government spending. Indeed, if both policies are pursued, instability drops from 2.4 to 1.1 incidents (a 54.2-percent decrease)—a larger effect than implementing each strategy alone. The results caution nondemocratic governments against either enacting political reforms or attempting repression. These regimes would be better served by simply trying to ride out their domestic problems than by trying to either quash or placate the opposition.

In summary, this analysis addresses the previously overlooked but important question of the relative success of state strategies for reducing domestic unrest. And it demonstrates that diversionary wars and spectacles generally do not work.

· · ·

Finding evidence of a general relationship between extractive capacity and the use of diversionary tactics—namely that pauper states and princely states may be equally likely to become involved in low-level spectacles but that pauper states are more likely to fight diversionary wars—is an important initial step

TABLE 3.5 Summary of results

Support?	Hypothesis
Yes	*Hypothesis 1*: Princely states and pauper states are equally likely to stage diversionary spectacles.
Yes	*Hypothesis 2*: Pauper states are more likely than princely states to fight diversionary wars.
No	*Hypothesis 3*: Interstate war reduces domestic unrest in democracies while increasing domestic unrest in nondemocracies.
No	*Hypothesis 4*: Repression increases domestic unrest.
Yes	*Hypothesis 5*: Moderate repression increases domestic unrest.
No	*Hypothesis 6*: In nondemocracies, moderate repression reduces domestic unrest. In democracies, repression increases domestic unrest.
Partial	*Hypothesis 7*: Political reforms increase domestic unrest.
Partial	*Hypothesis 8*: Economic liberalization reduces domestic unrest in the long term.
Partial	*Hypothesis 9*: Government social spending reduces domestic unrest.
Partial	*Hypothesis 10*: Pro-government foreign military interventions increase domestic unrest in the short run and reduce unrest in the long run.
No	*Hypothesis 11*: Pro-government foreign military interventions reduce domestic unrest.
No	*Hypothesis 12*: Muddling through reduces domestic unrest.
Yes	*Hypothesis 13*: Muddling through increases domestic unrest.

in evaluating the arguments presented in Chapter 2 (for a list of the quantitative results by hypothesis, see Table 3.5).

However, the statistics do not reveal the *process* by which extractive capacity affects a leader's decision-making calculus. Using a model of decision making based on the concept of policy substitutability, I outlined the main pathways by which leader preferences and extractive capacity interact to prompt unstable governments to use diversionary tactics. Evaluating whether extractive capacity influences government decisions along these causal pathways is best accomplished with the careful study of individual cases. Only a qualitative approach allows one to (1) construct the leader's policy ranking, from most-preferred to least-preferred strategy for addressing domestic unrest; (2) determine whether the preferred option was practicable, given the state's extractive capacity; and (3) demonstrate that the ability (or inability) to mobilize sufficient resources to fund the preferred policy contributed to the leader's decision whether to pursue that avenue. In the following chapters, therefore, I conduct in-depth case studies to investigate several of these causal pathways.

More specifically, I focus on the causal pathways that result in pauper states fighting diversionary wars, staging spectacles that do not escalate to war, and avoiding the use of diversionary tactics entirely. There is particular benefit in understanding the behavior of pauper states because, as the large-N analysis demonstrates, they are more likely than princely states to wage wars during periods of internal instability. Furthermore, the operation of extractive capacity is not easily detected in princely states, where resources function mainly as a permissive condition. In other words, wealthy governments may not explicitly discuss or even recognize how their resources open up the menu of options. They take for granted that a wide number of responses are affordable and focus on the merits of each. Instead, the role of extractive capacity is more apparent in pauper states, where the inability to mobilize societal resources powerfully and explicitly shapes the menu of available options for managing unrest, channeling actors away from their preferred response toward a less-desired policy.

I also conduct a comparative analysis of the cases selected to examine these pathways.[46] The aim is to increase our confidence in the set of factors that, I argue, influences whether pauper states use diversionary tactics and engage in diversionary spectacles that are especially likely to escalate. To help with the comparison, all of the case studies follow the same template.[47] After presenting the decision maker's policy ranking, I systematically identify the environmental factors that contributed to the government's final policy choice, either by enabling or limiting its ability to pursue the preferred responses to domestic unrest. This method reveals which conditions seem to correlate with changes in the policy outcome.

The first causal pathway I examine is the one most likely to culminate in a diversionary war (see Figure 3.4). Here, facing a lack of alternatives, a pauper state stages a spectacle, but mistakenly selects a high-risk target that retaliates, escalating the dispute into an unwanted war. To evaluate the plausibility of this logic, one must analyze a case in which a pauper state is believed to have initiated a diversionary war and then trace the actual causal process that led to the final policy choice.

One should note that the particular pathway followed in the case—including how the government ranked the options on the policy menu—was unknown at the time of case selection. And if I were to find, for example, that

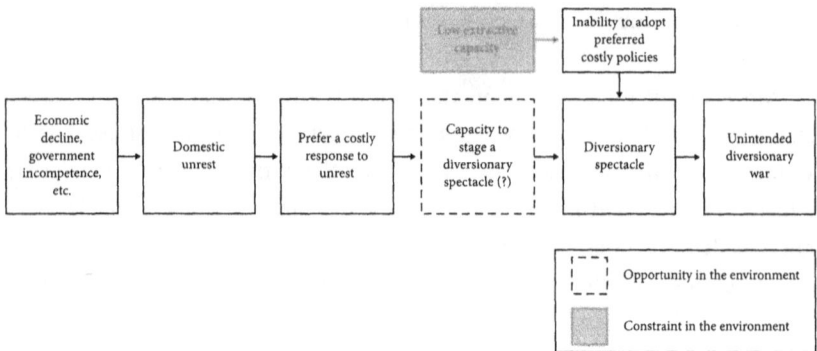

FIGURE 3.4 Causal pathway by which pauper states fight diversionary wars

the pauper state intended to fight a full-scale diversionary war, paying little heed to the cost of this policy response, the results would cast doubt on my argument.

I chose Argentina's invasion of the British Falkland Islands in 1982 for closer study because the governing junta was a pauper state and the case is widely—though not universally—regarded as an instance of diversionary war.[48] The Falklands War is also a crucial case, widely seen as a classic instance of diversionary war. In other words, it has "come to define, or at least to exemplify, a concept or theoretical outcome"—in this case the diversionary use of force.[49] Any new theory of diversionary war should produce an accurate explanation of this case. The results of the analysis are presented in Chapter 4.

In Chapter 5 I examine a diversionary spectacle orchestrated by a pauper state that did not escalate into a full-scale war—the U.S. government's anti-Mormon crusade in Utah in 1857. The basis for studying this type of case is twofold. It allows us to assess the plausibility of another of the proposed causal pathways. Figure 3.5 displays the two scenarios in which a pauper state stages a diversionary spectacle. One pathway is that the leader's preferred response to unrest is a spectacle, the government has the capacity to pursue this option, and the target puts up little resistance. Although the initiator is a pauper state, the target may be even weaker, or the target may have nothing to gain from a major military campaign.

The other pathway is that the state lacks the extractive capacity to implement the leader's preferred policies, pushing the government to stage a

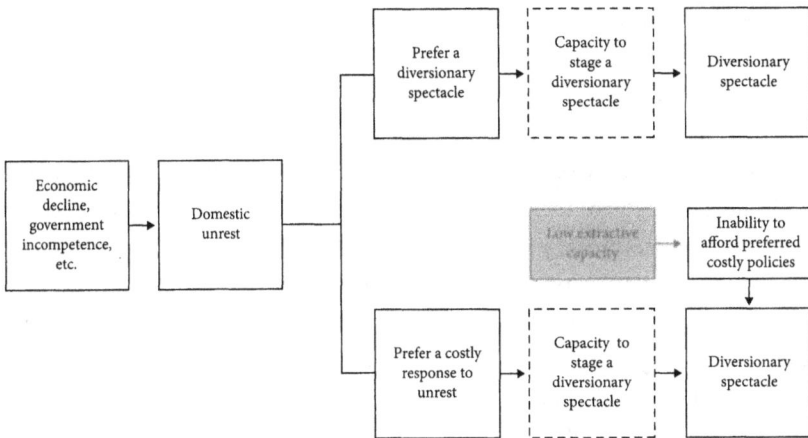

FIGURE 3.5 Causal pathways by which pauper states stage diversionary spectacles

diversionary spectacle, and, again, the target does not fight back. In this scenario, there is greater potential for an unintended escalation of the dispute as the leader, facing a rapid narrowing of options, is more likely to suffer from overconfidence and select a high-risk target. But a bias toward wishful thinking does not mean that these governments are doomed to choose high-risk targets. Only rarely will a leader wind up orchestrating a spectacle against a target that is both willing and able to fight a war, as the greater frequency of spectacles versus wars suggests.

I selected the U.S. military action against Mormon Utah for study because the government was a pauper state and the policy outcome was a suspected diversionary spectacle. Again, I did not know which (if either) of these causal pathways would play out in the case.

Examining this type of case offers another key advantage. It allows us to compare a case in which a spectacle staged by a pauper state remains a limited conflict with one that becomes a war, providing evidence of the variables that lead to escalation. We should find that the divergent outcomes are due in large part to the conditions that cause pauper states to miscalculate and select high-risk targets. In Chapter 2 I argue that when their core interests are imperiled and they have few alternative courses of action available, leaders are inclined to overestimate the chances that a policy will succeed. This may mean that they downplay the likelihood that a target will resist when they choose to stage a diversionary spectacle.

States do not always, or even usually, use diversionary tactics in response to domestic unrest. In Chapter 6 I examine three cases in which a pauper state adopted alternative strategies from the policy menu: French King Louis XVI's political reform measures to combat rising elite discontent in 1788, the Habsburg monarchy's request for Russian military intervention to extinguish the Hungarian revolution in 1849, and the Peruvian government's attempts to muddle through with a failing policy of repression against the Marxist movement Sendero Luminoso in 1988.[50]

Why study nonevents, or cases where leaders did not try to distract the public with smoke and mirrors? Although they are not discussed at length in Chapter 2, there is significant value in analyzing causal pathways that do not end in the use of diversionary tactics (see Figure 3.6). They afford additional opportunities to observe how leader preferences and extractive capacity together influence government decision making. If the government chooses not to orchestrate a spectacle, it may be because an alternative option is both higher on the leader's policy ranking and affordable, such as political reform, requesting foreign intervention, or muddling through. Or, alternatively, a diversionary spectacle is viewed as a more-attractive response to unrest

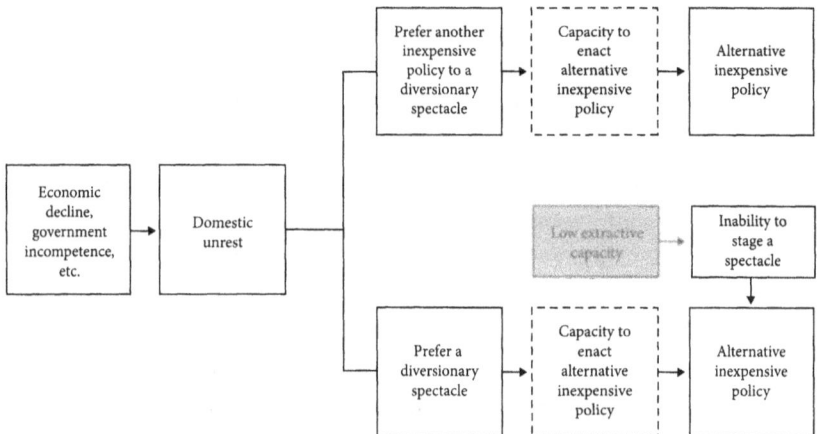

FIGURE 3.6 Causal pathways by which pauper states do not use diversionary tactics

but is impracticable—for example, there is no sufficiently low-cost target available—forcing the state to select another, less-palatable policy.

Importantly, these cases also allow us to explore why some pauper states fail to recognize that they are staging a diversionary spectacle against a high-risk target (i.e., exhibit a bias toward wishful thinking) while others correctly discern the absence of a low-cost target and avoid this policy option. I argue that when pauper states select their response to domestic unrest from an extremely limited menu of available responses, they are especially likely to miscalculate and stage diversionary spectacles against countries that ultimately fight back. However, I also hypothesize that desperate pauper states will shy away from using diversionary tactics if it would mean targeting an adversary with which it has a recent history of violent conflict. For these governments, experience may triumph over hope. If the leader considered, but ultimately chose not to provoke, a diversionary spectacle because the potential for a costly escalation was too great, we have an opportunity to investigate this logic.

Although the primary goal of the case studies is to examine how extractive capacity shapes government responses to unrest and explain the conflict decisions of pauper states, they have two further purposes. First, we can uncover additional environmental factors that close off the preferred responses of leaders to unrest and propel them toward less-attractive options. If extractive capacity is held constant and government policy choices vary across the cases, this may be because of differences in leader preferences (a factor included in the substitutability model). But it may also be because of new factors uncovered in the case that are either unique to that event or are potentially generalizable to other cases.

Second, the case studies may highlight reasons why diversions fail to distract attention from domestic ills. The statistics will not tell us *why* the use of diversionary tactics has a given effect on internal stability, and there is lack of theorizing about the efficacy of diversionary war in the extant literature. Therefore, the case studies are also used to generate new insight into when and why diversions are unsuccessful. We may find that differences between the Argentine public's response to the invasion of the Falkland Islands and the American public's response to the U.S. government's expedition against Mormon Utah correspond with, say, variation in the size of the military campaigns, the popularity of the missions, the outcome of the conflicts, and so on. That is, by comparing the cases we can generate new testable hypotheses.

Appendix: Descriptive Statistics

	Minimum	Maximum	Median	Mean	Standard deviation
MODELS OF THE CAUSES OF LOW-LEVEL SPECTACLES AND INTERSTATE WAR					
Low-level spectacles	0	1	0	0.271	0.445
Interstate war	0	1	0	0.016	0.127
Domestic unrest$_{t\text{-}1}$	0	2,160	2	20.792	96.774
Extractive capacity$_{t\text{-}1}$	−4.409	4.005	0.938	0.991	0.463
Democracy$_{t\text{-}1}$	0	1	0	0.302	0.459
Regime transition	−16	18	0	−0.349	3.940
National capabilities$_{t\text{-}1}$	0.00001	0.216	0.001	0.007	0.021
Enduring rivalry$_{t\text{-}1}$	0	1	0	0.328	0.470
Disputes$_{t\text{-}1}$	0	12.6	0.2	0.700	1.303
MODELS OF POLICY SUCCESS					
Domestic unrest	0	3,091	2	20.308	101.767
Domestic unrest$_{t\text{-}1}$	0	2,160	2	19.662	86.662
Interstate war$_{t\text{-}1}$	0	1	0	0.016	0.124
Low-level spectacle$_{t\text{-}1}$	0	1	0	0.282	0.450
Repression$_{t\text{-}1}$	0	266	2	8.126	17.470
Political reform$_{t\text{-}1}$	0	94	0	1.641	4.073
Government expenditures$_{t\text{-}1}$	15.709	27.268	20.292	20.453	2.136
Economic liberalization	−110.740	152.730	1.560	3.126	12.802
Foreign intervention$_{t\text{-}1}$	0	1	0	0.025	0.156
Population	5.568	13.824	8.996	9.045	1.413
Economic growth$_{t\text{-}1}$	−1.681	0.579	0.063	0.063	0.077
Ethnic fractionalization	0.001	0.925	0.325	0.388	0.288

4 A Diversionary War

Argentina's Invasion of the British Falkland Islands, 1982

O N APRIL 2, 1982, MORE THAN 1,000 ARGENTINE MARINES
landed on the British Falkland Islands in an early-morning raid
to reclaim the contested archipelago for Buenos Aires.[1] The Argentine forces
met little resistance from the small number of British troops stationed on the
sparsely inhabited islands. Shortly after the invasion, Argentina's president,
Leopoldo Galtieri, walked onto the balcony at Casa Rosada to announce the
dramatic victory. He was visibly moved by the cheering masses that gathered
to celebrate the news in the square below. Only days before, many of those in
the crowd had called for a swift end to military rule in Argentina and retribution for the countless victims of government brutality during the so-called
"dirty war."

Argentina's invasion of the Falklands Islands is often considered the ar-
chetypal case of diversionary war. Facing an unprecedented degree of domestic opposition to the regime, the junta sought to curry favor with the public
by launching a wildly popular mission to regain a historical territory. Yet no
studies of this conflict have explained why the embattled government chose to
use diversionary tactics instead of pursuing its preferred response to the internal turmoil—a combination of orthodox economic liberalism and repression
known as the Process for National Reorganization, or simply "the Process."

Using the policy substitutability approach, we see that Argentina's bid to
reclaim the Falklands was driven less by its inherent or perceived utility and
more by the fact that the government's preferred strategy was impracticable.

The Galtieri-led junta believed that one dimension of the Process was within its reach—economic liberalism. With enough time, reducing the size of the state and increasing foreign investment would repair the Argentine economy and lead to internal stability. But Buenos Aires could not afford the extensive repression required to keep the peace until the reform program paid dividends. Unable to suppress the opposition, the junta hatched a plan in January 1982 to win their allegiance, or at least distract their attention from the poor economy, by staging a diversionary spectacle in the Falkland Islands. The government would first attempt to acquire the Falklands through a negotiated settlement with Britain during bilateral talks held in February 1982. If the talks stalled, the junta planned to take the islands by force. Crucially, Galtieri was convinced that the British would not risk war over the Falklands, making the crisis seem at least a plausible, though not ideal, strategy for solving difficulties at home.

Two environmental factors contributed to this outcome. The first of these variables was the state's low extractive capacity, which has been overlooked in both the historical and international relations literature on the case. The government's severely limited ability to mobilize societal resources did not impede the junta's ability to adopt liberal economic reforms. After all, wage freezes, deregulation, and privatizing public enterprises were precisely the kind of measures that the Argentine pauper state could implement. But the junta could not afford to engage in the widespread repression of dissent. The second environmental factor was the perception that a low-cost, unifying target was available, making a diversionary spectacle possible.

The junta's mission to recover the Falkland Islands did not remain a low-cost spectacle, however. Instead of ceding control of the islands when Argentina invaded, British Prime Minister Margaret Thatcher "reacted like a lioness whose cubs were threatened," sending a task force of 44 warships and 10,000 ground troops to the South Atlantic.[2] The ensuing 74-day war resulted in a dual defeat for the junta—on the battlefield and at home. Soon after announcing the surrender of Argentine forces in the Falklands, Galtieri resigned from the presidency and was replaced as commander-in-chief of the army.

In Chapter 2 I argue that embattled pauper states rarely intend to fight full-scale diversionary wars, but instead engage in spectacles that escalate into sustained conflict. Environmental factors may close off their preferred strategies for managing domestic discontent, pushing them to select a less-attractive option from the policy menu. Facing a dire threat, such as growing civil unrest, and a narrowing of available responses, there is a tendency for leaders to overestimate the chances that the enemy will capitulate and the spectacle will succeed. However, the targets selected by pauper states are, on average, more likely to retaliate because they face a weak adversary. Together, these dynamics increase the odds that the spectacles provoked by resource-poor governments will escalate.

This case follows the predicted causal pathway (see Figure 4.1). The Argentine junta staged a diversionary spectacle because a low extractive capacity eliminated the preferred strategy, a combination of economic reform and repression. Fearing his ouster and unable to pursue the favored response to unrest, Galtieri grossly downplayed the risks associated with picking a fight with a nuclear-armed power. And unfortunately for the junta, Thatcher had both the will and the ability to roll back Argentina's gains in the Falklands. Galtieri's low-cost mission became an unwanted and costly war.

This chapter is divided into six sections. The first section outlines how rising domestic unrest threatened the survival of Argentina's military government, requiring immediate action by the junta. The second section describes how Galtieri ranked the options on the policy menu for managing domestic unrest, with his preferred response being a combination of economic reform and repression. The third section discusses the economic reforms implemented by Galtieri. The fourth section demonstrates that the state's low

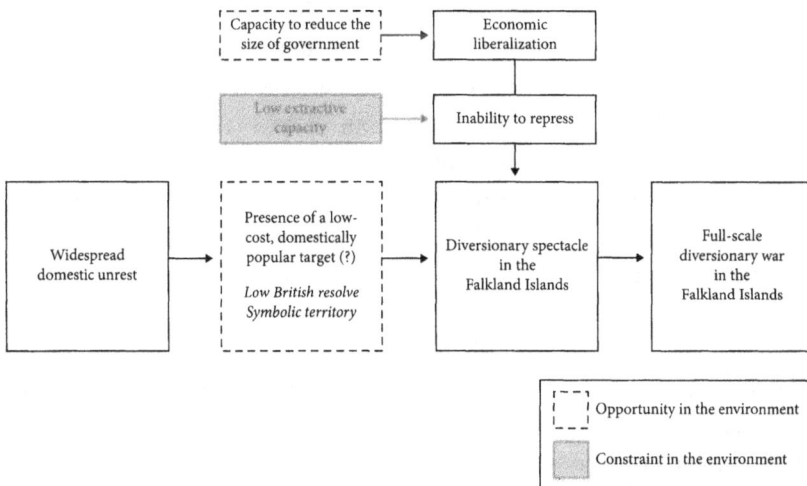

FIGURE 4.1 The Argentine junta's decision to invade the Falkland Islands, 1982

extractive capacity ruled out repression, pushing the Argentine government instead to orchestrate a diversionary spectacle. The fifth section contends that the junta provoked a crisis over the Falklands in order to distract a disgruntled public from a brutal regime and failing economy; that is, it was a genuine diversionary conflict. The final section reviews three alternative explanations for the junta's plan to reacquire the Falklands, each of which downplays the extent to which domestic unrest shaped the government's decision making. These arguments account for some aspects of the case, but they do not explain key elements, in particular the timing of the decision to recover the islands.

Social Strife in Argentina: An Existential Threat to the Ruling Junta

When Galtieri assumed the presidency in December 1981, he inherited an economy on the edge of collapse. From March 1980 to March 1981, more than 40 banks and investment firms declared bankruptcy. When the government attempted to reverse the economic decline by repeatedly devaluing the peso, inflation skyrocketed. Between June and July 1981, for example, the value fell from 4,200 to 7,800 pesos to the dollar.[3] The public outcry against the regime's poor handling of the economy was tremendous. Union leaders led the charge, reestablishing the General Confederation of Labor (CGT) and launching a series of high-profile strikes to decry the regime's liberal economic agenda and call for better wages, the right to engage in collective bargaining, and lower inflation. Business organizations and the domestic press also began, for the first time, openly criticizing the government's economic reform measures. For example, the media launched a barrage of fierce attacks on the junta's economy policy only days after Galtieri was sworn into office.

Galtieri's rise to power also coincided with unprecedented demands by many opposition groups for an immediate transition to democracy and compensation for victims of the dirty war. The Catholic church, which had initially adopted a policy of accommodation toward the junta, distanced itself from the government by publicly reaffirming its commitment to democracy and forming an alliance with the labor movement. Several political parties that had existed before the advent of military rule reorganized and founded the Multipartidaria, effectively ending the junta's ban on party activity. In addition to economic reforms, the coalition pushed for democratization.

Just days before Galtieri's inauguration, for example, the Multipartidaria published its boldest critique of military rule, provocatively titled "Before It Is Too Late," which called for an immediate return to civilian governance. At the same time, mothers of the victims of the dirty war gathered in increasing numbers in the Plaza de Mayo and demanded an explanation from the government for the disappearance of their children. These demonstrations came to the attention of the foreign press, other governments, and nongovernmental organizations. As a result, the military government was under mounting international pressure to improve its human rights record. In sum, union representatives, political parties, business leaders, the church, intellectuals, and human rights activists "formed a chorus of opposition that by the beginning of 1982 was difficult for the government to ignore."[4]

The public discontent encountered by the Galtieri presidency differed in two significant ways from the unrest that the junta had sought to contain since coming to power in 1976.[5] First, members of most sectors of society were openly expressing dissatisfaction with the performance of the military government, including groups that had previously backed the junta. Notably, this included the Catholic church and business leaders, essential sources of support for the regime. Second, the junta's opponents not only questioned the government's economic policies but also demanded that the junta step down and allow Argentina to democratize. Opposition was proliferating *horizontally*, with widening resistance, as well as *vertically*, with more-dramatic reform demands. As Juan Corradi notes, "[The] right of the regime to stay in power was called into question in a significant way for the first time, and by established groups."[6]

Thus, when Galtieri became president, the junta recognized the urgent need to manage its domestic problems; to ignore the opposition was "politically impossible" as the regime's "days were numbered."[7] During his inaugural speech, Galtieri himself acknowledged that "the time for words and promises is gone. I also know that words have lost their force and power to persuade. This is a time for firmness and action."[8] Given its collapsing political base, the junta had to do something—the question was, what?

Although the growing internal instability compelled action, it is insufficient to explain why Galtieri chose to liberalize the economy and engineer a diversionary spectacle to address his domestic problems instead of selecting another option from the policy menu.[9]

Galtieri's Preferred Strategies for Managing Domestic Unrest

To apply the substitutability approach to Argentina's decision to reclaim the Falkland Islands in January 1982, we must first establish how the key policy makers, in this case Galtieri, ranked the alternative options for addressing the unrest, from the most- to least-preferred response (see Figure 4.2). If there was a divergence between what the decision makers wanted to do and the strategy they actually chose, we can then identify which environmental factors, like a low extractive capacity, produced a policy substitution.

As leader of the hard-line faction of the military, Galtieri was fully committed to the political and economic program that the junta instituted following the overthrow of Isabel Perón, in 1976. The Process of National Reorganization, or "the Process," was chiefly a combination of liberal economic reform and state repression. When his immediate predecessor, Roberto Viola, allowed a limited opening of the political system, turning a blind eye when the labor unions and political parties reorganized, and shifted to expansionary economic policies, Galtieri "blocked or undermined every move" he made

Economic reform + Repression

Diversionary spectacle

Diversionary war

Muddling through

Political reform

Foreign intervention

FIGURE 4.2 President Leopoldo Galtieri's ranking of responses to domestic unrest

and then spearheaded a palace coup to assume the presidency.[10] As Gerardo Munck puts it, he "sought a 'return to the sources'—that is, to the military project as originally envisioned."[11] He was to be "savior of the Process."[12]

An orthodox economic policy was a tough sell when Galtieri came to power. It would necessitate deep cuts in defense spending and privatizing military-owned industries, potentially weakening the junta. And many elements of the reform program, especially reducing public expenditures and freezing wages, were unpopular with much of the public. But the president nevertheless "favored a return to neoclassical models" and believed that they, if implemented, would produce "economy recovery and social peace."[13]

For the Argentine junta, repression had always been the default strategy for dealing with domestic opponents—it was considered necessary to guarantee that the economic reform project was not derailed by, in particular, leftist elements. With the exception of Viola's short tenure in office, the military government had responded to any signs of protest with police violence.[14] This practice likely would have continued under Galtieri, who also preferred "a strong repressive state."[15] Two years before assuming the presidency, for example, he publicly affirmed that a heavy hand was required to combat the threat from left-wing subversives—as well as any potential sympathizers. Likening the enemies of military rule to a cancer, he stated: "[L]et nobody have any doubt that all evil will be extirpated; and to extirpate all evil, all cells will have to be extirpated, even those about which we are in doubt."[16]

If Galtieri could not use repression to push through his economic agenda, the next option on his policy ranking was likely a diversionary use of force to rally opinion by reclaiming the British Falkland Islands.[17] The president never revealed whether he saw diversion as an intrinsically attractive (or unattractive) strategy for managing unrest, which is to be expected given that the use of such tactics is generally seen as illegitimate.

However, Galtieri almost certainly would have preferred the use of diversionary tactics to limited political reform, as he was "in no hurry to steer the country towards a democratic path."[18] Like the members of the original junta that ousted Perón, he envisioned someday establishing an official political party that would represent the interests of the military and compete in open elections. Indeed, he imagined that he might helm the pro-military party when Argentina eventually transitioned to civilian rule.[19] But Galtieri had no intention of allowing even a small turn to democracy until he had realized his economic agenda, which he anticipated would take many years.[20]

Opening the political system was "unthinkable" as a solution to his current domestic troubles.[21] In May 1981, only six months before taking power, for example, Galtieri cautioned the public that, despite Viola's attempts to open a dialogue with opposition groups, "the ballot boxes are well guarded"—a remark all the more noteworthy because members of the military rarely spoke openly against the policies of the ruling junta.[22]

The least-attractive options for Galtieri were requesting foreign intervention and radical political reform. Neither of these options would have been deemed acceptable. By what conceivable path would the junta have invited foreign troops to repress the protestors or embraced immediate democratization? In all likelihood, the president would have preferred muddling through—itself a parlous course of action—to these obviously unattractive policies.

Therefore, it is reasonable to conclude that Galtieri would have seen a diversion as more palatable than political reform or inviting foreign intervention, but less attractive than economic reform and repression. Reclaiming the islands promised to dampen the unrest without requiring major concessions to internal adversaries or an external ally. But, of course, attempting a diversion was still risky: crises can escalate uncontrollably, and a defeat on the battlefield would certainly mean a loss of power at home (as Galtieri discovered). With an internal response to the unrest, such as repression, the junta could exert greater control over its destiny.

The question then becomes this: how did Galtieri weigh the advantages and disadvantages of a full-scale diversionary war versus the saber rattling of a diversionary spectacle? The key to generating a rally effect was recovering the historical territory—not killing British troops. Above all, Argentines were nationalists: "Rather than being characterized as anti-British, popular sentiment at that time is better described as anti-imperialist, or pro-Argentine."[23] For example, public displays of Anglophobia largely sprung up after fighting commenced in April 1982 but quickly dissipated after the hostilities ended.[24] Thus, whether the British simply surrendered the islands without a fight or after a bloody confrontation mattered much less than placing Argentine boots on sacred soil. And because the domestic political payoff from warring with Britain was not substantially greater, the junta would have preferred a low-cost mission to recover the islands—in other words, a diversionary spectacle.[25]

Given this ranking of preferences, it was the impracticability of repression that to a large extent explains the hawkish turn in Argentina's foreign policy.

I will explain below how this preferred alternative was eliminated from the Galtieri's menu of options, making economic reform, coupled with a diversionary spectacle, the junta's best hope for ending the unrest.

Choosing Economic Reform

Upon assuming the presidency, Galtieri put his economic plan into action, naming a new minister of economy, Roberto Alemán, who was "a devout exponent of pure economic liberalism" and "highly respected in financial circles for his orthodoxy."[26]

Alemán soon demonstrated his "fidelity to the original principles of the Proceso de Reorganización Nacional [i.e., the Process]."[27] Arguing that the military's economic policies had failed only because they had not been implemented with sufficient rigor and constancy, he immediately moved to freeze government wages, eliminate controls on the exchange market, and halt the provision of "non-essential" public services.[28] He further promised to reduce the money supply, privatize state enterprises, and lift protectionist measures shielding domestic industries from foreign competition—or, as he put it, to "deflate, deregulate and denationalize."[29] Although these harsh austerity measures received a cool welcome, Alemán assured the public: "The options are a bitter pill for the short term . . . or a worse pill of living with chaotic hyperinflation."[30] He also cautioned that "it was 'unrealistic' to think in terms of a full democracy until the economy had been put back in shape."[31]

Repression and the Argentine Pauper State

The question of why the junta chose to stage a diversionary spectacle and not to repress its opposition in order to buy time for its economic agenda to bear fruit is partly answered by examining how the state's low extractive capacity constrained the government's policy options.

There is little doubt that Argentina faced serious economic challenges when Galtieri took over the presidency, including soaring inflation, rising unemployment, and a rash of bank failures. In addition, government revenue from taxes was severely diminished. Monica Peralto-Ramos finds that the "ability of the state to cover its expenses with income from collected taxes was at the lowest level in twenty years."[32] A World Bank report on Argentina's tax system attributes the decline in government revenues to tax evasion,

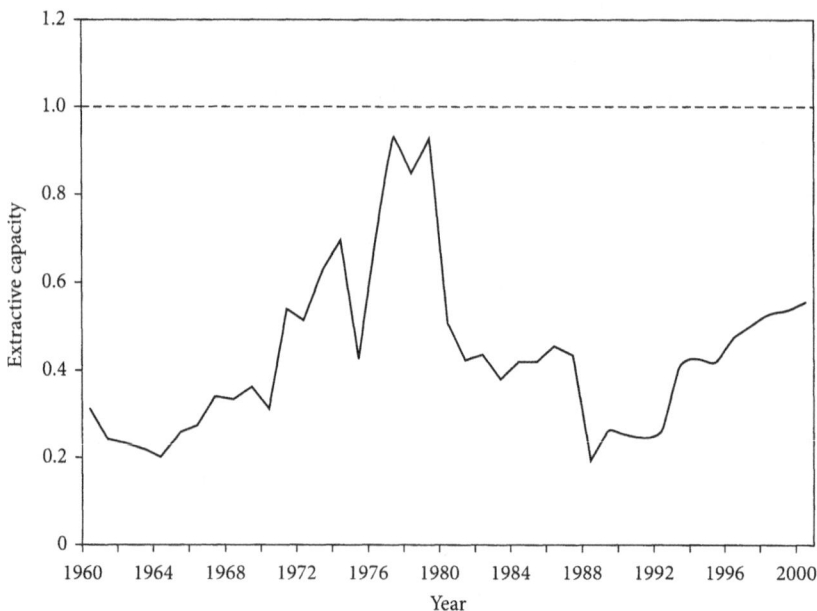

FIGURE 4.3 Argentina's extractive capacity, 1960–2000
SOURCE: Data from Kugler and Arbetman, "Relative Political Capacity."

inefficient tax administration, and rampant inflation: "Poor compliance, the proliferation of incentives and exemptions, and high inflation rates have affected revenue performance. . . . In 1981 and 1982, total revenues from all taxes fell sharply as a fraction of GDP."[33]

Jacek Kugler and Marina Arbetman's data on extractive capacity also confirm that Argentina was a severely impoverished pauper state in 1981 and 1982. Revenues were far short of the amount that theoretically could have been extracted from Argentina's economy (see Figure 4.3).[34]

Another indicator of the state's low extractive capacity during this period was the junta's increased efforts to find additional sources of revenue. For example, Alemán sought to increase government income by selling publicly owned businesses and taking out loans. The minister of the economy's decision to privatize state-owned industries was a reflection of a firm commitment to classical liberal economic principles, but it was also "designed to fulfill important short-run objectives such as acquiring badly needed cash from the sale of assets and attracting foreign investors."[35] By 1982, Argentina's public and private sectors had accumulated foreign debt equal to 60 percent of its gross national product (about $40 billion).[36] Interest payments on the debt (domestic and foreign) rose from 10 percent of the government budget in 1977 to 37 percent of the budget in 1982.[37] Moreover, half of Argentina's external debt was scheduled for repayment in 1983.[38] Simply put, the state was on the verge of insolvency.

The scarcity of revenue constrained the ability of the Galtieri-led junta to provide basic government services. In the words of one historian, the Argentine government had "insufficient resources for attending to society's multiple demands, from education to public health to the salaries of state employees."[39] Soon after his inauguration, the president begged the public for patience, arguing that although he wanted to improve the quality of government, the state's limited resources hampered his efforts:

> I profoundly believe in the importance of the state. A state that should not carry out what must and can be done by the private sector. . . . It is not a question of reducing the state to a minimum, but of giving it the necessary strength to carry out the great tasks that our republican organization has given it. Give it an authentic capability so that it can look after the educational and health sectors, the security of our people and the defense of our territory. So that it can expand and improve justice. . . . I will be hard, even miserly, in all management of public finances that are not channeled toward the high priorities that I have just mentioned.[40]

Importantly, the government's limited revenue also dramatically reduced its freedom of action in managing the rising unrest, eliminating the preferred option of sustained repression. Repression would have proved too costly if employed on a large scale and for a long period. The government had already struggled to finance the dirty war between 1976 and 1979, becoming heavily indebted in the process.[41] Another dirty war was out of the question. This was particularly true given the extent of the government's opposition when Galtieri came to power. Instead of just targeting left-wing subversives, as it had done during the dirty war, a policy of repression would have necessitated an expensive campaign of state violence against almost all sectors of society in late 1981 and 1982.[42] Cardoso, Kirschbaum, and van der Kooy report that Galtieri believed that a popular revolt would be "uncontrollable," suggesting that he knew the state did not have the capabilities to contain widespread unrest.[43] Consequently, Galtieri issued several "thinly veiled threats to wage another war against subversion" in the first months of his presidency, but he never carried them out.[44] The government instead subdued a handful of antigovernment demonstrations by the CGT but did not attempt to stamp out other signs of opposition, such as dismantling the Multipartidaria or preventing the mothers of the disappeared from gathering in the Plaza de Mayo.

Argentina's low extractive capacity was a necessary condition for the junta's decision to escalate its dispute with Britain over the Falkland Islands; if the government had been capable of extracting additional resources, it would have chosen the less-risky strategy of repressing its opposition. However, this more-desirable policy response was not on the menu of available options.

The Viability of a Diversionary Spectacle in the Falkland Islands

Because environmental factors hampered his ability to use repression, Galtieri faced a limited menu of alternative options for quelling the unrest, with a diversionary spectacle the most palatable of the remaining choices. However, staging a diversionary spectacle requires that a suitable target be available. Importantly, then, Galtieri perceived the mission to reclaim the Falklands to be not just domestically popular but also low cost: an ideal target for an embattled pauper state. This judgment might seem surprising given Britain's superior military and its close ties with the United States. However, the regime believed (wrongly) that London would not defend its territory and that Argentina's new alliance with the United States to fight communism in Latin America would guarantee Washington's support, or at least its neutrality, in the event of an invasion. The junta concluded that even if the February negotiations failed to deliver a settlement, it could seize the Falklands to rally the public and thereafter manage a diplomatic crisis with London without actually fighting a war.

A Historical Territory

In order for an international conflict to produce a rally effect, the government must select a target that will unify the citizenry behind the ruling elite. Foreign adventure will produce internal cohesion only if there is a consensus that the threat or use of force is justified. There is some evidence that many international conflicts produce a rally effect, or a temporary surge in support for the government. But if the government's primary motivation for provoking a crisis is a lasting improvement in public opinion, the government will prefer a mission where there is widespread support, such as reclaiming territory that has cultural or historical significance or defending the country against a known enemy.

The Falkland Islands may have had little strategic value—one observer likened the Argentine–British contest over the territory to "two bald men fighting over a comb"—but the mission to recover the Falkland Islands was a popular foreign policy goal in Argentina.[45] Indeed, it was perhaps the only policy that was supported by all sectors of Argentine society, including the junta's most avid critics. In the words of one Argentine, the "dispute has assumed the proportions of a national feeling going back to the childhood of every native of Argentina (without any political or class distinction) and uniting the national conscience in the knowledge of having been robbed and subjected to insult without apology."[46] This was evidenced by the public's reaction to the invasion in April 1982. Thousands of celebrants gathered in the Plaza de Mayo to demonstrate their support for the Argentine forces fighting for their "nation and for Jesus Christ" on the Falkland Islands.[47] Even a number of Montoneros, the left-wing guerillas targeted by the junta during the dirty war, were in the crowd, risking execution if they were discovered by the government.[48] In contrast, the Falklands would not have been a viable target for a diversionary spectacle if retaking the islands was a divisive issue or if the public was indifferent regarding their recovery.

The importance of finding a unifying target becomes evident if one compares the public's attitude toward the Falklands with its view of a potential war with Chile in 1978. While consolidating its rule and battling a left-wing insurgency, the junta briefly considered initiating a diversionary conflict with its neighbor and long-standing rival. The public's response to the possibility of a war with Chile was decidedly negative, however. For example, the Catholic church organized a series of public rallies against the war. In the end, the junta allowed the pope to arbitrate the dispute, in large part because of the public's strong objections to the war.

This pattern suggests that the junta would have abandoned its plans to regain the Falklands if it had not been a popular foreign policy goal, which is to say that the existence of a unifying target was a necessary but not sufficient condition for a diversionary spectacle. Obviously, this causal factor alone cannot explain why the junta committed to reclaiming the islands in January 1982, because the public had supported military action in the Falklands for decades.

British Resolve and the Likelihood of War

By the beginning of 1982, the junta had become "absolutely, viscerally, convinced that the British would not fight" if Argentina invaded the Falkland Islands.[49] During and after the war with Britain, Galtieri confessed that he had misjudged London's response, saying that "such a stormy reaction as was observed in the United Kingdom had not been foreseen."[50]

Several factors fed the junta's misperception that a diversionary spectacle against the British would be low risk.[51] In the months prior to the junta's decision to retake the Falklands, Britain announced the withdrawal of HMS *Endurance* from the South Atlantic, which was its only semipermanent naval presence in the region, and the closure of the British Antarctic Survey base, which was its only post on South Georgia and the South Sandwich Islands. In addition, while the dispute with Britain over the Falklands was often tense, it had never come to blows.

If one examines how Argentina prepared for and conducted the invasion in April, for example, there is ample evidence that the Argentine military was not anticipating a war with Britain. Although Argentina initially took the islands with a force of 1,400 troops, half of those sent were recently trained conscripts, and the junta kept its best-trained troops stationed along the Chilean border.[52] Furthermore, the admiral in charge of the campaign was instructed to send all but 500 troops back to Argentina in the days immediately after the invasion. The remaining force was charged with keeping order on the islands and not with defending the territory against a British assault.[53]

The junta's belief that Britain would not oppose an Argentine invasion of the islands profoundly affected its decision making in January 1982. Argentine leaders did not have to calculate the economic costs of fighting a war with Britain (surely high enough to deter an attack, given the government's perilous financial situation), whether additional resources could be mobilized if drawn into a lengthy war (dubious at best), or whether their military could defeat the British (hardly a certainty). Because it was entirely convinced that Britain would accept Argentina's occupation of the islands as a fait accompli, the junta devoted very little time to contingency planning for the possibility of a war with Britain.[54] The junta simply expected that "the military would have nothing to do after the invasion but drive up and down the streets of Port Stanley for the benefit of the media."[55] This was something a pauper state could cover. Simply put, if the junta had thought that Britain would fight for the islands, Argentina would not have considered an invasion.[56] As a representative of the Argentine navy said a few days prior to the invasion, "We can't stand more than 15 days of combat, let alone think of war."[57]

Britain's apparent lack of resolve made an invasion possible, but in the absence of a motivation for action, namely domestic unrest, Argentina would not have used force to reclaim the islands. Rather, Britain effectively had a veto over the invasion: it could have prevented Argentina from invading if it had strongly signaled its willingness to use force.[58] By declining to do so, Britain paved the way for an Argentine attack. It was a classic necessary, but not sufficient, condition.

American and Argentine Rapprochement

During Jimmy Carter's presidency, Argentina's relationship with the United States deteriorated significantly. For example, Carter imposed an arms embargo on Argentina in an effort to compel the junta to improve its human rights record. In the early days of the Reagan administration, however, U.S. policy toward Argentina became more conciliatory. This about-face resulted from President Ronald Reagan's desire to exploit the junta's strong anticommunist stance to combat the perceived Soviet threat in Latin America.[59] Reagan found a particularly receptive audience in Galtieri, who was flattered by the American president's attentions during the general's two lengthy visits to the United States in 1981.[60]

Argentina's decision to reclaim the Falklands, by force if necessary, was encouraged by the heady experience of being courted by the United States. There is considerable evidence that Galtieri's rapport with Reagan led to "an unrealistic sense of Argentina's comparative strategic importance in the world," with the president believing the United States would either support his efforts to recover the islands or, at a minimum, remain neutral.[61] In a January 1982 editorial published in La Prensa, Iglesias Rouco, who was closely connected to high-ranking government officials, stated that the junta anticipated the United States would side with Argentina in the event of an invasion: "[Buenos Aires is] searching for something beyond the mere recovery of a portion of its sovereignty. As far as we know, Washington understands it so, this being the reason why it has reportedly expressed its support for 'all of the actions' leading to the recovery [of the Falkland Islands], without excluding military actions."[62] Galtieri, who once described himself as America's

"pampered child," admitted he misperceived how the United States would respond to an invasion: "I didn't expect his [Reagan's] approval or support . . .
but I was sure that he would behave with balance and neutrality."[63]

It is improbable that Galtieri would have considered invading the Falklands if he believed the United States was prepared to offer Britain significant
support in the South Atlantic. Although many analysts prior to the war indicated that a British victory was far from assured, Argentina could hardly have
believed it would win if Washington aided Britain.[64] Thus, it follows that Argentina's calculations regarding the prudence of an invasion were influenced
by its expectations about the diplomatic effects of using force to reclaim the
Falklands. In other words, a point existed between the belief that an Argentine
invasion would be followed by diplomatic condemnation (which was almost
certain) and the belief that it would be followed by U.S. military support for
Britain (or indeed support by any other powerful state), where Buenos Aires
would no longer have considered the costs of an invasion to be acceptable. To
say that the junta's belief in the United States' strict neutrality was a necessary
condition for the war is perhaps too strong a claim. On the other hand, it was
necessary for the junta to believe the United States would not actively assist
Britain. In the end, however, the question of American neutrality is largely irrelevant. The foregoing discussion assumes that Argentina expected to fight a
war with Britain over the Falklands. It did not. Therefore, a more-accurate assessment of the causal importance of the United States' rapprochement with
Argentina is that it reinforced the junta's perception that the Falklands was a
low-risk target. Britain would be forced to acquiesce; the United States would
happily acquiesce.

Choosing a Diversionary Spectacle

Because environmental factors eliminated a preferred response to unrest—
sustained repression—the Argentine government resorted to orchestrating a
diversionary spectacle in the Falklands Islands.[65] In January 1982 the members of the junta committed to retake the islands.[66] The plan was to adopt
a tougher line in a forthcoming round of negotiations with Britain over the
Falklands scheduled for February, with the aim of pressuring London into
handing over control of the Falklands.[67] If diplomacy failed, they would seize
the islands in a limited military action.[68] Whether through negotiation or by
force of arms, the Falklands would be reunited with the homeland.

The overwhelming majority of scholars argue that the timing of the junta's decision to retake the islands is best explained by the unparalleled domestic opposition.[69] Unsurprisingly, Galtieri and the other members of the junta have publicly denied that they sought to reclaim the Falklands in order to produce a rally effect, but the facts suggest otherwise. In the early months of 1982, foreign correspondents in Argentina commented repeatedly that the junta's interest in reclaiming the islands was profoundly influenced by the worsening internal situation. For example, *Latin America Weekly Report* stated that Galtieri resolved to retake the Falklands soon after his ascension to power: "The link with internal politics is clear. . . . Galtieri feels that tough action over the Malvinas, for long a question of nationalist pride, could do wonders for his popularity."[70] More important still, Argentine journalists indicated that the junta's plan to reclaim the islands was connected with its declining popularity. For example, a lead article published in late January in *Conviccion,* a newspaper closely linked to the navy, said, "Right now . . . conditions are at their best. We have a decisive president and an excellent foreign minister. If, having won the war against terrorism, we recover the Malvinas, history will forgive the economic stupidities."[71] Similarly, three reporters from the daily newspaper *Clarín,* who interviewed many of the key players in the conflict and had access to confidential documents, maintained that social strife was a decisive factor in the junta's decision to retake the Falklands:

> Galtieri knew that he was arriving at the Casa Rosada with a country coming apart at the seams, with deep social divisions and a yearning for political change. . . . In particular, he felt that it would be essential to have some resounding triumph in order to give impetus to the military regime which was struggling to survive. . . . He placed much emphasis upon the Foreign Ministry, since he supposed that in foreign policy he might find a key to the success of his strategy.[72]

The British and American diplomats who attempted to negotiate an end to the crisis in April 1982 also concluded that managing the internal unrest had been the impetus behind the junta's efforts to take back the Falklands. For example, the British ambassador to the United States said that Galtieri "brought about the present occupation in order to distract public opinion from economic and political difficulties."[73] Reflecting on his efforts to mediate the dispute, U.S. Secretary of State Alexander Haig wrote that there "was a widespread impression that the junta was creating a foreign distraction to

give itself a respite from domestic economic problems, including severe inflation."[74] Therefore, the evidence points to the fact that the mass discontent in
Argentina was the primary motivation for the decision to regain control over
the Falklands.

Alternative Explanations

There are three prominent alternative explanations for the junta's plan to retake the Falklands. Each maintains that the main cause of the conflict was not
the escalating social unrest in Argentina. However, none can account for the
precise timing of the government's decision to reclaim the islands.

Chile and the Beagle Channel Dispute

Several studies of the Falklands War maintain that the junta's efforts to reacquire the islands were part of Argentina's grand strategy to achieve regional
dominance. In particular, historians have argued that it was partly a by-
product of the dispute between Argentina and neighboring Chile over the
ownership of three small islands located near the Beagle Channel. Argentina maintained that if it were not granted sovereignty over the islands, Chile
would have a significant foothold in the competition for control over the Antarctic Peninsula, would dominate the shipping route around Cape Horn, and
could control waters close to one of Argentina's key naval bases.[75] Thus, if
Argentina were not awarded the islands, it would affirm Chile's position as a
major power in the South Atlantic.

Historians have identified several reasons why the junta's concerns about
the outcome of the conflict with Chile influenced its decision to regain the
Falkland Islands. First, they contend that the junta believed that if Argentina
assumed control of the Falklands, it might strengthen its bargaining position
with Chile in the Beagle Channel dispute.[76] Chile and Argentina had managed
to avoid a military confrontation over the islands by accepting an eleventh-
hour offer by the Vatican to mediate the dispute. The Vatican considered the
matter for two years, then quietly informed Argentina that its judgment was
likely to favor Chile. Dissatisfied with this outcome, Argentina asked the Vatican to reconsider. Argentina's leaders reasoned that if they adopted a tougher
stance on the Falklands and demonstrated their readiness to use force to
achieve their objectives, the Vatican would offer concessions to Buenos Aires
over the Beagle Islands. Second, if the Vatican ultimately chose not to reverse

its decision, the junta hoped to compensate for its loss of the islands by recovering the Falklands.[77] Finally, the junta strived to reclaim the Falklands because it feared that Chile and the United Kingdom would form an alliance against Argentina; therefore, British influence in the region had to be diminished.[78]

These might appear to be a compelling series of mutually reinforcing arguments, but the evidence in their favor is limited. There is some indication that the Argentine navy believed that a victory in the Falklands would increase Argentina's leverage in the Beagle Channel dispute. An editorial in *Conviccion* hinted that "the taking of the Malvinas would actually help resolve the Beagle Channel issue since it would strengthen Argentina's negotiating hand."[79] In addition, Galtieri had long considered Chile to be a threat to Argentina's position in the regional balance of power, and Argentina's relations with Chile had reached a new low under his leadership.[80] Finally, in the weeks before the invasion of the Falklands, Britain received intelligence that Argentina's foreign minister, Nicanor Costa Mendez, was concerned that a peaceful resolution of the conflict over the Falkland Islands was unlikely if the outcome of the Vatican's mediation of the Beagle Channel dispute did not favor Argentina.[81] Therefore, one can safely conclude that managing the Chilean threat was a priority for Galtieri and that some members of the government believed the Beagle Channel and Falkland Islands disputes were linked.

On the other hand, there is no evidence that when the junta decided to retake the Falklands it was predominantly motivated by a desire to secure a positive papal decision in the Beagle Channel dispute. It hardly seems likely that the Vatican would have been favorably swayed by an unprovoked attack on the Falklands. There is also scant evidence that the junta sought the Falklands to compensate for the probable loss of the islands in the Beagle Channel. Indeed, tensions with Chile arguably led the junta to use more caution in regard to the Falklands, to avoid a spectacle on one front and a war on another. Finally, the junta's concerns about British–Chilean collusion had receded by January 1982. After London announced in June 1981 that it was withdrawing HMS *Endurance* from the South Atlantic, the junta concluded that its fears had probably been exaggerated.[82] Instead, the belief that Britain was increasingly uninterested in the region played a far more important role in the junta's decision to retake the islands. Furthermore, if the ties between Britain and Chile were becoming stronger, precipitating a crisis over the Falklands would not have severed them. Indeed, it is far more likely that if Argentina provoked a conflict with the United Kingdom, it would have pushed Chile and Britain closer together. Therefore, the fear of an alliance between Britain and Chile was either not a factor in the junta's decision making regarding the Falklands or one that made escalating the dispute with Britain over the islands less attractive.

Argentine Frustration with the Progress of Diplomacy

After seventeen years of formal negotiations over the Falkland Islands between Argentina and the United Kingdom, very little progress had been made. Richard Ned Lebow argues that mounting frustration with the diplomatic process—coupled with rising social unrest—led Buenos Aires to initiate a brinkmanship crisis, which he describes as "a confrontation in which one state knowingly challenges an important commitment of another with the expectation that its adversary will back down when challenged."[83] Lebow maintains that Britain's unwillingness to meet Argentine demands during talks in February 1982 convinced the embattled military government that the dispute could not be resolved diplomatically and that a new strategy was needed to pressure Britain to negotiate. The junta decided that by threatening an invasion, it might be able to blackmail London into ceding sovereignty over the islands. In Lebow's words, after the termination of the negotiations, "the generals set out upon a deliberate course of escalating tensions with Britain. Their strategy was to commit themselves step by step to military action in the expectation that this would succeed in eliciting some kind of British concession on sovereignty before they were compelled to act."[84]

Lebow maintains that the junta sent Britain signals that it would use force against the Falklands if no progress was made and began preparing public opinion for the possibility of an invasion. The brinkmanship failed, as London refused to concede the islands, putting Argentina's leaders in a difficult position. After promising the Argentine public that it was going to recover the islands, the junta was faced with a choice: it could back down and lose power or invade and risk war with Britain. In the end, the junta feared the public's wrath more than the wrath of London.

This argument nicely captures some of the dynamics that prevented the junta from withdrawing its troops from the Falklands after the April invasion. As Lebow suggests, the government was constrained by the tremendous outpouring of public support for the military action and, in particular, Galtieri's promise after the invasion that Argentina would "give battle" if Britain retaliated.[85]

But Lebow incorrectly asserts that the decision to invade (or rather to threaten to invade) was made in response to the failed talks in February and that the junta never intended to use force to recover the Falklands. The balance of evidence suggests that the junta had resolved to invade the islands if diplomacy did not deliver the islands to Argentina in January 1982, more than one month earlier than Lebow claims.[86] Therefore, the disappointing outcome of the talks could not have been a cause of the junta's decision to invade, except in the sense that a British capitulation would have averted military action. Thus, the invasion was not the unintended consequence of a failed attempt at initiating a brinkmanship crisis, as Lebow contends, but rather a deliberate choice.

In an important article on the causes of the Falklands War, Taylor Fravel similarly argues that the junta's decision to invade is largely explained by its failure to coerce Britain into ceding control over the islands, which he terms a "standard realist" interpretation of the case.[87] But, while Lebow allows for the possibility that growing domestic discontent with military rule contributed to the junta's decision to provoke a brinkmanship crisis, Fravel argues that internal factors played a minimal role. This argument is unconvincing for several reasons.

First, Fravel severely downplays the magnitude of the threat posed by rising unrest to the Galtieri regime. He acknowledges that Argentina's economy was floundering and there was mass unrest, but then notes that prior military governments had faced similar challenges and never used diversionary force—therefore, he argues, domestic variables cannot explain why the junta provoked a diversion in 1982. However, the survival of the Galtieri-led junta was in jeopardy because, for the first time, the military government had lost the support of groups on which it depended to stay in power, namely business elites and the Catholic church. Thus, to conclude that Galtieri did not fear removal from office is highly improbable—and runs counter to virtually every other historical analysis of the case.[88]

Second, Fravel overstates the importance of growing Argentine frustration with diplomacy in the junta's decision to escalate the crisis with Britain over the Falklands. To evaluate the causal importance of the negotiations with London we might consider the counterfactual: would Argentina have provoked a crisis with Britain over the Falkland Islands in 1982 even if negotiations had not stalled? The answer, almost certainly, is yes. With acute domestic problems, an inability to suppress the unrest, and an apparently low-risk target, a diversionary spectacle was highly likely.

Third and most importantly, Fravel's claim that the case is consistent with a standard realist argument is problematic. The significance of the Falklands to the Argentine nation goes well beyond the narrow realist logic. As Fravel's notes, the "standard realist model focuses on external threats and security challenges to national interests."[89] Yet the islands provided little strategic benefit to Buenos Aires. Rather, their value was to a large extent symbolic, as part of the historical homeland.

Bureaucratic Authoritarian Regimes and the Fragmentation of Military Rule

Jack Levy and Lily Vakili contend that the fragmentation of the Argentine junta was an important cause of its decision to reclaim the Falklands, arguing that bureaucratic authoritarian regimes, such as Argentina's military government, initiate international conflicts in response to domestic unrest when divisions emerge among the ruling elite. When such regimes are unified, they are insulated from domestic pressures because they can exclude the public from decision making. Thus, it follows that only when the regimes are fragmented and there is a "rupture in the self-imposed isolation" do their leaders feel compelled to respond to the public's demands.[90] In addition, when such a regime loses its unifying purpose, it may choose to initiate an international conflict to renew its sense of shared mission.

Levy and Vakili describe Galtieri's decision to recover the Falklands as a "classic instance of this pattern."[91] When the military came to power in 1976, it sought to rebuild the economy and rein in widespread domestic terrorism through the Process. During the first four years of military rule, the junta ruthlessly eliminated any traces of opposition. The dirty war was so effective that by 1980, "even isolated acts of terrorism seldom disturbed the peace."[92] The government's economic reforms were considerably less successful, and the Argentine economy was soon on the verge of collapse.

Initially, their shared commitment to economic reform and the war against leftist subversives enabled navy, air force, and army commanders to put aside competing bureaucratic interests. However, divisions within the junta deepened as the public began to demonstrate against the Process, demanding that the government repair the economy and account for the disappearance of thousands of Argentines during the dirty war. In other words, without a unifying mission, the military government was torn apart by factional infighting. By pursuing the Falklands, Levy and Vakili contend,

Galtieri sought to give the junta new purpose, creating, in effect, a rally within the government.

Historical accounts of the events prior to the Falklands War provide some support for Levy and Vakili's argument. In David Pion-Berlin's words, Galtieri's plan to retake the Falklands "was a desperate act designed to reunify a badly split institution."[93] The question remains, however, whether the fragmentation of the governing elite was a necessary condition for the junta's decision to reclaim the islands. Levy and Vakili contend that while the conflict over the Falklands was intended to address the social unrest in Argentina, the timing of the decision is best explained by the breakdown of the military government. That is, the Argentine government felt compelled to respond to the domestic unrest only after it splintered and was no longer insulated from domestic pressures. In order to evaluate the importance of elite fragmentation, therefore, one must consider whether the rising domestic unrest would have been threatening enough to compel a unified government to pursue the Falklands or, at least, to respond seriously in some way.

If there was one issue at the beginning of Galtieri's presidency of which every member of the government was acutely aware, it was the need for a strategy to address the public's increasingly insistent calls for political and economic reform. Not only did the public ask the government to ease its economic woes, but it also demanded the end of military rule. Thus, while there may have been an imperfect consensus among the members of the junta regarding which policies would revive the economy, they agreed that something had to be done in response to the public's dissatisfaction with military rule.[94] Indeed, the pressure to respond to the growing instability was so great that even a cohesive regime would have perceived it as a threat to its survival that needed immediate attention.[95] Furthermore, the breakdown of military rule was itself largely precipitated by the deepening social fragmentation. When domestic unrest resurfaced in 1981, the members of the junta initially could not agree on how best to respond, fracturing the government.[96] Therefore, Levy and Vakili overlook two factors: (1) elite divisions may result from domestic unrest, and (2) a united government will fear domestic unrest if it is sufficiently severe.

In any case, whether or not it was a necessary condition, the fragmentation of the governing elite was certainly insufficient to cause the junta's decision to regain the Falklands. Although this factor may help explain why the government felt compelled to address the mounting social unrest, it does not explain why the junta staged a diversionary spectacle instead of, for example, repressing its opposition. Levy and Vakili implicitly recognize elite fragmentation as insufficient when accounting for the junta's choice of a diversion over its alternatives by attempting in an ad hoc manner to explain why the junta did not suppress the unrest instead. For example, they mention that the government chose to initiate a diversionary conflict because of "the absence of viable alternatives" and suggest that repression was impossible because the resources to coerce the opposition were not available.[97] Thus, infighting made the junta more vulnerable to the public's demands for change, but it did not make a crisis over the Falklands inevitable.

Conclusion

The policy substitutability approach suggests the critical role played by a low extractive capacity in government decision making. Unable to afford their preferred strategy, pauper states are pushed toward adopting a less-attractive policy for managing unrest. In the Falklands case, a low extractive capacity compelled Galtieri to abandon his preferred solution to the junta's domestic problems. Though the president continued to pursue his economic agenda, he was forced to substitute a risky diversionary spectacle in place of repressing domestic opposition to the unpopular austerity measures. The Falkland Islands represented a seemingly ideal spectacle because the mission was perceived as being both inexpensive and likely to produce the desired domestic response.

This case demonstrates the effect of extractive capacity on leaders' responses to domestic unrest. The lack of resources did not interfere with the junta's ability to adopt liberal economic reforms, but it acted as a constraint in preventing the use of widespread repression. The analysis also reveals the role of another environmental factor. For leaders to stage diversionary spectacles, there must be an opportunity to provoke a crisis with a target where there is no expectation of sustained warfare and the mission is generally popular.

Because the junta's attempts to regain the Falklands resulted in a costly military campaign against British forces, this case also allows us to examine the conditions that lead pauper states to fight diversionary wars. As predicted, environmental factors eliminated the embattled junta's preferred strategy for managing growing internal instability, leading it to orchestrate a less-palatable diversionary spectacle. Facing a narrowing menu of options, Galtieri exhibited significant overconfidence in assessing Argentina's ability to reclaim the Falklands without provoking a military response from London—a misperception nurtured by Thatcher's decision to draw down Britain's military presence in the South Atlantic and a history of generally peaceful, if unproductive, negotiations over the islands.

In the next chapter I examine a case in which a pauper state staged a diversionary spectacle that did not become a full-scale war—the U.S. government's decision to send troops to install a non-Mormon territorial governor in Utah in 1857. This case study allows for further investigation of the effect of low extractive capacity on government decision making, and when compared with the Falklands crisis, it provides additional evidence of the factors that lead some spectacles, but not others, to escalate into costly wars.

5 A Diversionary Spectacle

The U.S. Government's Expedition to the Utah Territory,
1857–1858

IN 1848, HAVING SUCCESSFULLY ESTABLISHED A NEW ZION IN the unorganized territory of Utah, a member of the Mormon church reflected on the religious persecution that had prompted his fellow believers to seek refuge in the American West: "We now choose to make our homes in the Desert among Savages rather than try to live in the garden of the world surrounded by Christian Neighbors. . . . The Lord Almighty is preparing a scourage [*sic*] for this nation. The blood of the Saints is crying out from the ground for vengeance on that wicked nation."[1]

Joseph Smith founded the Mormon religion in 1830, after a divine vision revealed to him *The Book of Mormon* and God's new covenant with his chosen people, the Latter-Day Saints. With the Mormons widely despised as heretics, Smith led his followers on an odyssey through the Midwest. The Saints settled briefly in Ohio before migrating to Missouri—identified by Smith as the site of the Garden of Eden. Missourians were alarmed when Smith prophesied that, in preparation for the apocalypse, the Saints and the Indians would unite to destroy unbelievers and sinners, and then promised to wage a "war of extermination" against the Missouri people if they threatened his disciples.[2] Following a series of deadly clashes between the Mormons and Missourians, Smith was jailed on charges of treason, and his followers were ordered to leave the state.

The Mormons fled to Illinois, where they were soon joined by Smith after his escape from prison. The Saints, now more than 10,000 in number, were initially free from persecution. But tensions rose after Smith established an independent city-state under his rule, organized a militia, covertly introduced the practice of polygamy, or "plural marriage," and predicted the overthrow of the United States. The final straw was an attack by the Mormon militia on a newspaper critical of Smith's leadership, after which a warrant was issued for Smith's arrest on charges of fomenting a riot. When the prophet surrendered to authorities, a mob broke into the prison and assassinated Smith and his brother.

After escaping violence in Illinois in 1846, the Saints, led by Smith's successor, Brigham Young, journeyed to Utah to establish a new kingdom. By the end of 1848, more than 6,000 Mormons had made their home in the Great Basin.[3] Under the governorship of Young, Utah became a U.S. territory in 1850.

Migration to the West did not end the hostility between Mormonism and mainstream American opinion. Young created a Mormon theocracy in the Utah territory: his "word was law in matters both religious and secular."[4] He established a separate legal system and oversaw the selection of representatives to the territorial legislature. In 1852 the church leadership publicly confirmed its practice of plural marriage. Young's attempts to flout federal authority over the territory and promote the practice of polygamy gave rise to a series of political skirmishes between the church and the U.S. government.

In 1851 Young clashed with Washington-appointed officials over the proper jurisdiction of the federal courts in the territory. In 1853 Captain John Gunnison and seven of his command, who were in Utah on a federal expedition to map a route for the Pacific railroad, were murdered by a party of Indians. When Young failed to investigate the Gunnison massacre, the federal government sent Lieutenant Colonel Edward Steptoe, along with several hundred soldiers and civilians, to investigate rumors that the Mormons had instigated the attack. In 1855 Steptoe, angered by the Mormons' treatment of his soldiers and Young's handling of the massacre, urged the federal government to select a new territorial governor. Despite repeated calls by the public for action against the Mormons, each successive crisis was resolved peaceably.

In the spring of 1857, the Mormon church and Washington locked horns again. Several federally appointed officials fled Utah, claiming that Young exercised tyrannical leadership over the territory, leaving them unable to enforce the law without fearing for their safety. In response, President James Buchanan, less than three months into his term of office, unveiled a plan to send federal troops to coerce Young into resigning and allowing a non-Mormon to assume the governorship. As the president averred in his annual report to Congress, "[T]here no longer remains any government in Utah but the despotism of Brigham Young. This being the condition of affairs in the Territory, I could not mistake the path of duty."[5]

During the summer and fall of 1857, 1,300 federal troops were redeployed from postings throughout the Midwest to Utah. As the army trickled into eastern Utah Territory, they were harassed by Mormon militiamen, who delayed their advance by destroying the federal supply wagons. Unable to reach Salt Lake City before winter, the expedition was forced to encamp in Fort Bridger, more than 100 miles from Salt Lake City, and wait for fair weather and additional supplies. In December 1857, Buchanan petitioned Congress for additional funds to escalate his crusade against the Mormon church after the spring thaw. But when Congress delayed a decision on his request, Buchanan was forced to offer Young a peace settlement. By the time the army marched into Salt Lake City in June 1858, Young and the federal government had resolved the dispute. Brigham Young agreed to step aside as governor, but his followers would be pardoned if they submitted to federal authority.

How can we explain Buchanan's use of force in Utah? The primary concern on the president's mind was not Young and the Mormon church but Kansas, where a virtual civil war had broken out over the territory's future as a slave state or a free state. Buchanan planned to resolve the crisis by admitting Kansas to the Union as a free state. But he feared this outcome would split the Democratic Party, enable the hated "Black" Republican Party to dominate the North, and trigger southern secession from the Union. To settle the Kansas issue peaceably, the president needed time to put the pieces of his plan into action. A diversionary use of force against the Mormons promised to solve his problems. A military campaign in Utah would rally domestic opinion in the North and South and buy his administration some breathing room. Utah was an ideal diversionary target because militant abolitionists and fire-breathing secessionists alike hated the Mormons. Illinois Senator Stephen Douglas spoke for most Americans when he described the Mormons as a "loathsome, disgusting ulcer."[6] Excising this ulcer would stop the bleeding in Kansas.

Many historians argue that Buchanan's anti-Mormon crusade was a diversionary use of force. But the Utah expedition has been entirely ignored by international relations scholars—even in the literature on the diversionary theory of war. One reason for this neglect is that the use of force in 1857 was not a classic interstate conflict, like the Falklands War (see Chapter 4).

Indeed, because Utah was a U.S. territory rather than an independent country, the case could be considered an instance of diversionary repression rather
than diversionary conflict. But the anti-Mormon crusade was closer to the
classic model of interstate conflict than it at first appears. The Mormon regime in Utah was a recalcitrant territorial government, with its own separate
court system and independent militia. As one historian put it, Young was "in
sovereign control of his own flock."[7] For many Americans, the Mormons were
a state within a state.

The Utah expedition affords us an opportunity to investigate a case in
which a pauper state staged a diversionary spectacle that did not escalate into
a full-scale war. In Chapter 2 I outline two causal pathways that can result in
this outcome. In the first pathway a spectacle is the decision maker's preferred
response to domestic unrest, the state has the capacity to pursue this option,
and the target puts up limited resistance. In the second the decision maker
engineers a diversionary spectacle because the government lacks the capacity
to implement preferred policies, and, again, the target does not fight back.
This case roughly follows the first pathway—with a few notable departures.

Buchanan's preferred strategy for managing the growing tumult over the
expansion of slavery was limited political reform. He hoped to engineer a
moderate political compromise in which Kansas's status on the slavery issue
would be decided via a popular vote. Buchanan believed that a sufficiently
large percentage of Americans—northern Democrats, a majority of southern
Democrats, and even some Republicans—would be satisfied by this solution,
making his preferred policy of limited political reform practicable. Why then
did the president end up also staging a diversionary spectacle in Utah?

The answer was political opportunism. When Brigham Young, in the
spring of 1857, renewed his objection to federal interference in the governance
of the territory, Buchanan saw the possibility for a diversionary use of force
to boost his domestic support. At this point, the United States' low extractive
capacity played a critical role. The president would likely have preferred to
authorize a large-scale diversionary war to destroy the Mormon church and
generate a more-robust rally effect. But a war in Utah was too expensive for
the American pauper state. Congress's commitment to limited government
and Buchanan's own election promise to reduce federal spending precluded
an expensive campaign against Young and his disciples. Buchanan therefore moved to his next available option on the policy menu: a limited use of
force as a diversionary spectacle. Because it was widely believed that support

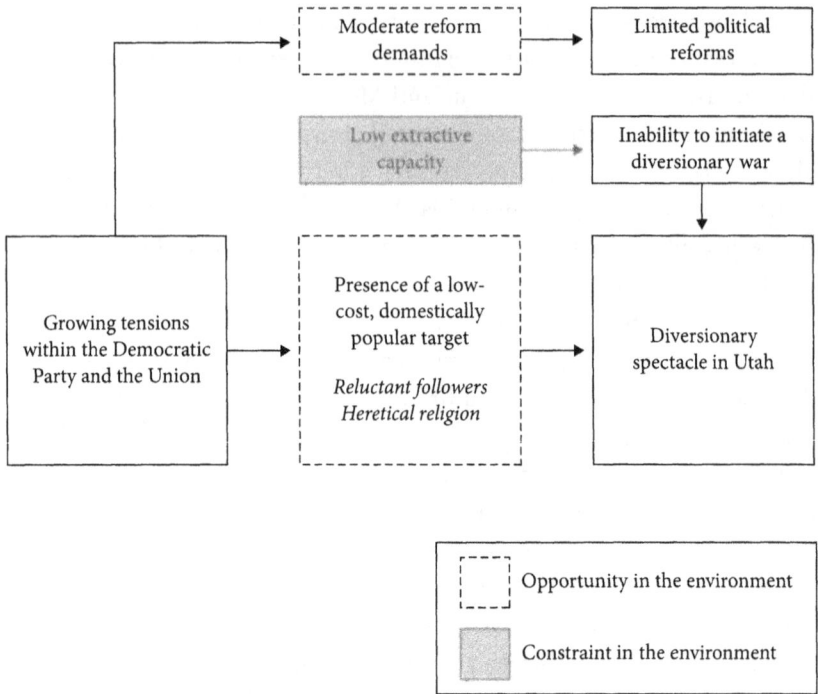

FIGURE 5.1 The U.S. government's decision to send troops to Utah, 1857

in Utah for Young was shallow, even a small-scale operation would force the Mormon governor to step aside. Therefore, an expedition against Utah was a perfect diversionary spectacle: a low-cost, highly symbolic military adventure that promised to drown out the domestic squabbles threatening the Union (see Figure 5.1). Buchanan's course would busy giddy minds with the anti-Mormon quarrel and thereby waste memories of the former dispute in Kansas.

Thus, in line with the first causal pathway, Buchanan used diversionary tactics because he saw them as a valuable strategy for managing domestic unrest. That is, he was not driven to stage a diversion because environmental factors eliminated his preferred response to the domestic instability (though he would have opted for a war over a spectacle). But, in a slight deviation from this pathway, the president orchestrated a diversionary spectacle to supplement his preferred response, political reform, and did so only because an ideal opportunity for a diversion unexpectedly emerged.

This case, when considered alongside Argentina's invasion of the Falkland Islands, also points to the conditions that may prevent diversionary spectacles from escalating into full-scale wars. In the Falklands case, the junta engaged in wishful thinking and underestimated the odds that the target would fight a war. In the Mormon case, we also find some evidence of wishful thinking. The Buchanan administration had positive illusions about the ease of the spectacle, underestimating the support for the church among rank-and-file members and not anticipating nonviolent forms of resistance. But Buchanan did not exhibit wishful thinking regarding the likelihood of war: he expected the Mormon military to avoid engaging federal troops, and he was correct. Indeed, the key reason that the Utah expedition did not escalate into a major military campaign was the determination of Young to avoid a full-scale war with the U.S. Army.

This chapter is laid out as follows. The first section discusses why the dispute over Kansas threatened the survival of the Democratic Party and potentially the country, necessitating a response by the Buchanan administration. The second section describes Buchanan's ranking of the options on the policy menu, arguing that his preferred response to events in Kansas was limited political reform. The third section explains why the president believed a political solution to his troubles in Kansas was practicable. The fourth section contends that when an opportunity to use diversionary force against the Mormons emerged, the federal government's low extractive capacity eliminated the option of a full-scale war to defeat the church, pushing Buchanan toward the less-attractive option of a diversionary spectacle. The fifth section presents evidence that Buchanan sent the expedition to Mormon Utah in order to distract the public from the controversy over Kansas.

Slavery and "Bleeding Kansas": A Threat to the Democratic Party and the Union

When Buchanan won the presidency in 1856, there was a growing sense that the American experiment might not survive the divisions over slavery between the northern free states and the southern slave states. In historian Philip Klein's assessment, the election, "for the first time in American history, had probed down to the bedrock question of union or disunion; survival or disruption. The cliché of editors and orators had become the *bona fide* statement of the fundamental problem: the Union *was* in danger."[8] The greatest source of domestic instability was the status of slavery in the newly organized western territories of the United States. It was a zero-sum struggle: each new slave state or free state would tip the sectional balance of power.

The primary battleground lay in the territory of Kansas, where destruction had replaced debate. The question of whether the territory would enter the Union as a free state or a slave state triggered a guerrilla war among its settlers, widening the breach between North and South, and threatening to destroy the Democratic Party. The gravity of the crisis was not lost on Buchanan. He believed that piloting the country safely through the storm would be "the greatest trial of his life."[9] "God save the Union!" Buchanan wrote shortly before winning the presidential election. "I do not want to survive it."[10]

In 1854 Congress passed the Kansas–Nebraska Act, which was based on the principle of popular sovereignty, where a majority of residents had the right to decide whether slavery would be permitted in the Kansas and Nebraska territories. This represented a significant deviation from the Missouri Compromise of 1820, where slavery had been prohibited in the territories of the Louisiana Purchase north of the 36′30″ latitude, except for the planned state of Missouri. The sponsors of popular sovereignty believed that the democratic process could peaceably resolve the question of whether Kansas and Nebraska would admit slaves. They were wrong.

Kansas became ground zero in the sectional divide, as proslavery and antislavery groups sought to build a majority and win the elections that would determine the territory's fate. Concerned that the steady influx of settlers from New England and the Midwest had shifted the balance in favor of a free-state outcome, proslavery Kansans encouraged sympathetic "border ruffians" from Missouri to vote illegally in Kansas's elections. By 1856, two rival territorial governments had emerged. One, based in Lecompton, was proslavery and passed a draconian slave code that, for example, mandated the death penalty for fomenting a slave rebellion or assisting a runaway slave. It was backed by President Franklin Pierce, who chose to overlook the massive voter fraud. The other government, based in Topeka, was antislavery, reflecting the wishes of a clear majority of settlers.

In the spring of 1856, a posse of Missourians attacked the antislavery stronghold of Lawrence, Kansas. Armed with a five-cannon battery, the proslavery militia marched on Lawrence, looting stores, stables, and homes, destroying the offices of two newspapers, and burning a hotel and the free-soil governor's home.[11] The "sack of Lawrence" marked the beginning of a "three-cornered" guerilla war with, in the words of one observer, "free-state men on one side, proslavery men on the other, and Uncle Sam's men pretending to keep the peace, but not able to do it."[12] The death toll was in the hundreds and the damage to property in the millions of dollars.[13] In a desperate effort to dampen the unrest, Washington appointed a new territorial governor, John Geary, and sent additional federal troops to Kansas. Through skillful diplomacy and brute force, Geary "succeeded in returning the struggle in Kansas to the arena of politics, not war"—just as Buchanan won the presidential election for the Democratic Party in November 1856.[14]

The Buchanan administration was confronted with a daunting challenge: how could Kansas attain statehood with a constitution that would be acceptable to a majority of the settlers and the broader American public? Surveying the political landscape, Buchanan faced an exceptionally complex and divided set of constituencies. Uniting these rival groups would have tested a man of much superior leadership ability.

Events in Kansas reverberated far beyond the territory. Washington's willingness to accept fraudulent election results, in combination with the violence against free-staters, energized the young Republican Party. Formed in 1854, the Republican Party was united by its opposition to the "slave power," that is, the cabal of southern slaveholders bent on extending the reach of slavery and creating a permanent proslavery majority.[15] A minority of Republicans were abolitionists committed to rolling back slavery where it existed, but most were free-soilers who sought more limited goals, to contain slavery and prevent its advance into the territories.

Republicans had never accepted the Kansas–Nebraska Act or the principle of popular sovereignty, which they saw as a mechanism for expanding the number of slave states. Nevertheless, they hoped to limit the damage from popular sovereignty by building an antislavery majority in Kansas to admit the territory to the Union as a free state. For Republicans, the refusal of proslavery forces to accept the will of the majority in Kansas confirmed the South's contempt for democracy. Bleeding Kansas was also a tailor-made opportunity to brand the Democratic-controlled federal government as a pawn of the slave interests, which had disregarded the political rights of a majority of settlers in Kansas in order to open the territory to slavery.[16]

The turmoil in Kansas highlighted and deepened tensions within the Democratic Party. Proslavery southern Democrats believed that the institution of slavery should be permitted and protected in every territory—if not the entire Union. Washington did not have the power to exclude slavery from any territories or to prevent any territory from joining the Union as a slave state. Quite the opposite: Congress had an obligation to enforce the property rights of slaveholders, for example, by passing legislation requiring the return of escaped slaves. Like their Republican counterparts in the North, the southern Democrats were at best nominally committed to the principle of popular sovereignty. They supported the democratic process, unless it produced an unfavorable result.[17]

The southern wing of the Democratic Party viewed Kansas as a test of the party's "readiness, as well as ability, to protect southern interests within the Union."[18] Because Kansas had been designated a free territory under the Missouri Compromise of 1820, southern Democrats viewed the Kansas–Nebraska Act as a modest win for southern rights. Popular sovereignty provided an opportunity for the expansion of slavery. But frustration grew with the arrival of each new wave of free-soil settlers, who seemed poised to deliver a free state if the democratic process ran its course. As a congressman from South Carolina wrote in the spring of 1857, "The admission of Kansas into the Union as a slave state is now a point of honor. . . . The fate of the South is to be decided with the Kansas issue."[19] Ignoring the illegality of the election process, southern Democrats threw their weight behind the proslavery legislature and expected the national party leadership to do the same. Indeed, several southern extremists in Congress, the so-called fire-eaters, hinted at secession if Kansas did not become a slave state.

At first glance, northern Democrats held an unusually principled position, being committed to popular sovereignty. They joined southern Democrats in denouncing the antislavery agitation of Republicans as a threat to the Union and maintaining that it was the responsibility of voters, not Congress, to decide whether a territory or state permitted slavery. Unlike the southern wing of the party, however, northern Democrats were willing to accept the outcome of popular sovereignty, whether it was a victory for the free-soil or proslavery forces. They were anti-antislavery, rather than proslavery stalwarts.

This commitment to principle was in truth a desperate bid to paper over the cracks in the party and the nation. Most northern Democrats preferred free labor to slave labor but, in the interest of remaining a united party, were careful to speak of its economic benefits, rather than its moral superiority.[20] A smaller faction was explicitly free-soil, hoping to preserve the western territories for white labor. In any case, whether a state voted Democratic, they argued, mattered more than whether it was free or slave. Popular sovereignty promised to defuse the slavery debate by "making it a 'local' decision."[21]

Northern Democrats wanted to grant Kansas statehood immediately, whether slave or free, seeing it as the "quickest way to end the abolitionist furor in the North and the secessionist clamor in the South."[22] They also hoped that a swift and fair resolution to the conflict—that is, ensuring an honest vote on a state constitution—would convince Kansans to vote Democratic. About half of the settlers who opposed slavery in the territory were free-soil Democrats. If they could be prevented from allying with the Republican Party—and if the party could retain the support of proslavery Democrats—Kansas might enter the Union as a Democratic state.[23] The worst-case scenario would be for Buchanan to allow the proslavery legislature to achieve statehood with a proslavery constitution over the protests of the free-state majority.[24] It would furnish the Republicans with yet more evidence of slave power's sway over the Democratic Party and discredit popular sovereignty.

Buchanan did not have long to plan his strategy for Kansas. Even as he was sworn into office, new troubles brewed in the territory. In February 1857 the proslavery territorial legislature in Lecompton embarked on a scheme to admit Kansas as a slave state. The legislature passed a bill authorizing a convention of elected delegates to draft a state constitution. The result of this process was not in doubt. The measure charged proslavery sheriffs with registering voters, who would then select the convention delegates, and granted proslavery county commissioners the power to appoint election judges.[25] The bill also did not require a referendum on the constitution. Outraged by the apparent efforts of what he labeled the "felon legislature" to rig the convention process, Governor Geary vetoed the bill.[26] The legislature immediately overrode his veto. Unable to overturn the bill and facing death threats from proslavery extremists, the governor resigned. In a portent of the way Kansas would bedevil his presidency, Geary's resignation occurred on the very day of Buchanan's inauguration.

Kansas was the critical challenge for Buchanan's administration. How the president handled its bid for statehood would determine whether the Democratic Party survived as a national organization. Here, Buchanan was caught on the horns of a dilemma. If he sided with the northern wing of the party and guaranteed majority rule in Kansas, he would anger proslavery southerners. If Buchanan aligned himself with southern Democrats and supported

the Lecompton convention, he would alienate northern Democrats. To sub-
vert popular sovereignty would push northern voters into the arms of the Republican Party and widen national divisions.[27] Southerners regarded a major
electoral victory for the Republicans as a "mortal threat" to slavery.[28] Indeed,
many southern Democrats spoke of secession if a Republican won the White
House. During the 1856 presidential election, for example, Virginia Senator
James Mason vowed that if the Republican candidate prevailed, "one course
remains for the South: Immediate, absolute, and eternal separation."[29] Buchanan took this particular threat seriously, declaring: "The Union is in danger and the people everywhere begin to know it."[30] But how could he save the
Union without sacrificing the Democratic Party in the North?

Buchanan's Preferred Strategy to Resolve the Conflict Over Kansas

The Kansas crisis had the potential to fracture the Democratic Party and the
Union, and necessitated a governmental response. But the crisis is not sufficient to explain why Buchanan pursued a political solution, accompanied
by a diversionary spectacle in Utah, instead of enacting alternative responses.

To apply the policy substitutability approach to Buchanan's decision to
orchestrate a diversionary spectacle in Utah, we must first identify the president's ranking of preferred strategies for addressing the dispute over Kansas
(see Figure 5.2). Such an exercise is challenging because nowhere does Buchanan leave an explicit record of his preferences. Indeed, he was "instinc-
tively reticent" and avoided documenting his thoughts at crucial moments.[31]
Further, during his White House years, no one among the president's advisors
recorded the content of cabinet meetings or his daily activities. Consequently,
historians have relied heavily on the voluminous correspondence between the
president and a handful of close advisors to discern his motives.[32] Using the
available evidence, we can make a plausible case about the relative attraction
of menu options and reveal how environmental factors winnowed down the
available choices.

Buchanan's preferred policy option to calm the furor over Kansas was
limited political reform. It was predictable that the president would think
in terms of political reform to overcome sectional division, given the history of negotiated deals such as the Missouri Compromise of 1820 and the
Compromise of 1850. But it was also in his character. Long before occupying

Limited political reform

Diversionary war

Diversionary spectacle

Muddling through

Radical political reform

Repression

Foreign intervention

FIGURE 5.2 President James Buchanan's ranking of responses to domestic unrest

the White House, Buchanan reflected on the traits of a successful American president. Military officers, he asserted, should never hold the presidency, for they "lacked the instinct to consider opposing opinions and negotiate compromises."[33] A lawyer "who was neither jealous of his power nor 'irritable and quarrelsome' in his personality" was better suited to the office.[34] A lawyer by training, Buchanan was almost certainly describing himself. During his diplomatic career, he "had always shown a talent for shifting positions under political stress, and the balancing of issues had been a major part of his success"; he was a pragmatist, a "canny wheeler-dealer."[35] As a presidential candidate, Buchanan believed that his skill at finding common ground among rival views would appeal to voters weary of sectarian bickering.[36] He sought to project "an image of Union-saving conservatism as an alternative to Republican extremism."[37] Buchanan promised voters that he would "restore the same harmony among the sister States which prevailed before this apple of discord, in the form of slavery agitation, had been cast into their midst."[38] This apparent equanimity helped Buchanan capture the presidency.[39]

Buchanan entered office committed to ending the conflict over Kansas through a political compromise. Indeed, he had staked his presidency on it.

Buchanan sought to guide the ship of state between the Scylla of Republican radicalism and the Charybdis of southern extremism. On the one hand, the president was "a northern man with southern principles."[40] Although he hailed from Pennsylvania, his sympathies clearly lay with the southern Democrats.[41] For example, Buchanan believed that there was a constitutional right to own slaves and strongly supported the 1857 Dred Scott Supreme Court decision allowing slavery in all western territories. In Buchanan's view, the agenda of the Republican Party was to "strike a mortal blow against the South" and tear the country apart.[42] He asserted: "Republicans must be, as they can be with justice, boldly assailed as disunionists, and this charge must be reiterated again and again."[43] By the end of his term in office, Buchanan would be strongly identified with the South, having used his executive powers to push a fraudulent proslavery Lecompton constitution through Congress.[44]

On the other hand, during the first days of his presidency, Buchanan adopted a relatively moderate tone. He viewed southern extremists, the fire-eaters, who habitually threatened secession when faced with any perceived challenge to slavery, as a threat to the Union on par with the Republican Party. In other words, his goal was to "destroy the subversive league of northern fanatics *and* southern rebels."[45] He objected to the attempts of fire-eaters to use any method, however illegal, to guarantee that Kansas would become a slave state. Buchanan implicitly rebuked the southern extremists in his inaugural address: "[I]t is the imperative and indispensable duty of the government of the United States to secure to every resident inhabitant [of Kansas] the free and independent expression of his opinion by his vote. This sacred right of each individual must be preserved."[46]

Because the president saw himself as a conciliator, he was committed to finding a broadly acceptable compromise for Kansas. Enacting radical political reforms to placate Republicans, namely legislation prohibiting the westward spread of slavery or abolition, was unacceptable. Also unacceptable was the position of the fire-eaters, who wanted Buchanan to guarantee that Kansas would become a slave state.[47] Instead, the president hoped to resolve the dispute over slavery in Kansas on the basis of popular sovereignty, allowing the territory to become a free state. This plan would appease northern Democrats by allowing a fair election in Kansas. Buchanan also hoped to placate proslavery southerners with the promise that even if free-staters prevailed in Kansas, a fair outcome would increase support for the Democratic Party among Kansans and preserve Democratic dominance in Congress.

Buchanan's favored strategy for managing the conflict over slavery was limited political reform. But there is also reason to believe that the president saw the diversionary use of force as an inherently attractive strategy that could accompany and strengthen efforts to avoid civil war through political action. There is no smoking gun, or document, laying out Buchanan's preference for diversion. But this is hardly surprising given that, in advance of assuming the presidency, there was no obvious target suitable for rallying public opinion. The Mormon problem waxed and waned over time, and it was serendipitous that it waxed in the spring of 1857, when Young defied federal authority, providing the president with an opportunity to use diversionary force.

It was common during this period for political elites to contemplate, even quite openly, a diversionary war. William MacKinnon observes in his history of the Utah expedition that to consider waging a diversionary war "seems fantastic in terms of the gravity and irresponsibility of such a notion, but nineteenth-century politics were awash with such schemes or least speculation about them."[48] And Walter MacDougall describes Buchanan's temperament as being suited to the use of diversionary tactics; the president "decidedly favored the dodge over the fix" when it came to the national slavery debate.[49]

Would Buchanan have been more inclined toward a diversionary war or a diversionary spectacle in Utah? A full-scale war against the Mormons would have required sending a large contingent of federal troops, for example, to oust Young, crush the church, rescue the women trapped in polygamous marriages, and install a friendly territorial governor—with the expectation of bloodshed. A diversionary spectacle was instead a show of force, requiring a smaller force and more limited aims: to coerce Young into stepping down without engaging the Mormon militia.

Seen through the lens of Kansas, a full-scale assault on Utah was inherently more attractive than a small-scale military expedition. The rally effect was likely to become more pronounced in proportion to the scale of the assault. Calls for a "holy war" to eliminate the Mormon heresy were commonplace in newspapers, public speeches, pamphlets, and even novels.[50] For example, an editorial in the *New York Daily Times* advocated that Mormons "be utterly exterminated."[51] The commanding officer of the Utah expedition, General William Selby Harney, similarly suggested that to solve the Mormon problem, "he would capture Brigham Young and the twelve apostles and execute them in a summary manner and winter in the temple of the Latter-day Saints."[52]

The severity of the crisis in Kansas required a maximal diversion and a substantial rally effect to provide Buchanan the necessary political breathing room. In 1857 the United States was careering toward a civil war that would be resolved only after 600,000 men had died. For a nation fixated on events in Kansas, a spectacle in Utah would offer a modest diversion. To be confident of rallying northern and southern opinion, full-scale war must be unleashed. American blood must be spilled on American soil.

Why, then, did Buchanan favor a diversionary war over a spectacle, while the Argentine junta likely favored a spectacle over a war in the Falkland Islands in 1982? (See Chapter 4.) Part of the difference lies in the nature of the missions. In the Argentine case, the goal was to regain a historical territory and return it to the homeland. If this could be achieved with a mere show of force, then all the better. After all, conflict with the British was only a means to an end. But in the U.S. case, the aim was to defeat the Mormon church in a dramatic fashion. War against the polygamists was an end in itself. With the Falklands, the rally effect came from having Argentine boots on sacred soil. With the Mormons, the rallying came from eradicating a despised adversary on the battlefield.

Although the precise allure of using diversionary tactics is difficult to establish, we can confidently say that it was less attractive than limited political reform and more palatable than the other options on the policy menu: radical political reform, repression, and foreign intervention. Radical political reform in this context would have meant either appeasing the Republicans or the southern extremists. Both policies would have further destabilized if not permanently divided the country and were anathema to Buchanan in the spring of 1857.

Repression was also inherently unattractive to a leader who saw himself as a uniter, not a divider. But if Buchanan had placed this option higher on his policy ranking, he would have found it difficult to implement successfully, given the democratic political system in which he operated. Indeed, repression would almost certainly have sparked complete catastrophe. The president eventually did send a small contingent of federal troops to Kansas, authorized to keep the peace while his political compromise was put into place.[53] But if Buchanan had dispatched troops to Kansas to impose a settlement on the territory, it may have led to wider conflict or even disunion. Using force to make Kansas a free state would have angered both wings of the Democratic Party— the northern Democrats because it was at odds with popular sovereignty and the southern Democrats because, instead of protecting the peculiar institution, the federal government had blocked slavery from spreading. At the same time, foisting slavery on Kansas at the point of a bayonet, with no semblance of a democratic process, would have enraged Republicans and in all likelihood prompted many northern Democrats to switch parties.

Foreign intervention was not even contemplated. For a country that established the Monroe Doctrine and was intent on evicting the European powers from North America as it expanded westward, and certainly for Buchanan, who was an ardent champion of Manifest Destiny, inviting another country to send troops was undoubtedly at or near the bottom of his policy ranking.[54]

In summary, Buchanan would have preferred to muddle through rather than adopt any of these remaining options on the menu. Indeed, when the Republican candidate Abraham Lincoln won the 1860 presidential election and seven southern states left the Union, Buchanan chose to muddle through with halfhearted attempts at a limited political compromise, even though "the odds were poor" that such a strategy would "create even a temporary sectional truce."[55] Buchanan asserted that although secession was illegal, the Constitution did not grant him the power to use force against the rebellious states—a response favored by militant Republicans. Instead, Buchanan sought to appease southern Democrats by proposing a constitutional amendment that would recognize the property rights of slave owners in the southern states and would protect slavery in the territories, an idea that gained little traction.

In the remainder of the chapter I will explain why Buchanan believed that limited political reform was practicable in the spring of 1857 and briefly describe the compromise he pursued for Kansas. I will then demonstrate how, when the troubles in Utah provided an opportunity for diversionary action, a low extractive capacity eliminated a full-scale war against the Mormons from Buchanan's menu of options, pushing his administration instead toward a low-cost diversionary spectacle.

Choosing Political Reform: Buchanan's Plan for Kansas

Buchanan was convinced that extremists—abolitionists and southern secessionists—threatened the Union, but he also believed that they represented a minority of Americans. Ending the unrest through political reform was practicable. The president sought to isolate the vocal antislavery voters in the North and fire-eaters in the South, while appealing to the silent majority who remained pro-Union and open to political compromise. Buchanan's policy for Kansas threaded the needle by (1) supporting the northern Democratic position that popular sovereignty should decide the status of slavery in the territory; (2) appealing to free-soil Democrats and Republicans by guaranteeing a fair vote, meaning that the territory would join the Union as a free state; and (3) assuring southerners that even if they outlawed slavery, Kansans would vote Democratic, particularly if the president could swiftly restore order and democracy to the territory.[56]

In practice, Buchanan's policy centered on the selection of a new territorial governor, one who would ensure that any state constitution be submitted to an honest vote and would work to build support for the Democratic Party in Kansas.[57] His choice, Robert J. Walker, appeared perfectly suited to accomplish these potentially contradictory goals. He was a nationally respected, proslavery southern Democrat, but he also promised to uphold popular sovereignty in Kansas and accepted that free-staters would prevail in a fair election.[58]

The initial challenge for Walker was to convince free-state Kansans to participate in the constitutional convention process, even though the territorial legislature had attempted to exclude them from it. The governor designate hoped that because many of the free-soilers were avowed Democrats, they could be persuaded to put aside past wrongs and ally with the proslavery Democrats to "make Kansas a free Democratic state in preference to a Black Republican and abolitionist state."[59] Walker assumed (wrongly, as it turned out) that the proslavery settlers would concede his argument that the climate in Kansas was ill suited to slavery and accept their defeat gracefully, allowing the majority to bring Kansas into the Union as a free state.

For Buchanan, the challenge was to hold the national Democratic Party together while his plan for Kansas was realized. The northern wing of the party could be mollified relatively quickly. Because the election of convention delegates would occur within a month of the governor's arrival, it would soon become clear whether Walker would allow, as he put it, "the actual bona fide residents of the Territory of Kansas, by a fair and regular vote, unaffected by fraud or violence . . . in adopting their State constitution, to decide for themselves what shall be their social institutions."[60] However, southern Democrats had to be patient optimists. It would be a long wait before a decision to abandon Kansas to the free-state majority might bear fruit. And even then, it was not at all certain that Kansans would vote Democratic in national elections.

As Walker departed for Kansas in mid-April, Buchanan and partisans of all stripes believed that the governor's success was vital to the survival of the Democratic Party and possibly the country. As one Philadelphia newspaper accurately observed, "The eyes of the whole Union are fixed on him."[61]

The American Pauper State and Diversionary War

Buchanan believed that it was possible to construct a political compromise for Kansas that would unify Democrats and marginalize extremists. Buchanan also saw an opportunity to strengthen these efforts by using diversionary tactics in Utah to distract the public from domestic divisions. But here the president was unable to pursue the strategy with the highest utility for distracting the public—a diversionary war to defeat the Mormon church. Instead, the government's inability to efficiently mobilize the resources needed to pay for an extended campaign forced Buchanan to reduce the scale and aims of the Utah expedition, and pursue instead a diversionary spectacle.

The antebellum U.S. state was weak, in the words of one historian, "a mere shell."[62] The federal government was restricted to a narrow set of activities, such as mail delivery, the collection of customs duties, and a small standing army for defense. Its ability to extract the monies to pay for these activities was severely circumscribed.[63] Economic historian John Wallis has tallied U.S. government revenue (federal, state, and local) as a percentage of the gross national product (GNP) in the nineteenth and twentieth centuries (see Figure 5.3). Between 1840 and 1860, revenue at all levels of government was only four to five percent of GNP. And in 1850, for example, federal revenue accounted for less than half of the total amount extracted. Per capita federal government revenues actually fell slightly between 1800 ($1.96) and 1850 ($1.93).[64]

Washington's ability to raise revenues was constrained by the long-standing commitment of Americans to limited government. The public might have disagreed on the institution of slavery, but there was a virtual consensus on the need to limit the reach of the federal government: "For at least the first century under the Constitution, the American political tradition was one of very limited government—limited, above all, as far as the federal government was concerned. Americans of the generations of Jefferson, Jackson, and Lincoln demanded little of the federal government and had low expectations of it."[65]

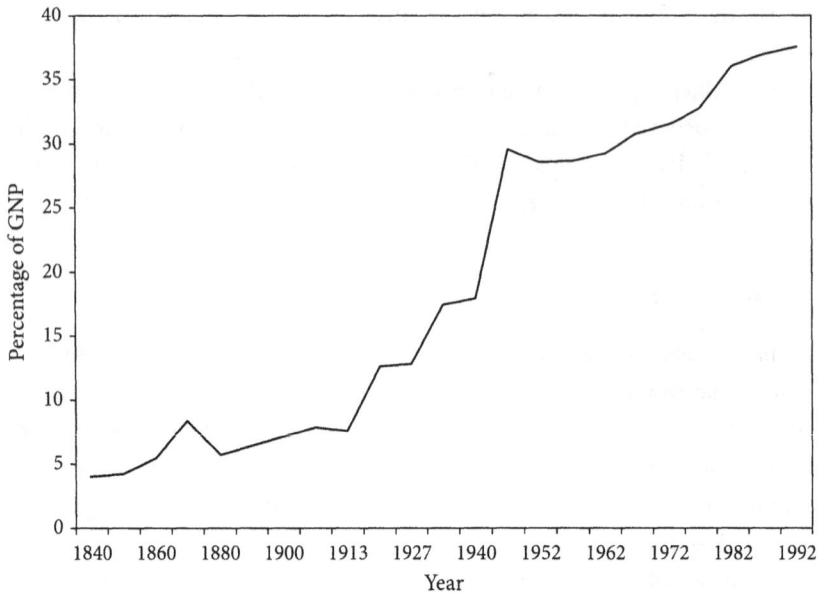

FIGURE 5.3 Government (federal, state, and local) revenue as a percentage of GNP
SOURCE: Data from Wallis, "American Government Finance in the Long Run," 65.

The Constitution restricted the capacity of the federal government to raise revenue from the public. Washington could collect indirect taxes, but only state and local authorities could tax property, the source of most American wealth. And when the federal government exercised even these limited powers, it often faced a recalcitrant public. For example, the government was forced to abandon excise duties due to taxpayer opposition. As a result, federal income came almost exclusively from import tariffs.[66] Tariffs were relatively popular because they protected domestic industry. But even here, critics feared that a government with access to resources would commit mischief. On occasions when tariffs produced "an unwelcome surplus," the federal government was compelled to reduce them further.[67] As Buchanan entered the White House, for example, there was a movement to reduce taxes on imports in response to perceived excesses in government income, which resulted in a general reduction of the tariff level.[68]

As a Democrat, Buchanan's ability to increase government income was particularly constrained. In a culture that celebrated a pauper state, the

Democrats were the party of extremely limited government. Buchanan campaigned on a platform of fiscal frugality.[69] The president declared in his inaugural address that a matter of more practical importance than slavery was the treasury surplus, which he argued "almost necessarily gives birth to extravagant legislation" and "wild schemes of expenditure."[70]

Limitations on the federal government's ability to raise revenue severely restricted Buchanan's diversionary options, preventing the administration from fully rallying opinion with a substantive anti-Mormon operation. Simply put, Buchanan lacked the resources to launch a major campaign in the spring of 1857. At the time, the entire federal army consisted of around 13,000 troops, spread across the vast western territories.[71] And funding even this peacetime force represented about 28 percent of federal expenditures.[72] With a weak hand to play, the president was forced to choose a diversionary spectacle over a more expensive, but also likely more-effective, diversionary war. Although limited force with limited objectives would produce a limited rally effect, it still might give Buchanan some additional room for maneuver in Kansas.

In May 1857 the president authorized a contingent of 2,500 troops as a "show of military force" to coerce Young into stepping down and ensure that his replacement, Alfred Cumming, "was accepted and respected" as the territory's new governor.[73] Winfield Scott, the commanding general of the army, worried that this force would be inadequate given the estimated 4,000 men in the Mormon militia, some of whom were veterans of the Mexican-American War.[74] He also doubted whether so many soldiers could be moved from their current postings. Scott's aide-de-camp cautioned: "The lateness of the season, the dispersed condition of the troops and the smallness of their numbers available, have seemed to present elements of difficulty, if not hazard, in this expedition."[75] (He was correct in his assessment, as the president was unable to assemble more than 1,300 troops to send to Utah in 1857—the mounted troops of the Second Dragoons had been marked for duty in Utah but were kept in Kansas to help Walker keep the peace until September 1857.[76]) However, Buchanan was undeterred because, as we will see, he believed that the limited aim of ousting Young could be accomplished without having to engage the Mormon militia and, therefore, was within his means.

The effect of a low extractive capacity on Buchanan's decision making became evident as the mission progressed and threatened to escalate from a spectacle closer to a war. Although there was no direct military confrontation, the Mormon militia impeded and harassed federal troops as they journeyed to Utah, destroying supply wagons, stampeding livestock, and burning grass along their route. Supplying and then resupplying the expedition quickly depleted the treasury.[77] The president confronted the difficult choice of abandoning the mission and provoking the public's ire or trying to wring resources out of Congress to intensify the campaign into a full-scale military operation. Indicating that Buchanan was attracted to the maximum military option available, the president chose escalation.

Buchanan may have believed that public anger over the misdeeds of Young's militia—including its raids on the expedition's supply train and the Mountain Meadows Massacre, in which 120 emigrants passing through Utah to settle in California were murdered by a party of Mormon militiamen and Indian auxiliaries—would make it harder for Congress to withhold the revenues required by the military to defeat the church.[78] His administration made an enthusiastic case for further action against the Mormons. In his annual report to Congress for 1857, Secretary of War John B. Floyd averred: "However anxiously the government might desire to avoid a collision with this or any other community of people under its jurisdiction, yet it is not possible for it to postpone the duty of reducing to subordination a rebellious fraternity."[79]

Indeed, instead of simply asking for resources to continue the current mission, the president pressed for an expansion of the operation into a bona fide war. Cap in hand, Buchanan beseeched Congress for revenues not only to replenish the empty treasury but also finance four new regiments for the Utah expedition—that is, an additional 4,000 soldiers.[80] In another sign of the president's desire to widen the aims of the campaign, the War Department began preparations to send a year's worth of supplies to the territory, while also considering a plan to send troops from the West Coast to "crush all resistance."[81]

Buchanan struggled in vain against the restraints of the U.S. pauper state. Congress balked at the spiraling cost of the expedition and flatly denied the president's request for new regiments.[82] Both Republicans and Democrats also opposed the deficiency appropriations bill, accusing the president of profligacy. A North Carolina Democrat described the spending on Utah as "monstrous and entirely unjustified."[83] Across the aisle, a Republican from Illinois charged the Buchanan administration with wasting public money on "its favorite pet contractors."[84] Congress delayed the bill for months, forcing a despairing Buchanan to hastily offer peace terms to Young. The Mormons were granted pardon on condition of future cooperation with federal authority.[85]

The low extractive capacity of the U.S. government was a necessary condition to explain the limited scope of the Utah expedition. If Buchanan had been capable of extracting additional resources, he would likely have ordered a war to defeat the Mormon church. Unfortunately for the president, this more-desirable policy response was not on the menu of available options, as Buchanan was reminded when he tried and failed to mobilize funds from Congress.

The Viability of a Diversionary Spectacle in Mormon Utah

When resurgent troubles in Utah provided an opportunity to use diversionary tactics, the government's low extractive capacity eliminated the option of a diversionary war, pushing the president toward staging a lower-cost spectacle. The viability of a spectacle now hinged on a second environmental factor: the nature of the target. A limited operation could hope to succeed only if resistance would be minimal, and a rally effect could be anticipated. Many potential targets would have failed either or both of these tests, removing the option of a diversionary spectacle entirely. Crucially, Buchanan believed that Young's regime was fundamentally weak and that the Mormons were widely hated, meaning that even a small-scale operation could successfully remove Young from the Utah governorship and provide significant political benefits. A diversionary spectacle remained on the table.

Heresy, Moral Iniquity, and Tyranny

In 1857 the Mormon church was a highly symbolic target, and any military operation against the Mormons could be expected to generate national applause. At this time, Americans were "almost unanimous in their hostility toward the church."[86] Mormonism was reviled as a heretical religion and an affront to Christian morality, particularly after 1852, when the Mormon church publicly admitted and defended the practice of polygamy. As the *San Joaquin Republican* put it, Mormonism was a "monstrous combination of superstition, ignorance and debauchery" and Young "the arch imposter, tyrant and debauchee."[87] Anti-Mormon sentiment also stemmed from the conviction that Young rejected federal authority and aimed to establish an independent theocracy in Utah. Detractors suspected the governor of trying to build a Mormon empire in the West or even topple the federal government.[88] Young's reported acts of sedition included expelling federal judges, defying federal law when it contradicted church rulings, and inciting Indian violence against the United States.

There were also rumors that the governor, in an effort to inspire a Mormon Reformation, had resurrected the doctrine of "blood atonement," or the belief that someone who commits an egregious sin can gain eternal salvation only through his or her death. As one of the perpetrators of the Mountain Meadows massacre put it, the "right thing to do with a sinner who did not repent and obey the [Church] Council, was to take the life of the offending party, and thus save his everlasting soul."[89] Unsurprisingly, this practice was seen as a direct threat to the non-Mormon residents of Utah.[90]

For Buchanan, the main virtue of anti-Mormonism was that it crossed party lines: "Mormonism was a political issue of a kind rarely encountered in 1857, because, with few exceptions, Northerners and Southerners, whether Democrats, Republicans, or Americans, could unite wholeheartedly in condemning it."[91] The Republican Party included an anti-polygamy plank in its 1856 presidential platform, proclaiming that it was the "right and duty of Congress to prohibit in the territories those twin relics of barbarism—polygamy and slavery."[92] Proslavery southern Democrats also reviled the Mormon church. For example, the *Richmond Enquirer* asserted that Mormonism was "revolting alike to civilization and law" and rejected the use of popular sovereignty in Utah until the church abandoned its "barbarous code of laws."[93] In the name of popular sovereignty and religious freedom, some northern Democrats had initially defended the right of Mormons to practice polygamy. But by the mid-1850s, they too had climbed aboard the anti-Mormon bandwagon. Even the foremost advocate of popular sovereignty, Stephen Douglas, denounced the Mormons as "outlaws" and "alien enemies," deserving of punishment by Washington.[94]

Brigham Young's Reluctant Followers
The Buchanan administration also believed that a low-cost diversionary spectacle was practicable because the Mormons would not resist the army's efforts to replace Young with a non-Mormon governor.[95] Two assumptions underpinned this assessment. First, the administration believed that although Young might have been willing to do battle with Washington, rank-and-file Mormons were not prepared to commit treason by opposing federal authority in the territory. In the words of the secretary of war, "It was hardly within the

line of reasonable probability that these people would put themselves beyond the pale of reconciliation with the government by acts of unprovoked, open, and wanton rebellion."[96]

Second, the prevailing view was that support for Young's rule was shallow. Buchanan saw the governor as a despot and assumed that his disciples agreed.[97] This conclusion was reinforced by the accounts of non-Mormon visitors to Utah, who found that there was considerable "dissatisfaction with Brigham Young's satrapy" and "many Saints would welcome rescue."[98] The press also advanced this opinion. As the *New York Daily Times* reported, "one-third or half of the Mormons, who are disgusted with Brigham's tyranny, would rise against him were they protected by the United States troops."[99] The Mormons would greet the army as liberators.

The expedition authorized by Buchanan in May 1857 was premised on the belief that the mere sight of federal troops marching into Salt Lake City would either intimidate Young into abdicating his throne or perhaps embolden the Mormons to depose him. Not only was the force sent to Utah relatively small, but the War Department also specifically ordered the campaign commander not to "attack any body of citizens whatever" unless "the ordinary course of judicial proceedings, and the power vested in the United States marshals and other proper officers, [are] inadequate for the preservation of the public peace and due execution of the laws."[100] The Mormon church therefore represented a uniquely favorable target: strong enough in its demonic influence that the use of force would garner widespread praise, weak enough that Young's regime would topple like a house of cards.

Choosing a Diversionary Spectacle

The government's low extractive capacity eliminated the option of a diversionary war, while the nature of the target allowed a diversionary spectacle. Although the stars aligned in favor of a diversionary use of force, does the evidence show that, in fact, this was Buchanan's motivation? In other words, were tensions within the Democratic Party and the Union, which had been exacerbated by the turmoil in Kansas, a necessary condition for the president's decision to dispatch troops to Utah?

The evidence of a diversionary motivation for the Utah expedition is considerable. Primary documents, as well as the sequence and timing of events, point to Buchanan's desire to generate a rally effect as a central cause of the campaign. As a result, many historians agree that the expedition was intended as a diversion. Relative to the great events transpiring elsewhere, Utah was a sideshow for Buchanan. But he hoped to make it the main show.

In the early months of 1857, Mormon Utah reemerged in the national news when several non-Mormon officials appointed by the federal government to serve in Utah were forced to flee the territory after facing threats of violence from the church. The highest-profile incident involved a territorial Supreme Court judge, W. W. Drummond, who claimed that his life had been threatened when he attempted to uphold the authority of the federal courts. Before leaving Utah, Drummond sent Buchanan and his cabinet a letter detailing Young's treacheries and asserting that the territory was in a state of rebellion: "[I]t is impossible for us to enforce the laws in this Territory. Every man here holds his life at the will of Brigham Young."[101] The judge also sent his missive to the *New York Herald*, where it was promptly published. Soon after, on March 30, Drummond resigned his post, asserting (again in a published letter): "[Since] Young received his appointment as governor, it is noonday madness and folly to attempt to administer the law in that Territory. The officers are insulted, harassed, and murdered for doing their duty, and not recognizing Brigham Young as the only law-giver and law-maker on earth."[102] His broadsides outraged the public, prompting calls for Young's immediate removal and military action against the church.

At the same time, unbeknownst to Congress and the press, Buchanan's cabinet received additional correspondence from federal appointees in Utah, including the other two members of the territorial Supreme Court, expressing concerns about Young's government. In January 1857 the Mormon-dominated Utah legislature passed several resolutions that seemed to challenge federal authority over the territory. One such resolution stated: "[W]e will resist any attempt of Government Officials to set at naught our Territorial laws, or to impose upon us those which are inapplicable and of right not in force in this Territory."[103] Confronted with Young's truculence and an increasingly indignant public, Buchanan resolved to appoint a new governor for Utah and, in early April, began the search for a replacement.[104]

Utah was a thorn in the administration's side, and in the absence of events in Kansas, Buchanan would likely have felt impelled to craft a policy response. The question was this: what kind of policy? Importantly, the president initially held off making a decision about whether to send troops to the territory. Indeed, through March and April, Buchanan appears to have been uncertain about the wisdom of a military intervention.[105] In May, however, the War Department began planning for an expedition to Utah in earnest, signaling a clear shift in the president's policy toward the territory.[106] By the end of the month, the expedition "had moved from the status of speculation to reality," and the administration announced it would send 2,500 troops to Utah.[107] What explains the hawkish turn in Buchanan's policy?

At the end of April, Buchanan juggled simultaneous crises in Utah and Kansas. As the president was considering whether to send troops to Utah, Walker was en route to the Kansas territory to assume the governorship. The country waited to learn whether Walker could guide Kansas to statehood without engendering further violence. At this critical juncture for U.S. policy toward both territories, Buchanan received a letter from a trusted friend, Robert Tyler, who was the eldest son of former president John Tyler, as well as a leading southern Democrat and a member of Buchanan's inner circle. Historian David Williams contends that Tyler "doubtless exercised considerable influence upon Buchanan."[108] From the late 1840s through the end of the Civil War, Tyler was a regular correspondent with Buchanan. In a letter dated January 18, 1855, for example, Buchanan wrote: "You have always held a very high place in my regard, quite as high as that of any other friend, and I have been happy to believe that this feeling has been cordially reciprocated on your part."[109] Even while Buchanan was in office, when his secretary often handled his correspondence, the president personally read and responded to Tyler's letters, often several times a week. Indeed, Tyler frequently visited the White House.[110]

Buchanan also owed his friend a political debt. Tyler had played a vital role in securing for Buchanan the Democratic Party's nomination in the 1856 election. In Buchanan's judgment, few had done more than Tyler to "elevate me to my present position and . . . I am personally attached to him very warmly."[111] In appreciation, Buchanan sought to award him a cabinet post and, when unable to do so, offered him the position of minister to Switzerland (Tyler declined).[112] Later, in the fall of 1857, Tyler would help to convince the president to break his promise to Walker and send the proslavery Lecompton constitution to Congress for approval, even though the free-state majority had boycotted a referendum on the articles pertaining to slavery.[113]

On April 27, Tyler wrote to Buchanan at some length about the president's troubles in Utah, making the case for military invention—specifically on the grounds that it would be useful for diverting public attention from the conflict over Kansas:

The public mind is becoming greatly excited on the subject of *Mormonism*. The Popular Idea is rapidly maturing that Mormonism (already felt slightly in our large Northern cities) should be put down and utterly extirpated. *I believe that we can supersede the Negro-Mania with the almost universal excitement of an Anti-Mormon Crusade.* Certainly it is a subject which concerns *all* Religious Bodies & reaches every man's fireside with a peculiar interest. Should you, with your accustomed grip, seize this question with a strong, fearless & resolute hand, the Country I am sure will rally to you with an earnest enthusiasm & the pipings of Abolitionism will hardly be heard amidst the thunders of the storm we shall raise. . . . The eyes & ears of the Nation may be made to find so much interest in Utah as to forget Kansas.[114]

The president's receipt of this letter immediately preceded—and likely precipitated—the decision to send a military expedition to Utah.[115]

It is also noteworthy that Buchanan grasped the sword based on very limited intelligence. Indeed, the president acted "without even making a minimal inquiry" into the veracity of the accusations made by Drummond and his colleagues.[116] As the *New York Daily Times* commented in the spring of 1858, "An army was sent to chastise rebels before it was clearly ascertained whether or not there were any rebels to chastise."[117] Indeed, in January 1858, when Congress asked for a full accounting of the evidence that the Buchanan administration had collected to justify a military intervention in Utah, the president required several weeks to assemble the report. The resulting dossier was a "hodge-podge" of documents, many of which were actually acquired by the president *after* his decision to send troops had been made.[118] The fact that the president rushed to use force without receiving the necessary intelligence suggests a desire to take advantage of propitious timing, by announcing a planned expedition to Utah within days of Walker's inaugural gubernatorial address in Kansas.

Many historians agree that Buchanan's anti-Mormon crusade was intended as a diversionary spectacle.[119] For example, in his history of the Utah expedition, Will Bagley writes: "Of all the complex difficulties facing the new administration, the Mormon problem offered the most tempting political opportunity and promised the most beguiling of solutions—military action, a course that might unify the nation in a popular crusade against the evils of Mormonism."[120] Similarly, in her biography of Buchanan, Jean Baker contends that the president authorized a military expedition because there was "much to gain by deflecting attention from an emerging crisis over slavery in the territory of Kansas."[121]

There is not universal agreement regarding Buchanan's motives, however. An alternative interpretation of Buchanan's decision making is that the extent of Young's rebelliousness and the magnitude of anti-Mormon sentiment within the public would have necessitated a firm response by the federal government, even in the absence of the troubles in Kansas. In other words, the use of force was "almost mandatory."[122] Certainly, as argued above, the popularity of a mission against the Mormons was a necessary condition for the expedition. Given his worries over the intensifying sectional conflict, Buchanan would never have risked exacerbating tensions with an unpopular military adventure in Utah.

However, events in Utah were not a sufficient explanation for the expedition. There were many similarly grave disputes involving the Mormon church before and after 1857: in 1851, 1853, 1855, 1871, 1874, 1882, and 1887. But only Buchanan sent the army to coerce compliance from the church.[123] In the fall of 1851, for example, shortly after Utah became a territory, several federal appointees clashed with Young over polygamy, the jurisdiction of the federal court, the legality of territorial elections, and the dispersal of federal money. In frustration, the officials returned to Washington with tales of the governor's tyranny and demands for military action. The so-called "runaway-officials" affair caused a "national uproar."[124] And it appeared for a time that the furor might result in a military expedition to remove Young from power, as opinion "flowed strongly against the Mormons."[125] However, the White House and Congress were circumspect in their response, carefully weighing the evidence against Young. After much deliberation, Washington ultimately sided with the church. There was no concurrent crisis over slavery and consequently fewer incentives to quickly escalate the dispute.[126]

In the absence of bleeding Kansas, the most likely scenario in 1857 is that events would have unraveled in a similar manner to 1851. Cooler heads would have prevailed, drawn-out discussions would have given the Mormon church the opportunity to press its case, and most likely a compromise solution would have been negotiated. And no one would have been surprised if the conflict in 1857 had been resolved without the use of force. This solution would have been perfectly in line with previous responses to troubles in Utah. But the bloodshed in Kansas raised temperatures and heightened the administration's willingness to gamble.

This pattern suggests that the crisis in Kansas was a necessary condition for the Utah expedition. Successive conflicts between Mormon Utah and Washington produced public outrage followed by demands for swift military action against the church. But each time, with the exception of 1857, the president in power—from Millard Fillmore to Grover Cleveland—chose to negotiate a compromise with the church, allowing public anger to abate. If, as historian Philip Klein asserts, "Mormon defiance of federal authority was traditional," why did only the dispute in 1857 result in military action?[127] The answer is found in the wider context in which Buchanan acted—the growing sectional conflict triggered by the dispute over Kansas.

Conclusion

In the spring of 1857 the president deviated from the traditional policy of resolving crises with the Mormon church with a negotiated deal, by sending troops to Utah. Given the paucity of direct evidence available about Buchanan's thinking, we must be cautious in our conclusions about his motivations. However, a strong case exists that Buchanan sought to distract the public from troubles in Kansas. A spectacle in Utah might rally opinion and grant more time to negotiate a settlement of the slavery issue. In the main, therefore, the case follows the causal pathway in which a pauper state uses diversionary tactics because the leader has both the desire and ability to select this option from the policy menu.

Applying the policy substitutability approach to this case reveals the effect of several environmental factors on Buchanan's decision making. First, the president's belief that a large percentage of Americans were committed to preserving the Union and open to compromise allowed the president to pursue his preferred policy of limited political reform. Second, a low extractive capacity closed off the option of a full-scale war against the Mormon church, propelling Buchanan toward the less-expensive and somewhat less-attractive option of a diversionary spectacle. Finally, Buchanan's perception that a low-cost, domestically popular mission against Mormon Utah was possible provided him with the occasion to stage a diversionary spectacle.

In contrasting the 1850s and the 1980s, we can see that extractive capacity and the availability of a suitable target also contributed to Argentina's decision to retake the Falkland Islands. But these environmental factors restricted the freedom of action of the junta far more than the U.S. government in the

1850s. While Buchanan was able to implement his preferred responses to the dispute over Kansas (with the caveat that he likely saw a diversionary war in Utah as more attractive than a spectacle), Argentine President Leopoldo Galtieri was compelled to forgo his top-ranked strategy for managing the internal instability.

However, both governments ultimately selected a diversionary spectacle from the policy menu. The question then is why, if Buchanan and Galtieri each believed they were orchestrating low-cost spectacles, the anti-Mormon crusade remained a limited conflict while the Falklands invasion became a full-scale war. The Buchanan administration did not exhibit the same degree of overconfidence when evaluating the potential cost of sending troops to install a non-Mormon governor in Utah. The president underestimated the willingness of rank-and-file Mormons to resist federal authority, but he was correct in concluding that they would not risk a major military campaign. While Young had a penchant for bellicose rhetoric, he knew the Mormon militia could not defeat the U.S. Army and avoided a war with federal forces.[128] All told, the federal army outnumbered and outgunned the Mormon militia. The governor first instructed his followers not to directly engage federal troops as they marched into Utah.[129] And later, when the army was poised to enter Salt Lake City in the spring of 1858, Young accepted Buchanan's peace settlement, even though it meant handing over the governorship of Utah to a non-Mormon.[130]

Having examined the conditions that lead pauper states to use diversionary tactics, I turn in the next chapter to the question of why some resource-poor governments, even those that would prefer to stage a diversion in response to growing internal tensions, select an alternative option from the policy menu.

6 The Road Not Taken

When Pauper States Do Not Use Diversionary Tactics

THIS CHAPTER EXAMINES THREE CASES IN WHICH PAUPER states chose not to use diversionary tactics in response to escalating social strife: the French monarchy's decision to call the Estates General in 1788, the Habsburg monarchy's request for Russian aid in suppressing the Hungarian revolution in 1849, and the Peruvian government's decision to muddle through with a failed policy of repression in 1988.

This analysis reveals how preferences and environmental factors combine to produce outcomes other than a diversionary spectacle or war. In each case, a low extractive capacity closed off preferred responses to unrest, pushing the government toward less-palatable options on the policy menu. Indeed, the decision makers in all of these regimes would likely have preferred the use of diversionary tactics to the strategy that they adopted, meaning that the impracticability of a diversion was a necessary condition for their final policy choice.

The cases also provide evidence of the conditions that allow some pauper states to avoid the Falklands trap—that is, provoking a diversionary spectacle against a target that escalates the conflict into a costly full-scale war. In Chapter 2 I argue that when environmental factors eliminate several options on the policy menu and the government faces a significant threat to its core interests, decision makers are likely to overestimate the chances that the policy they select will succeed. In the case of diversionary spectacles, the bias toward wishful thinking leads actors to downplay the probability that a target will resist.

Pauper states can escape this fate if they have a recent history of significant conflict with the target. It is more difficult to succumb to positive illusions when past hostilities are fresh in one's memory. In two of the cases—France in 1788 and Peru in 1988—the governments chose to forgo a diversionary spectacle because of the absence of a sufficiently low-cost target, a reality underscored by the fact that they had recently fought bloody campaigns against their main adversaries. The Habsburg monarchy faced a more basic obstacle to using diversionary force in 1849—the absence of a widely popular adversary to engage. In this case, Vienna's experience in ruling a multiethnic empire that was often deeply divided on matters of foreign policy helped to inoculate the government against the wishful-thinking bias.

Political Reform: King Louis XVI in Prerevolutionary France

The period from 1787 to 1788 in France is widely described as the "prerevolution."[1] But, at the time, the future of the guillotine and the levée en masse was still unknown. Instead, a combination of financial problems and a restive nobility seemed to presage a period of conflict and bargaining within France's elite, after which the ancien régime would continue much as before.

The absolutist French monarchy has been described as a "conglomeration of mostly centuries-old, sometimes thousand-year-old elements, none of which was ever discarded."[2] During the reign of King Louis XVI, however, a debate about the country's fundamental political institutions began in earnest. In August 1786 the king's minister of finance, Charles-Alexandre de Calonne, informed Louis XVI that the state was nearing bankruptcy and urged reform of the "whole public order" to right the monarchy's financial ship.[3] To replenish the regime's dwindling coffers, Calonne, with Louis XVI's full support, proposed a package of ambitious administrative and fiscal reforms in the fall of 1786. The centerpiece of the reform program was a land tax to be paid by all property owners, regardless of class, which would be assessed by a new tiered system of assemblies located at the parish, district, and provincial levels. To ensure that the tax assessments were not rigged to favor the nobility, wealthy landowners from any order—clergy, nobility, and lay commoners—could participate in the assemblies.

Calonne advised Louis XVI to summon an Assembly of Notables to consult on the monarchy's financial difficulties and endorse the reform program.

Because the king handpicked its members, the finance minister expected the reforms to pass through the Assembly with ease, investing his plans with "a convincing show of national support."[4] Calonne calculated that the support of the Notables would prevent the reform program from being derailed by the parlements, or the thirteen regional courts staffed by a hereditary class of magistrates, which by tradition registered royal edicts, including new taxes. The magistrates interpreted the right of registration to mean that they approved sovereign legislation and could remove or modify provisions that were inconsistent with legal precedent and "the abstract principles of justice, reason and virtue."[5] In practice, the parlements impeded the monarchy mainly through the tactic of delay, stretching out the process of registration indefinitely to pressure the king to revise or withdraw unpopular legislation.[6]

During Calonne's tenure, the parlements had become increasingly obstructionist. They made it "virtually impossible" to impose new levies, forcing the government to rely on loans.[7] And in 1784 and 1785, disturbed by the monarchy's profligacy, the preeminent court, the parlement of Paris, repeatedly objected to royal borrowing and only reluctantly registered loans to keep the regime afloat.[8] Calonne concluded that not only were the parlements certain to resist a land tax that challenged the noble tax privileges, but they were also unlikely to approve another loan for 1786. Thus, the finance minister sought to outflank the recalcitrant parlements by securing the support of the Assembly of Notables.[9]

However, the Notables surprised the crown by almost unanimously rejecting the measures and forcing Calonne's dismissal. They objected to the king's reforms not only because the land tax challenged their fiscal privilege but also because of the authoritarian manner by which the monarchy's finances, including the reform program, had been handled—evidence, they thought, of an "arbitrary or despotic government."[10]

Unable to win over the Assembly of Notables, the king's first minister, Loménie de Brienne, sent a revised reform program directly to the parlements for registration in the fall of 1787. The magistrates proved to be as unyielding as the Notables, however. Angered by the crown's attempt to circumvent them, the parlements refused to register the edict for the general land tax, insisting that only a representative body could authorize new levies. Louis XVI thus faced a "growing chorus of calls" to summon the long dormant Estates General, an elected consultative assembly comprising delegates from the three orders.[11]

In May 1788, after months of political wrangling, the monarchy moved to bridle the parlements. The crown announced that it would transfer the right of registration from the parlements to a new plenary court, whose members would be chosen by the king, and directed the magistrates to recess indefinitely. The "coup d'état," as the May edicts were dubbed, provoked widespread discontent, as the clergy and nobility made common cause in opposing the state.[12] After enduring more than two months of unrest in the révolte nobiliaire, which included riots in some provinces, the king relented: on August 8, 1788, he set the first meeting of the Estates General for May 1 of the following year.

Why did Louis XVI respond to the unrest by pledging political reform rather than pursuing his preferred options of muddling through or using diversionary tactics? Environmental factors ruled out these more-attractive responses to the social instability, propelling the government toward its decision to convoke the Estates General (see Figure 6.1). The monarchy's low extractive capacity eliminated both muddling through and diversionary war as

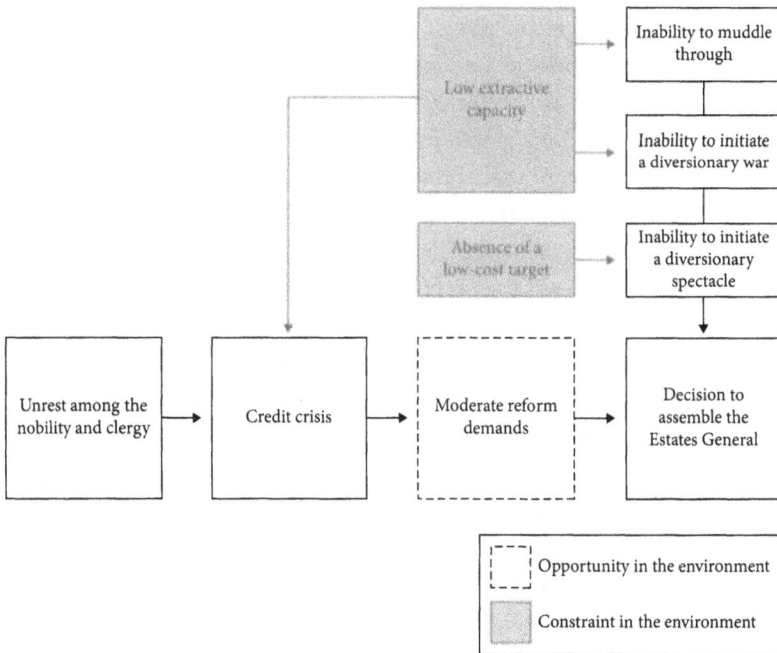

FIGURE 6.1 The French monarchy's decision to assemble the Estates General, 1788

viable policy responses, while the absence of a low-cost target rendered moot the option of staging a diversionary spectacle. Meanwhile, Louis XVI's belief that the Estates General would produce only modest change allowed the king to pursue this avenue. Through a process of elimination, the rather unpalatable option of political reform rose to the top of the menu of available policies.

The Révolte Nobiliaire of 1788

The coup d'état of May 1788, which subverted the power of the parlements, immediately produced widespread disorder. Indeed, the "system broke down completely."[13] With only two exceptions, the parlements declared the king's laws invalid and renewed their demand for the Estates General. In some cases the magistrates not only condemned the laws but also published polemics against the king's ministers, for example, describing them as "abettors of despotism."[14] In Pau, residents flooded the provincial governor's palace and forced him to allow the parlement to reassemble. In Rennes, the nobility organized large demonstrations in support of their parlement, causing the frightened governor to flee the province. In Grenoble, crowds of commoners refused to allow the parlement to vacate the city and sacked the governor's mansion. On the so-called "day of tiles," the citizens of Grenoble used tiles from the rooftops to pelt the soldiers sent to restore order.

The main lever by which the nobility and clergy exerted pressure on the monarchy was fiscal. In response to the May edicts, the nobility organized a massive tax strike, meaning that the "already bleak financial prospects of the Crown were made considerably worse."[15] Many of the nobles selected by the monarchy to serve on the new plenary court also refused to cooperate, frustrating the regime's efforts to pass taxes without the consent of the parlements.

In July the Assembly of the Clergy, the church's treasury, decreed that it would not pay the 8 million livres requested by the state as part of the reform package of 1787—instead, it would give the monarchy only 1.8 million livres. Breaking with a tradition of loyalty to the crown, the Assembly beseeched the king: "When the first Order of the state finds itself the only one able to speak; when a public outcry urges it to carry the will of all the others to the foot of your throne . . . it is shameful to be quiet. . . . Do not deprive yourself any longer of [the parlements'] lights."[16]

The instability, and the monarchy's lack of money, contributed to a severe credit crisis. The government struggled to negotiate loans to cover its expenditures.[17] And in early August, Brienne informed Louis XVI that the royal treasury was (again) empty. Indeed, the monarchy suspended payments on many outstanding loans on August 16. The ancien régime was staring bankruptcy in the face.

The collapse of the monarchy's finances necessitated swift action by the state. As historian Alfred Cobban concludes, the king's predicament was sufficiently dire that "no government could ignore it."[18]

King Louis XVI's Preferred Strategy to End the Révolte Nobiliaire

Louis XVI's preferred response to the unrest in the summer of 1788 was to muddle through. In other words, he wanted to weather the instability long enough to enact the judicial reforms outlined in the May edicts (see Figure 6.2). The edicts, which established a pro-monarchy plenary court with the power to sanction new taxes, would guarantee the king a steady income. And with his finances bolstered, Louis XVI could more easily resist future demands for political reform. In a perfect world, therefore, the monarchy would buy time and keep the protestors at bay with vague promises of future political reform and very limited repression—for example, deploying troops to disperse the most violent protests. Muddling through also suited Louis XVI's personality: as his brother once remarked, persuading the king to make a decision, especially to take drastic action, was akin to "vainly trying to hold together a set of well-oiled billiard balls."[19]

The next option on Louis XVI's policy ranking was likely the use of diversionary tactics. The king and his ministers did not discuss the advantages of using diversionary force in the summer of 1788 because, as we will see, they had known for some time that environmental factors precluded this policy choice. But it is probable that Louis XVI would have preferred this option to the alternatives on the policy menu.

Earlier, in September 1787, as the monarchy tangled with the parlements over registering the land tax, there was a serious debate at Versailles about using a diversionary war to rally the nobility around the regime. The opportunity for a diversionary war surfaced when Prussian forces, with the support of the British government, invaded the Dutch Republic, a French ally. Several of the king's advisors urged Louis XVI to repel the Anglo–Prussian coalition on the grounds that it would have "diverted abroad that turbulence of opinion which was convulsing France and which urgently required occupation outside the country if were not to provoke an explosion at home."[20] The minister for the navy, the Marquis de Castries, counseled the king: "Present

Muddling through

Diversionary war

Diversionary spectacle

Limited political reform

Radical political reform

Repression

Foreign intervention

FIGURE 6.2 King Louis XVI's ranking of responses to domestic unrest

the idea of *la gloire* to Frenchmen and you will effect the most useful . . . diversion from the present turmoil."[21] Importantly, the policy was rejected because of the regime's low extractive capacity—not because a diversionary war was intrinsically unattractive.

If a successful diversion depended on winning "gloire" for France, as Castries suggested, we can also surmise that Louis XVI would have preferred a full-scale diversionary war to a more-limited diversionary spectacle. There was significantly less prestige to be gained from saber rattling or hurling barbs at France's great power neighbors than scoring a victory on the battlefield.

But a diversion of any kind—as long as there was some hope of increasing noble support for the monarchy—was more attractive than granting the opposition's demands for political reform. Louis XVI embraced minor political reforms when he deemed them necessary to strengthen the monarchy, such as summoning the Assembly of Notables. As historian P. M. Jones puts it, he "displayed a readiness to harness innovative reform to the business of government," principally to increase the monarchy's extractive capacity.[22] That said, Louis XVI abhorred the idea of making France a constitutional monarchy like Britain.[23] He was unwavering in his commitment to absolutism and "was not prepared to concede any substantial change."[24] During the first thirteen years of his reign, Louis XVI consistently spurned any reforms that might curb his power. For example, the idea of an Estates General had been "a constant rallying cry" among the aristocracy for more than a year before he reluctantly acquiesced in August 1788.[25]

This prompts the question: because Louis XVI was firmly committed to preserving the absolutist monarchy, did he prefer repression to political reform? More specifically, would the king have favored ending the révolte nobiliaire through extensive repression, such as imprisoning all clergy and nobility agitating against the crown, rather than by conceding to the opposition's demands for reform?

Almost certainly not. On the one hand, repression was a tried and true response to domestic unrest for the Bourbon monarchy. In 1775, even before his official coronation, Louis XVI brutally suppressed peasant uprisings over the price of bread during the "flour war." And in the year before the May edicts, he forced the closing of political clubs and discussion societies, moved to stamp out publications critical of the monarchy, ordered the arrest of seditious magistrates, and bullied the parlements into registering royal edicts—for example, sending the uncooperative parlement of Paris into exile for several months.[26]

On the other, Louis XVI had a lifelong fascination with British history and was anxious to avoid the mistakes of Charles I, who was executed for warring against his people.[27] As a confidant of the king once observed, "If it came to using it, he could never decide to draw the sword against his subjects."[28] For example, Louis XVI refused to use force to dissolve the National Assembly when its members vowed to draft a national constitution for France in June 1789.[29] Indeed, the king instructed the commander of the troops stationed in Paris only to keep the peace: "[T]ake the very greatest care not to get into a quarrel with or to engage in any combat with the people, unless they are inclined to arson or to commit riot or pillage which threatens the safety of the citizen."[30]

There is evidence that Louis XVI later considered repression after he was asked to support policies that he believed imperiled his eternal salvation. The king reluctantly accepted reforms that significantly limited his influence over the legislature, and approved the *Declaration on the Rights of Man*. But in 1790 the National Constituent Assembly introduced the Civil Constitution for the Clergy, declaring that Catholic bishops and priests would be popularly

elected. The Civil Constitution "presented Louis XVI with the most profound moral dilemma of his life . . . he was being asked to compromise his
personal faith."[31] The king determined that he could not stand behind the
Civil Constitution—his support for it was a "mortal sin."[32] The royal family
fled Paris.

But all of this was in the future. For Louis XVI to consider repression required far more provocative actions than the nobles and clergy were demanding in 1788. At this time the king distinguished between maintaining public
order and using large-scale violence to compel loyalty from his subjects. The
former was a requirement of government; the latter was impermissible. Extensive repression was near the bottom of his policy ranking.

The least-preferred option was foreign military intervention. Allowing an
ally to subdue the révolte nobiliaire would quite literally have been to make
war on the king's subjects and, therefore, would surely have been rejected by
Louis XVI. Above all, for a monarch who viewed himself as the "arbiter of Europe," foreign intervention would have been a national disgrace.[33] If anything,
the king was bent on convincing his neighbors that the unrest posed no threat
to the regime.

If muddling through and the use of diversionary force were Louis XVI's
preferred responses to instability, why did he agree to call the Estates General
in August 1788?

Muddling Through, Diversionary War, and the French Pauper State

Alexis de Tocqueville wrote of the French monarchy's finances: "I do not hesi-
tate to say that no private individual could escape ruin if he conducted his
affairs as the great monarch in all his glory managed the public business."[34]
Despite an economy "rich enough to meet its debts," the crown had insufficient revenues to pay its expenditures.[35] The financial problem was "rooted in
the very structures of Old Regime state and society" as the "traditional fiscal
institutions of the French state proved manifestly inadequate to the growing
needs of its government."[36] In particular, the monarchy relied on a "faulty
system of revenue collection."[37] The regime was not only saddled by a grossly
inefficient and corrupt tax system, but lay commoners also bore much of the
tax burden, with the wealthiest subjects, the nobility and clergy, exempt from
many direct taxes.[38] Unable to efficiently mobilize societal resources through
taxation, the monarchy relied on loans to cover budgetary shortfalls. But

because the French kings had a history of defaulting on their debt and tax revenues were unreliable, credit could be difficult to obtain and expensive. By the late 1780s, Louis XVI had accumulated large debts, requiring more than 50 percent of government income to service them.[39] France, the land of the Sun King, had become a pauper state.

The monarchy's low extractive capacity made it impossible for Louis XVI to muddle through during the summer of 1788, as he would have preferred. The structural weakness of the French pauper state provided the nobility and clergy with considerable leverage over the monarchy, enabling regime opponents to hold the crown ransom by withholding taxes and refusing to pass new levies. In turn, the difficulties of tax collection meant that creditors balked at providing new funds, sparking a full-blown credit crisis.

By ruling out the option of muddling through, a low extractive capacity was a necessary condition for Louis XVI's decision to call the Estates General. In a counterfactual, if the French monarchy had been a princely state in 1788, or even a wealthier pauper state, the nobles would have been less able to compel the government to reform by impeding its ability to tax. Their demands would have fallen on deaf ears.

The regime's low extractive capacity also ruled out a diversionary war. In 1787, when the monarchy considered intervening in the Dutch crisis to rally opinion, Brienne strongly cautioned the king against committing troops because "such an option was for France financially impossible."[40] As the Austrian ambassador to France, Comte de Mercy-Argenteau, commented after the denouement of the Dutch affair: "It is not credible that the Versailles ministry, in such straits, would risk getting involved in a war that would make bankruptcy inevitable."[41] And because the monarchy's finances only continued to worsen, a war would have been even further beyond the king's reach one year later: "Louis XVI could no longer afford the stakes of the game he had played in international politics since [assuming the throne in] 1774."[42]

Thus, the government's low extractive capacity was a necessary condition for the monarchy to call the Estates General in 1788. If the regime's access to resources had been greater, the king would have either muddled through or possibly initiated a diversionary war.[43]

The Impracticability of a Diversionary Spectacle

The monarchy might have been able to afford the next option on the policy menu: a low-cost diversionary spectacle. And *low-cost* was the operative term:

the monarchy's finances in 1788 made even limited military intervention too risky. France's retreat from great power politics was nearly total: the monarchy abandoned its alliance commitments, cut or suspended all foreign subsidies, and even abdicated its role as the arbiter of European disputes. As one French aristocrat observed, Louis XVI became a "nullity" in international affairs.[44] Or, as the Swedish ambassador to France put it, the king "is nothing."[45] The only affordable diversionary action was a symbolically unifying military operation with no prospect of sustained resistance.

Such a target simply did not exist in 1788. France's chief rival and most likely target for a diversion was Britain. And the French crown was painfully aware of the cost of doing battle with London, as the war over the American colonies had concluded only five years earlier. Although the conflict ended in a victory for France, it had come at great expense—the war cost more than France's three prior wars combined.[46] Moreover, Louis XVI believed that Britain was looking for an opportunity to recoup its losses. In particular, he was haunted by the fear that "England would take advantage of France's internal weakness to renew the [American] colonial war."[47]

Nature of the Reform Demands

The elimination of muddling through and the use of diversionary tactics left political reform as the highest-ranked option on the policy menu. But for this response to be viable, it was necessary that the reform demands of the elite be moderate. The monarchy's decision to call the Estates General was undoubtedly a risk. The consequences were unpredictable because the assembly had not met since 1615.[48] But buying off the nobles with political reforms in August 1788 seemed unlikely to threaten the monarchy. Only with the benefit of hindsight does the calling of the Estates General appear as the first step toward the creation of the French Republic. If summoning the Estates General had clearly presaged an end to Louis's rule—or if the opposition explicitly sought to end the monarchy—then the king would have avoided political reform and given more thought to repression.

Choosing Political Reform: Louis XVI's Decision to Call the Estates General

The regime began the crisis by pursuing the preferred option of muddling through. One month into the révolte nobiliaire, in June 1788, Brienne invited Frenchmen of any order to provide the crown with suggestions regarding a possible structure for the Estates General. The move was largely a ploy to "gain time" because it was clear that the monarchy "had not yet decided to call the Estates General in the near future, especially when it would precede the completion of the [May] reforms."[49] As Brienne advised Louis XVI, "Do not seem to be very far from convening your subjects [in the Estates General], but delay the convocation as long as you can; your authority can only lose by it, and your kingdom gain very little."[50]

The credit crisis of late July upended the crown's plan to play for time. The lack of resources forced the government to respond quickly, and eliminated muddling through and diversionary war as available options, until "the drowning government of Louis XVI grasped at any available straw."[51] In early August, Brienne announced that the monarchy would halt its efforts to create the plenary court and convoke the Estates General on May 1, 1789. The first minister hoped that by allowing the representative assembly to monitor the state's finances, he would rehabilitate the crown's credit. The maneuver ultimately failed: the monarchy halted payments on royal loans, and Brienne resigned.

Louis XVI "took a very gloomy view of the future" but comforted himself with the thought that by making political concessions to his opponents, he would avoid the fate of Charles I.[52] A lack of resources removed the "let them eat cake" option, so the king chose the unpalatable but still digestible policy of political reform.

Foreign Intervention: The Habsburg Monarchy and the Hungarian Revolution of 1848–1849

In the spring of 1848, the multinational Habsburg empire—described by one observer as a bird "made up of borrowed feathers"—threatened to disintegrate.[53] Indeed, as successive provinces succumbed to revolution, the very survival of the monarchy was in doubt. Revolution spread across Europe in 1848. But no country suffered such profound disruption as Austria: "[F]or months the future of a European great power appeared to hang in the balance."[54]

Among the most serious challenges to the monarchy came from the Kingdom of Hungary, which was incorporated into the Habsburg empire at the end of the seventeenth century but retained its own historic constitution and Diet. Inspired by the revolution against King Louis Philippe in France, Hungarian firebrand Lajos Kossuth denounced the absolutist Austrian monarchy on March 3, 1848, as "the pestilential air which breathes on us from the charnel-house of Vienna, an air which dulls our nerves and paralyses our spirit."[55] He demanded greater autonomy for Hungary, including control over its own finances, and a new constitution for the empire. News of Kossuth's oration provoked mass demonstrations in Vienna against the government, in particular the long-serving, conservative minister-president, Prince Clemens von Metternich, who presided over the crown's advisory council of ministers. Fearing revolution but reluctant to let loose imperial troops on the protestors, the court buckled, dismissed Metternich, and pledged to reform the monarchy. Kossuth, emboldened by Metternich's resignation, pressed the regime for further concessions, most notably the right to assemble an independent national guard, loyal only to the Hungarian constitution. After weeks of foot-dragging, the crown capitulated on April 11, allowing Hungary substantial autonomy from Vienna.

The court sanctioned the so-called "April Laws" in part because Emperor Ferdinand I was a weak and pliable leader who was disposed to grant the demands of any petitioner who gained his ear, but mainly because subduing Hungary by force of arms was not an option.[56] Much of the army was tied up in Lombardy–Venetia, the empire's northern Italian territories. Imperial troops were fighting to regain control of Venetia, which had been lost after a local nationalist uprising. And King Charles Albert of neighboring Piedmont–Sardinia had invaded Lombardy with the hope of adding the province to his dominions. Protecting Habsburg Italy was "absolutely crucial for the survival of the Monarchy," as it was one of the wealthiest regions in an impecunious empire, supplying between one-quarter and one-third of its income.[57]

With the crown distracted by instability in northern Italy and Vienna, Hungary set about building the honvédség, or "home defense force," assuring the emperor that its purpose was only to defend the kingdom against the threat from disgruntled ethnic minorities within Hungary, especially the Croats. When the Hungarian Diet resisted sending troops to reinforce Habsburg forces fighting in Italy, it fueled suspicions that Hungary was intent on declaring independence. The fires of Croat nationalism would be dampened only so that the blaze of Hungarian nationalism could be further fueled.

The monarchy took steps to rein in the renegade province in mid-July 1848. Alexander Bach, a zealous advocate for centralization, was appointed to the council of ministers. And a Habsburg victory over the Piedmontese–Sardinian army in Lombardy on August 8 gave renewed hope that order could be restored elsewhere.[58] With new leadership and additional capabilities potentially freed up by the success in Italy, the time appeared "ripe to move against Hungary."[59] The monarchy declared the April Laws illegal and threw its support behind Josip Jellačić, the commander of Habsburg troops in Croatia, who was preparing a military campaign to liberate Croat territory from Hungarian control.

In early October 1848 the monarchy's bid to reassert imperial rule over Hungary was interrupted by a major resurgence of unrest in Vienna, prompting the court to flee the city. The crown, abandoning its prior reluctance to repress the Viennese, ordered Field Marshal Alfred Windischgrätz to wrest the capital from the revolutionaries. With the aid of Jellačić, whose forces had rallied near Vienna after meeting stiff resistance from the honvédség, the field marshal laid siege to the city. The revolutionaries, outnumbered by imperial troops, begged Hungary to offer aid. Although initially reluctant to send the honvédség into Austria for fear of imperial reprisals against Hungary, Budapest soon threw its lot in with the Viennese rebels. After less than two weeks of fighting, however, the imperial army subdued the rebellion and drove the Hungarians into retreat.

With Vienna and northern Italy quiet, and Hungary's disloyalty transparent, the crown looked to more-dramatic means of quelling the Hungarian insurrection. A camarilla of counterrevolutionaries orchestrated a shake-up in the council of ministers, promoting leaders committed to centralizing the empire, and convinced Ferdinand to abdicate in favor of his nephew, Francis Joseph, who promised to be a more-resolute defender of the absolutist monarchy.[60] With the hawks in charge, Windischgrätz marched into Hungary leading a force of 52,000 troops on December 16, 1848.[61]

Fighting the Hungarians on Hungarian soil proved to be a very different experience from the battles outside Vienna. Between February and April 1849, the honvédség repeatedly bested the imperial army, culminating in Hungary's declaration of independence from the Habsburg empire on April 14. Facing desperate circumstances, the monarchy played its final card, requesting military assistance from Russia's conservative tsar, Nicholas I, on May 1, 1849. With the aid of Russian troops, the Habsburgs reestablished imperial control over the rebellious kingdom and embarked on a campaign of brutal repression, executing or imprisoning revolutionary leaders, military officers, and those merely suspected of sedition.

Why did the Habsburg monarchy respond to the unrest by requesting Russian intervention rather than pursue the preferred option of repression or

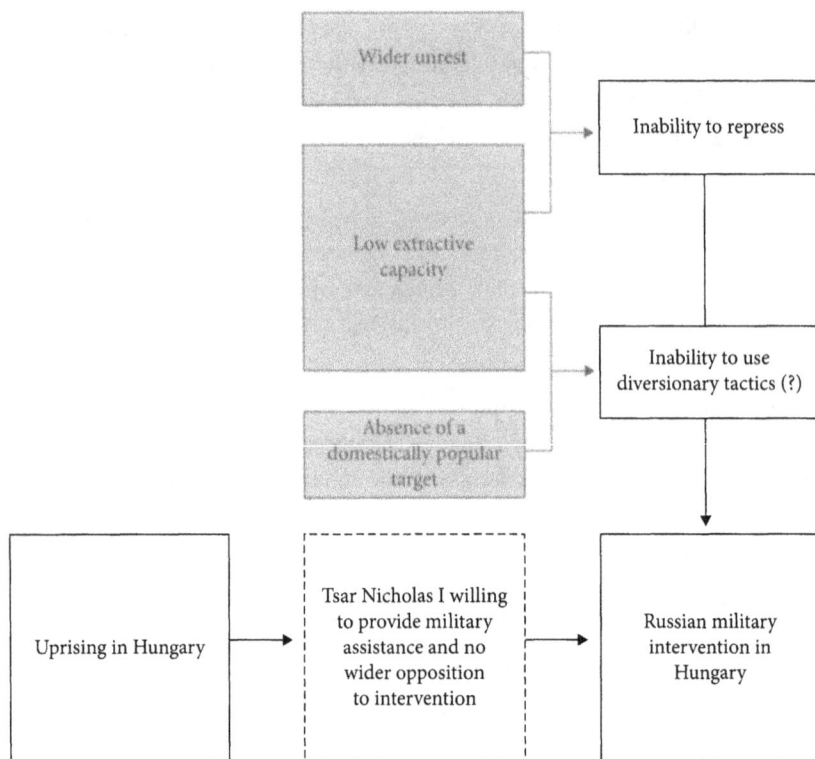

FIGURE 6.3 The Habsburg monarchy's decision to request Russian intervention in Hungary, 1849

possibly the use of diversionary tactics? (See Figure 6.3.) Environmental factors, including costly fighting in northern Italy and the regime's low extractive capacity, prevented the Habsburgs from continuing to repress Hungary. And the absence of a widely popular, low-cost target ruled out a diversion. Fortunately for the monarchy, the Russian tsar saw the dominoes of revolution falling toward his empire and was eager to offer his repressive services.

The Habsburg Monarchy's Preferred Response to the Hungarian Revolution

In the spring of 1849 the Habsburgs faced a key decision point. Unrest throughout the empire was a potentially fatal threat to the monarchy. Under the leadership of Ferdinand, the Hungarian kingdom had achieved nearly complete autonomy from the crown, threatening the integrity of the empire and interrupting the flow of taxes and soldiers from the province to the

Repression

Diversionary war/spectacle (?)

Foreign intervention

Muddling through

Limited political reform

Radical political reform

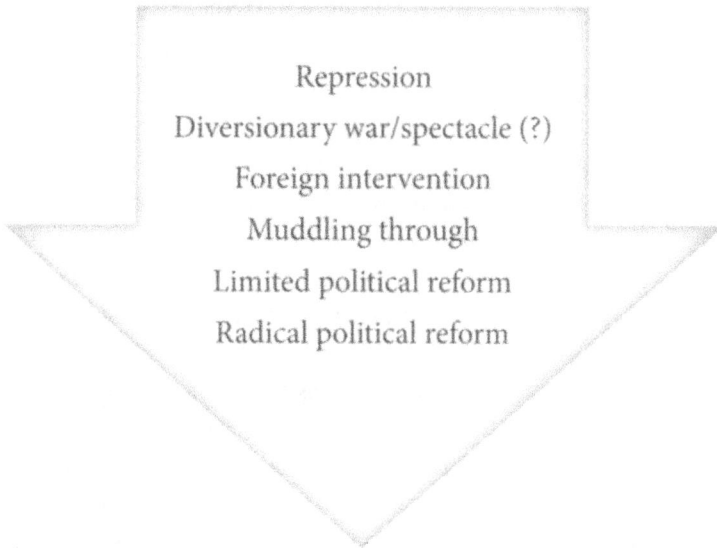

FIGURE 6.4 Prince Felix zu Schwarzenberg's ranking of responses to domestic unrest

imperial capital. After restoring order to Vienna and northern Italy in the fall of 1848, the Habsburg monarchy under Francis Joseph marched on Budapest, only to face military defeat. The question for Francis Joseph and his council of ministers was whether to accept the April Laws and allow Hungary to remain virtually independent or to adopt an alternate, less accommodating response from the menu of policy options.

Only eighteen years old upon assuming the throne, Francis Joseph relied heavily on the advice of Austria's minister-president, Prince Felix zu Schwarzenberg. Acting as Francis Joseph's "guardian" and "teacher," Schwarzenberg directed imperial policy during the early years of the emperor's reign.[62] The minister-president's goal was not only to end the Hungarian rebellion but also to integrate the kingdom fully into the Austrian empire, rescinding its historical right to be governed by a separate constitution.[63] That is, he sought to "construct a new monarchical order on the ruins of revolution" in which Vienna would become "the nucleus of a unitary Habsburg monarchy."[64]

Schwarzenberg's preferred strategy to secure Habsburg control over Hungary was repression (see Figure 6.4). Historian Gunther Rothenberg writes that in order "to create a unitary, centralized Austrian state," the prince believed that the kingdom of "Hungary had to be totally conquered and any possible military or political opposition had to be eliminated."[65] Indeed, soon after learning of his appointment as minister-president, Schwarzenberg wrote that his government's primary aim would be the "[s]uppression of the revolt everywhere and at any price, [and] preservation of the privileges of the dynasty over against all usurpations of the revolution."[66] Eleven months into his administration, Schwarzenberg spoke even more frankly about his wishes for Hungary: "The Hungarian nobles [behind the unrest] have always been rebels and are still rebels.—They must be annihilated, yes, be done away with forever."[67] Simply put, the Hungarian revolution should end by force of arms.

Schwarzenberg's second preference was likely foreign intervention. Requesting Russian aid to address internal troubles was unbecoming to a great power: "Every government may have to fight against rebels. . . . That does not damage their reputation. . . . But when they document their incapacity to restore order within their own house by calling in foreign assistance, they lose all credit, both domestic and foreign."[68]

However, this course of action was preferable to offering concessions to the Hungarian rebels. After all, Schwarzenberg had been appointed as minister-president because he was reputed to possess the iron hand needed to rescue the Habsburg dynasty from dissolution. Upon taking the helm of state, the prince criticized his predecessors for being too quick to concede to the enemies of the monarchy: "The government lacked leadership, unity, and energy of action. . . . [It was] a symbol of incapacity, a plaything for passions, a tool of the revolutionary party, neglecting its primary and most important duty of opposing that party."[69] He averred that "the word 'concessions' would never be one which his ministry urged from the lips of Austria's emperor."[70] Therefore, historian Kenneth Rock concludes: "[M]onarchist, authoritarian, and soldier by nature, the Habsburg minister would not—as his ministerial colleagues would not—compromise with the Magyar [Hungarian] insurgents."[71]

If there was no opportunity for foreign intervention, it is likely that Schwarzenberg would have favored muddling through with repression over granting Hungary even limited autonomy. Schwarzenberg simply "refused to countenance any alternative to the integration of Hungary into the rest of the monarchy," placing any degree of political reform—from limited federalism to complete autonomy for the kingdom—at the bottom of his policy ranking.[72]

Where did Schwarzenberg rank the use of diversionary tactics as a possible response to the Hungarian revolution? In this case, the answer is unclear.

There is no direct evidence that Schwarzenberg considered provoking a diversionary war or spectacle during the instability of 1848–1849 or that Francis Joseph ever contemplated a diversion during his reign. Observers speculated that the Second Schleswig–Holstein War of 1864 and the Austro–Prussian War of 1866 resulted, at least in part, from the emperor's desire to generate popular support for the monarchy. In 1864, for example, an Austrian officer suggested that Francis Joseph "invaded Schleswig-Holstein more to restore faith in military rule at home than to liberate Austria's so-called 'brothers on the Eider.'"[73] Similarly, in 1866 the semiofficial *Ostdeutsche Post* touted the impending war with Prussia as "a family affair uniting all parties and nationalities" in the empire.[74] But because there is little evidence that the emperor or any other imperial advisor discussed the wisdom of a diversionary use of force during the Hungarian revolution, we can only speculate as to how the monarch might have weighed the merits of this option on the policy menu. We can conclude with some confidence that a diversion was ranked higher than political reform for the simple reason that reform was viewed as utterly abhorrent. We can also say that a diversion was ranked lower than repression, which was the clear favored option for the monarchy. What we cannot say with any confidence is whether the use of diversionary tactics was ranked higher or lower than foreign intervention. But as we will see, environmental factors enabled the choice of foreign intervention and eliminated a diversionary war or spectacle.

If Schwarzenberg preferred to counter the Hungarian revolution with repression, why did the monarchy request Russian intervention in May 1849?

Repression and the Habsburg Pauper State
The low extractive capacity of the Habsburg Empire eliminated the preferred option of repression and moved foreign intervention to the top of the available policy ranking. By 1848, the monarchy operated on a "threadbare budget" and faced chronic shortfalls in revenue.[75] Indeed, historian Steven Beller concludes: "The main problem of the Habsburg Monarchy in the Vormärz (the period before March 1848) was that there was never enough money or resources for Austria to either fulfill its foreign policy responsibilities, or invest in building an effective domestic regime."[76]

The Achilles' heel of the monarchy was its inability to access societal resources, and for decades, state revenues had been "grossly insufficient to meet her expenditure."[77] The crown avoided increasing tax levels, for fear of stoking unrest, and lacked the capacity to compel its subjects to pay existing levies.[78] Raising revenues in Hungary was particularly troublesome as it required the cooperation of the Diet, where delegates flexed their muscle by making the passage of new taxes conditional on political concessions.

To compensate for "a lack of ready money," Austria became heavily indebted.[79] In 1847, for example, interest on state debt consumed 28 percent of the monarchy's annual income—nearly the amount the crown collected in direct taxation.[80] Only three months before the outbreak of revolution, the Rothschilds' private banking house in Vienna provided the latest in a long line of loans to rescue the empire from bankruptcy. While the terms of the loan were negotiated, Austria's finance minister offered this prescient warning regarding the monarchy's treasury: "Unfortunately, when this sum is spent there will be nothing left to deal with any new misfortune which may arise . . . I feel it to be my duty to make the grave statement that we are on the verge of an abyss."[81] On the eve of revolution, the Habsburg empire was a pauper state.

The crown's financial problems handicapped its ability to pursue the preferred policy of repression. The monarchy continually struggled to fund the imperial forces fighting in Hungary. Indeed, among Schwarzenberg's first acts after sending troops to the kingdom was to request a loan from Russia to pay for the campaign—which the tsar denied. Most importantly, when imperial troops were forced into retreat in the winter and spring of 1849, the crown could not afford to raise new forces.[82] For example, the Habsburg commander in Hungary confessed to Schwarzenberg that the imperial army was losing ground because he lacked reserves: "I no longer command the means of rescue."[83]

The monarchy's predicament was made especially plain after Russia agreed to intervene in Hungary in May 1849. In exchange for providing military assistance, Nicholas I asked the Habsburgs to refund the cost of supplying, transporting, and providing medical care for Russian troops in Hungary. However, an Austrian official stationed in Hungary reported to Vienna that he could not satisfy Russia's supply needs due to "a shortage of money."[84] As he put it in a letter to Schwarzenberg, "with nothing it was only possible to achieve nothing."[85]

If the crown had not faced a wider rebellion, especially the war in northern Italy, the Habsburg pauper state might have successfully financed repression in Hungary. Although the army was "run down" due to "repeated economic cuts" even before the unrest of 1848, the monarchy had the ability to put down a small to moderate amount of unrest—the degree of instability that was present in Hungary in the early days of the uprising—with relative ease.[86] The crown was sidetracked by events in Italy and therefore failed to nip the Hungarian crisis in the bud, when the nationalist movement was still relatively weak. Furthermore, the prolonged fighting in Italy limited the forces available for military action in Hungary. A significant military presence remained in the Italian territories (and elsewhere) through the spring of 1849 to prevent further unrest.[87] Thus, as historian Robert Kann contends, the "Habsburg armies save for the Italian crisis would probably have been able to put down the Hungarian insurrection so speedily and decisively that Russian intervention would not have become necessary."[88]

In sum, the monarchy's inability to extract the resources necessary to pay for additional troops, coupled with the scope of the unrest in the empire, foreclosed the court's preferred option of repressing the Hungarian revolution. If its access to resources had been greater and/or the unrest in the empire lower, the crown likely would have been able to quash the rebellion in Hungary before turning to the tsar.

The Impracticability of Diversionary Tactics

While it is not clear where diversionary war fell in the policy ranking, the monarchy's low extractive capacity also removed this option. Simply put, the crown lacked the resources to fight a major military campaign against any of its great power neighbors—each of which was at least as powerful as Austria.[89] Even a brief conflict would have pushed the Habsburgs into bankruptcy.[90]

If diversionary war were not already eliminated by Vienna's lack of resources, the absence of a plausible target signaled the death knell for foreign adventure. There was no available target with the potential to rally the regime's opponents around the flag. The empire, and Hungary in particular, comprised a myriad of ethnic and religious groups, many of which were longstanding rivals.[91] For example, historian F. R. Bridge concludes: "[I]t was simply impossible to devise a [foreign] policy that would have a hope of being acceptable to 'public opinion,' so various were the strands of which it was composed—from . . . the Czechs, who advocated alignment with Russia, to the Magyars and Poles, who abhorred such an idea, and the Germans, who demanded an alignment with Berlin."[92] There was no equivalent of the Falkland Islands or the Mormons as a potential adversary to rally opinion. Thus, the constant challenge of making foreign policy in a fractious multiethnic empire meant that the monarchy was unlikely to suffer from false illusions regarding its ability to provoke a successful diversionary war or spectacle. Of course, if foreign intervention was the preferred alternative, then the diversionary option would have been rendered moot.

The Viability of Foreign Intervention in 1849

Foreign intervention was practicable in the spring of 1849 because of another environmental factor: the availability of a repressive partner. In the spring of 1849, two states offered their services in quelling the revolt in Hungary: Prussia and Russia. Prussia made its assistance conditional on assuming the dominant position in the German Confederation.[93] Given that increasing the empire's influence in Germany was a top foreign policy goal, Schwarzenberg declined the proposal.

However, Russia's Tsar Nicholas I was willing to provide troops without demanding any meaningful concessions in return. Nicholas offered such favorable terms because he had every interest in propping up the Habsburg monarchy. The tsar feared that the unrest in Hungary (and elsewhere in the empire) would be contagious, rousing revolutionary fervor in Russia's neighboring provinces, especially Poland. The Habsburgs were "an essential barrier against the spread of western liberalism to the borders of his empire."[94] As the tsar wrote to a Russian general on April 20, 1849, "I must admit I have no burning desire to intervene in the whole affair. I foresee only envy, malice, and ingratitude, and I really would not interfere if the shirt were not closer to me than the coat . . . [the] rascals in Hungary [are] not only the enemies of Austria but also the enemies of order and tranquility in the entire world."[95]

One possible obstacle to a Russian intervention in Hungary could have been the expectation of a hostile international response, particularly from the liberal governments in Britain and republican France. Although Britain and France predictably found the prospect of Russian interference in Hungary distasteful, they did not actively oppose it.[96] France offered only mild protests, having just intervened in Rome to restore the pope. Russia was also able to win France's support by recognizing the new revolutionary government in Paris—ironically, on the same day that the tsar's troops marched into Hungary. Although British public opinion favored Kossuth and the revolutionaries, Lord Henry Palmerston, Britain's foreign secretary, believed that the disintegration of the Habsburg empire would disrupt the European balance of power.[97] As a result, Palmerston instructed the British chargé d'affaires in Russia to express no formal opinion on the intervention. But quietly, he urged Nicolas to limit the disruption and "finish with them [the Hungarians] quickly."[98]

Together, these environmental conditions made foreign intervention possible. An ally was willing to aid the crown in return for limited compensation, and international opinion supported, or at least did not oppose, the scheme. The second-ranked policy option was viable.

Choosing Foreign Intervention

After months of defeat at the hands of the Hungarians in the winter and spring of 1849, Schwarzenberg determined that imperial forces were inadequate for crushing the revolution and moved to secure Russian assistance. Francis Joseph wrote that we "would never take this step if our own forces were sufficient."[99] On May 1 the emperor officially requested Russian intervention, urging the tsar to join "with resolute firmness the holy struggle of the social order against anarchy."[100] Nicholas immediately obliged.

Requesting Russian intervention was, as Schwarzenberg once put it, a "moral defeat" for the Habsburg monarchy.[101] And the minister-president made every effort to minimize the significance of Nicholas's contribution—for example, referring to the Russian troops in Hungary as "auxiliary" forces and Habsburg "reserves."[102] But with repression impracticable, foreign intervention was the most attractive of the available options on the policy menu. As the U.S. chargé d'affaires in Vienna, William Stiles, observed, the crown "feared Russia much, but they feared liberal opinions more; as the least of two evils, conquest was preferred to conciliation, and the intervention of Russia was asked."[103]

Muddling Through: Peru and Sendero Luminoso

The Maoist party Sendero Luminoso first caught the attention of the Peruvian government in May 1980, when its followers burned ballot boxes and hung dogs, bearing cardboard signs accusing China's Deng Xiaoping of betraying the Marxist cause, from streetlights.[104] Embracing the Maoist dictum that "political power grows out of the barrel of a gun," the revolutionaries declared these acts the opening salvo in an insurgency aimed to topple the state. Peru's newly elected president, Fernando Belaúnde Terry, dismissed the group as little more than "cattle thieves" and "political pranksters."[105] When his successor, Alan García Pérez, assumed the presidency five years later, however, the fight against Sendero had claimed the lives of more than 175 military and police personnel and 2,500 civilians.[106] Defeating the rebels had risen to the top of the government's agenda, but the administration resorted to muddling through the instability because environmental factors eliminated a host of preferred alternatives.

Asserting that its members were capable of "childish acts of delinquency" but not substantive violence, the Belaúnde administration initially ignored Sendero Luminoso.[107] It was, at most, a matter for the local police. Sendero capitalized on the government's inertia during this period, building a solid base of support among the peasants of the Ayacucho region, who were drawn to its program of poverty reduction, debt relief, land redistribution, and anticorruption. Attacks by the Senderistas subsequently became more frequent, widespread, and destructive. By December 1982, the president began to take the movement seriously. After Sendero perpetrated several highly publicized incidents in Lima, including the bombing of electrical towers that caused a citywide blackout, Belaúnde ceded control over counterinsurgency strategy to the military.[108] Given the "total war" methods preferred by the armed forces, this meant violence against both Senderistas and noncombatants.[109] Belaúnde was untroubled by the reports of civilian casualties during the military's campaign. Upon receiving a scathing review of his human rights record from Amnesty International and Americas Watch, the president claimed to have pitched them unceremoniously in a wastebasket.[110]

The military's tactics proved markedly unsuccessful. Arbitrary searches, torture, and extrajudicial executions lost the hearts and minds of the peasantry to the Senderistas. By the end of Belaúnde's term in office, Sendero was well into what its leaders termed the third stage of revolution—expanding the guerrilla war from rural to urban areas of Peru. More than half of the reported terrorist acts now occurred outside of Ayacucho.[111] In particular, Sendero was gathering momentum in the coca-producing Huallaga Valley and Lima itself. The frequency of attacks also increased, from 219 in 1980 to 2,050 in 1985.[112] Belaúnde's failure to restore order eroded the public's confidence in his administration. The president's approval rating dropped from 70 percent in 1980 to less than 20 percent by early 1983.[113]

In 1985 Alan García assumed the presidency, pledging to combat Sendero with a new strategy that combined economic reform with targeted repression. García's reform program would funnel development aid to communities in the impoverished highlands, where support for Sendero was most deeply rooted. In so doing, he would win over Sendero's peasant sympathizers and weaken the movement. García also promised to improve the military's human rights record by ensuring that it targeted Senderistas and not civilians.

García introduced his economic policies with great fanfare, but they were soon abandoned. The few reforms implemented by his administration, such as a loan program for agricultural producers, were starved of funds and ineffective, while other proposals simply withered on the vine. Aside from some success in limiting attacks on noncombatants, the military also failed to subdue Sendero, which was conducting operations throughout the country and had established a base of operations in Lima. In mid-1988, discouraged and "out of ideas," the government began to shift greater responsibility for combating the unrest to paramilitary groups and allowed attacks against civilians again to climb. The president displayed little confidence that the new strategy of decentralized repression would work.[114] The Peruvian government's policy was a classic example of muddling through.

Why in 1988 did García begin to muddle through with a failing policy of decentralized repression, when any number of alternative policies—such as economic reform, limited political reform, targeted repression of the guerrillas, or a diversionary use of force—would have been preferable (see Figure 6.5)? The state's low extractive capacity undermined the president's efforts to enact economic reforms and implement a policy of targeted repression. It also ruled out the possibility of a diversionary war. Sendero's endgame—that is, its desire "to destroy all established civil institutions"—unsurprisingly eliminated limited political reform as a viable response.[115] Finally, the lack of a low-cost, domestically popular target and an ally willing to provide military assistance made a diversionary spectacle and foreign intervention impracticable.

Alan García's Preferred Response to Sendero Luminoso

Sendero violence showed no signs of flagging after García took office in 1985. During the first three years of the García administration, there were nearly 5,000 incidents of political violence in which more than 2,500 civilians and 600 police and military personnel were killed.[116] During this period, Sendero also stepped up its efforts to assassinate national and local politicians, foreign and domestic businesspeople, and aid workers. Senderistas killed a number of mayors in the departments of Pasco, Junín, and Lima, and by the end of 1988, 104 mayors and 224 council members had resigned after receiving death threats.[117] Several political parties questioned whether they would be able to

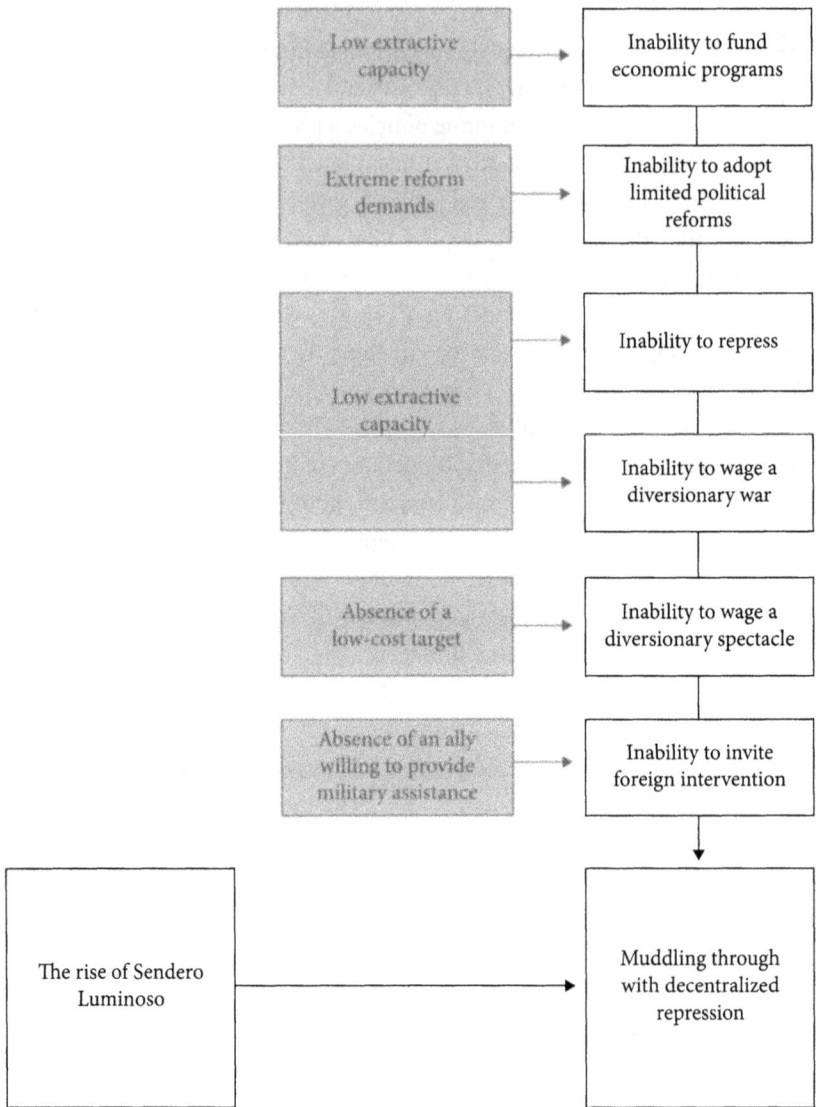

FIGURE 6.5 The Peruvian government's decision to muddle through, 1988

The boxes in the figure read:

- Low extractive capacity → Inability to fund economic programs
- Extreme reform demands → Inability to adopt limited political reforms
- Low extractive capacity → Inability to repress
- Low extractive capacity → Inability to wage a diversionary war
- Absence of a low-cost target → Inability to wage a diversionary spectacle
- Absence of an ally willing to provide military assistance → Inability to invite foreign intervention
- The rise of Sendero Luminoso → Muddling through with decentralized repression

Economic reform
Limited political reform
Repression
Diversionary war
Diversionary spectacle
Foreign intervention
Muddling through
Radical political reform

FIGURE 6.6 President Alan García's ranking of responses to domestic unrest

recruit candidates for future elections. Given the rapid escalation of violence, the García administration was under increasing pressure to rethink its handling of the unrest.[118]

In 1988 García's preferred response to the rise of Sendero Luminoso was to co-opt the Senderistas with a combination of economic and limited political reform (see Figure 6.6). As a member of the center–left party American Popular Revolutionary Alliance (APRA), he was committed to economic development. García was the president, as he put it, of "the other 70 percent" of the population, or the "agricultural and peasant sectors, the unemployed and street vendors, the provincial inhabitants, and the shantytown residents."[119] But García also believed that poverty reduction was the key to combating Sendero. Peasant communities not only gave aid and comfort to the Senderistas, but a significant percentage of Sendero's foot soldiers were also peasants.[120] They were attracted to Sendero's message of economic equality, mainly out of disillusionment with the government's poor record in providing development assistance to the highlands. Therefore, García's preference was to address the needs of the impoverished peasant communities and deny the rebels their base of support—that is, to catch the fish by draining the pond.

The García administration was also open to dampening the unrest with limited political reform. At first glance, Sendero and APRA seemed, if not political brothers, at least cousins. They were both leftist movements. Indeed, historically, APRA was also committed to revolutionary change—although of a populist rather than Marxist variety. In its not-too-distant past, APRA had even used violence against the state.[121] Furthermore, the extreme left wing of APRA, particularly young party members who were impatient with evolutionary economic reform, supported elements of Sendero's message and tactics.[122] On occasion, therefore, García would applaud Sendero's activities in order to appeal to the APRA youth. In one speech, for example, he said: "Mistaken or not, the *senderista* has what we do not have: mystique and dedication. . . . These are people that merit our respect and my personal admiration because they are, like it or not, militants."[123] Despite his "penchant for radical rhetoric," however, García generally sought to play within the rules of the existing democratic system.[124] Thus, while he was reluctant to countenance radical political change, he likely would have accepted a turn toward socialism.

If a political compromise were not tenable, García's next preferred response was to couple economic reform with targeted repression against the Maoist guerrillas. Belaúnde had granted the military complete operational autonomy over the counterinsurgency and turned a blind eye when civilians were targeted. Hundreds, if not thousands, of Peruvians disappeared during the five years of his presidency.[125] During his inaugural address, therefore, García declared that he would reform the military's practices. Minimizing collateral damage in the fight against Sendero would become a priority, and military officers responsible for human rights violations would be held accountable. The president would, in his words, "fight subversion with resolute firmness" but also with a "respect for the law and for human rights."[126]

The next option on García's policy ranking may have been a diversionary use of force. Although there is no direct evidence that he considered a diversion during his term in office, the president was certainly aware that an international conflict could rally the public around his government. In January 1981, for example, Peru and its long-standing rival, Ecuador, came to blows when the Peruvian military discovered that the Ecuadorans had secretly erected several outposts in contested territory along the Amazon River, which they then refused to surrender. After five days of fighting and nearly 200 fatalities, Peruvian forces pushed Ecuadoran troops back across the border.

Belaúnde's popularity soared as a result of the conflict, and the dispute marked the high-water mark of public support for his administration.[127] Indeed, the timing of the conflict may have been influenced by domestic political concerns. The Peruvian government had known of the outposts for several months before it protested, and Belaúnde's decision to expel the Ecuadoran forces coincided with rumors that the labor unions were planning a large strike—which was subsequently called off because of the hostilities with Ecuador.

In any case, it is certainly plausible that García would have seen a diversion as a potentially useful strategy for increasing public support for his regime—particularly if he could have, say, soundly defeated Ecuador. And he likely would have viewed this policy as preferable to the remaining unpalatable alternatives on the menu—foreign intervention, muddling through, and radical political reform.

Requesting foreign military assistance in the fight against Sendero was probably a less-attractive option than a diversionary use of force. García sought to "change Peru's image from that of an unimportant player on the international scene to that of an active participant in international politics, defending human rights, fighting against drugs and supporting peace-keeping measures on the sub-continent."[128] Asking for international intervention did not comport with the "broad activist role for Peru in world affairs" that he imagined.[129] In particular, García was loath to accept substantial military aid from the United States, which he described in his inaugural address as the "richest and most imperialist country on earth."[130] He openly opposed the United States' aid to the contras in Nicaragua, stating on several occasions that he would break ties with any government that attempted to oust the Sandinista regime.[131]

Muddling through was near the bottom of García's policy ranking, being preferred only to granting Sendero's demands for radical political reform. Muddling through in this context meant ignoring any systematic attempt to end the unrest in Peruvian society. Instead, the government would adopt a strategy designed simply to keep the regime in office for as long as possible.

The García administration ended up selecting one of the least-preferred alternatives when it began muddling through in 1988. The regime authorized paramilitary groups to police Sendero and stopped holding the military accountable for human rights violations. This policy was not chosen because it held out the prospect of defeating Sendero—but rather because doing something was better than doing nothing. Why did García choose a response to the unrest that was near the bottom of his policy ranking?

Economic Reform, Repression, Diversionary War, and the Peruvian Pauper State

The regime's low extractive capacity eliminated several preferred policy alternatives, namely economic reform, repression, and diversionary war. Certainly, the government's poverty partly reflected the broader crisis in the Peruvian economy after 1987. But the economic downturn served only to highlight the administration's inability to raise revenue. Despite higher than usual economic growth in the first two years of García's presidency, state revenues had actually declined substantially.[132] By the end of García's term in office, government tax receipts as a percentage of GNP were the lowest of any country in the region.[133]

The Peruvian state's persistent struggle to mobilize societal resources was mainly a product of its grossly inefficient and corrupt tax administration and rampant tax evasion.[134] Not only did the government lack the administrative capacity to detect cheating—a scarcity of auditors meant that the average business would face inspection once every 55 years—but the penalties for nonpayment were also low.[135] Government revenue during García's presidency also suffered from an expansion in the informal economy, especially in the production of illegal drugs. Indeed, much of the improvement in the economy during the first two years of the García administration was driven by the informal sector and especially the export of cocaine to the United States. By the mid-1980s, the informal economy made up about one-third of the workforce.[136] Because narco-traffickers, like Al Capone in the 1930s, are also tax evaders, the government was forced to rely on a small number of legitimate businesses for much of its income.[137] In 1987, for example, 60 percent of tax receipts came from 24 of Peru's largest firms, most of which were state owned.[138]

García was unable to make up for the deficit by borrowing. Among his first acts as president was to unilaterally reduce the country's debt service payments, an initiative motivated in large part by the need to conserve state revenue for domestic projects.[139] But the decision also damaged the government's credit rating, causing the supply of foreign and domestic loans to dry up.

Peru's status as a pauper state during this period is confirmed by Kugler and Arbetman's extractive capacity data. They calculate that the Peruvian government's revenues were well below the amount that could have been extracted given the size of the national economy (see Figure 6.7).

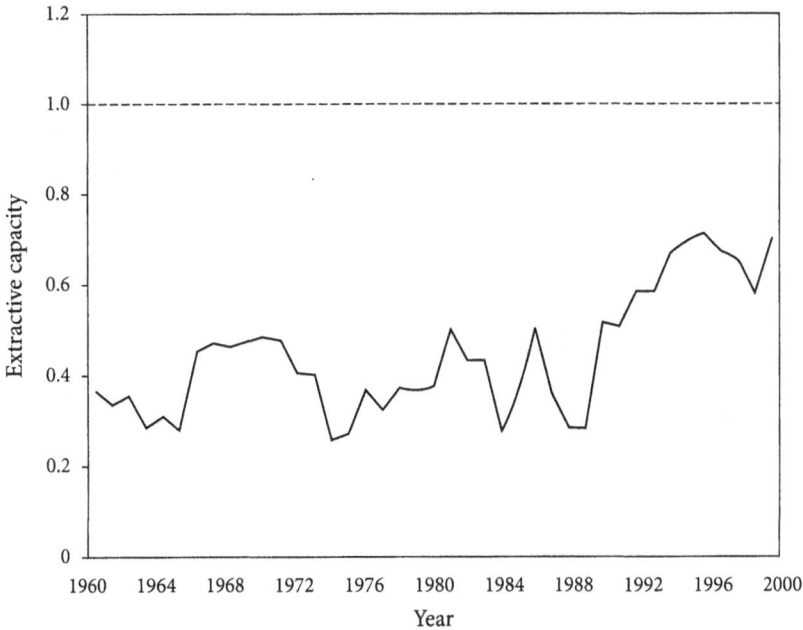

FIGURE 6.7 Peru's extractive capacity, 1960–2000
SOURCE: Data from Kugler and Arbetman, "Relative Political Capacity."

García's preferred strategy for tackling Sendero—economic reform in the impoverished Andean highlands—was derailed by the state's low extractive capacity. His reform initiatives, which included low-interest loans and agricultural assistance, "had a high fiscal cost" and were soon crippled by a lack of funding.[140] As John Crabtree concludes, "Without an effective overhaul of the tax system, it was inappropriate to think that the [García] government would be able to intervene more in pursuit of economic development or greater social equity."[141] Deborah Poole and Gerardo Rénique similarly find that García's proposals for economic development "became mired down" because he "lacked the resources to carry out such ambitious programmes."[142] It was apparent by the beginning of 1987, even before the economic crisis, that García could not fund his reform agenda, and the plans were abandoned.[143] The president could not win hearts and minds without dollars and cents.

The Peruvian state's low extractive capacity also helped to eliminate the option of targeted repression. García enjoyed some initial success in curbing the military's excesses. In an unprecedented move, he forced the resignation of three of the military's highest-ranking officials, including the president of the joint command, for their role in a 1985 massacre of more than sixty peasants in Ayacucho.

But targeted repression requires considerable revenues to be effective. It is much more costly to hunt down well-armed guerrillas hiding in the mountains than to target immobile and undefended peasant villages. The military's lack of financial resources undermined its ability to subdue the unrest.[144] Indeed, Sendero extracted revenues to fund its activities with greater ease than did the García administration. By 1986, the Senderistas had formed an alliance with the coca growers in northern Peru and collected "taxes" in exchange for providing protection against government officials, unscrupulous buyers, and Sendero itself.[145] Amply funded by the drug trade, Sendero neared a "strategic equilibrium" with the Peruvian military.[146] The Senderistas began "attacking military installations and ambushing police and army patrols with impunity."[147]

After the financial crisis of 1988, the military's ability to repress Sendero was in a virtual free fall. Reductions in salaries led to difficulties attracting new recruits and a decline in morale. There was a "virtual stampede" of resignations among officers and desertions among enlisted soldiers.[148] And the military's capabilities had degraded to the point where, for example, most of its helicopters had been grounded due to a lack of fuel and spare parts.[149] It was clear that the armed forces were "unable to halt the growth, let alone defeat, the *Sendero Luminoso*."[150]

The Peruvian pauper state also reduced the government's ability to wage a diversionary war. The most likely target for rallying opinion was Ecuador. Indeed, of all the conflicts in Latin America, it was the only one "marked by the expression of nationalist hatred."[151] And regular skirmishes along the Peruvian–Ecuadoran border meant that it would have been fairly easy for García to find a pretext for conflict.[152] However, while a war "looked cheap" in 1981 under Belaúnde, it was a much riskier prospect seven years later.[153] The Peruvian defense budget had steadily declined over García's presidency, and the balance of capabilities no longer clearly favored Peru.[154] Provoking a war with Ecuador was essentially off the table.

The Extent of Sendero Luminoso's Political Reform Demands

This left political reform as a potential option, but unfortunately there was little room for compromise with the extremists of Sendero Luminoso. Founded in the early 1960s by Abimael Guzmán, a philosophy professor at San

Cristóbal de Huamanga University in Ayacucho, Sendero espoused a revolutionary ideology heavily indebted to "Gang of Four" Maoism. And its followers were prepared to wage guerrilla war against the Peruvian government.

Unlike similar movements in the region, Sendero never attempted to organize the peasants for nonviolent protest with the hope of encouraging the state to undertake political or economic reforms.[155] Rather, from its inception it was committed to the destruction of the existing social order. As James Rochlin writes, "The group was not satisfied with obtaining only a quotient of power, or with becoming an important voice among others in political debates. SL [Sendero Luminoso] strove for absolute and dictatorial power through state control."[156] The Senderistas were also distinguished by their ideological dogmatism: "Such was the importance of ideology to Sendero that it became virtually a religion, a set of unquestionable and immutable doctrinal precepts."[157] Given the movement's ideological rigidity and extremist demands, as well as García's commitment to democracy, there was no mutually acceptable political compromise possible.

The Impracticability of a Diversionary Spectacle
A diversionary spectacle was also not on García's menu of available responses to Sendero Luminoso. There was no guarantee that a conflict with Ecuador would have a low cost. Saber rattling sufficient to rally the public around the García administration could easily escalate into a prolonged and unaffordable conflict—as Peru's deadly clash with Ecuador in 1981 had demonstrated. And Quito was bent on overturning the 1942 Rio Protocol Settlement that denied it access to the Amazon River, and was looking for an opening to recover the lost territory. Ecuador would likely have seen a conflict provoked by Peru as an ideal opportunity to press its case for a more favorable territorial outcome.[158] Thus, with violent skirmishes occurring at regular intervals over the preceding decades, it would have been difficult for García to fall prey to wishful thinking regarding the feasibility of a low-cost diversionary spectacle against Ecuador.

The Impracticability of Foreign Intervention
With viable options dwindling, why did García not ask an ally to help put down the unrest in 1988? The answer is simply that no state was both willing and able to intervene. The one country in South America that had sufficient capabilities to intervene against Sendero and a history of military cooperation with Peru was Argentina.[159] Although Belaúnde had sided with Argentina

during the 1982 Falklands War, Buenos Aires was unlikely to return the favor by sending ground troops to combat Sendero guerrillas.[160] The president of Argentina, Raul Alfonsín, had been elected on a promise to investigate the previous juntas' actions against leftist insurgents during the dirty war of the 1970s and early 1980s. Therefore, he was unlikely to aid in Peru's own "dirty war" against Sendero.[161]

Outside of South America, the most likely candidate for military assistance was the United States. Washington not only had the capability to make a decisive intervention in the war against the leftist Senderistas, but it also had an interest in combating the insurgency because of its partnership with the narco-traffickers exporting cocaine to the United States. Indeed, García did receive limited military and economic assistance from the United States during the late 1980s.[162] Although this aid was intended for drug enforcement, some funds were diverted to finance the campaign against Sendero.[163]

That said, the priority of the U.S. government was not the war against the Senderistas but rather the eradication of coca crops. Consequently, its aid to Lima grew only slowly between 1985 and 1989.[164] Furthermore, in 1988 the Reagan administration was recovering from the Iran–Contra scandal, a product, in part, of U.S. intervention in Latin America, and would have had little appetite for putting U.S. ground troops in Peru in such an unfavorable domestic climate. Given that the United States was unwilling to intervene against Sendero—and given García's own opposition to American meddling in the region—U.S. foreign intervention in Peru was not an option.

Peru was left to fight the guerrillas alone, and this reality ensured that García would play his final card of muddling through.

Choosing to Muddle Through with Decentralized Repression

In 1988, because of a "lack of viable alternative strategies," García was pushed toward a policy of decentralized repression.[165] That is, the president enlisted the aid of paramilitary groups in the fight against Sendero. The government began arming civil defense groups in peasant communities, known as *rondas*. They had briefly been used under Belaúnde to scout and flush out Sendero bases in the highlands, but the practice was "largely disastrous."[166] The final straw for the policy came after one patrol assassinated eight journalists in the town of Uchuraccay, prompting the Belaúnde administration to disavow the use of *rondas* in response to public pressure. Given their poor track record, the García administration's "increased reliance on *rondas*," as Philip Mauceri argues, was "perhaps the clearest indicator of the declining ability, if not the willingness, of the government and the military to assert their authority."[167]

Further evidence of the government's "turn to more desperate tactics" was the emergence of the commando Rodrigo Franco, a right-wing paramilitary with ties to APRA and especially García's interior minister.[168] The death squad assassinated Sendero sympathizers, as well as leftist political leaders, human rights activists, and journalists.

With the shift to decentralized repression, civilian deaths jumped from around 500 in 1987 to 665 in 1988 and 1,017 in 1989—numbers on par with those of the Belaúnde administration era.[169] In effect, García had returned to the strategy of Belaúnde—repression with little regard for human rights. The difference was that Belaúnde selected this option thinking it might work, while the García administration was essentially muddling through. When governments cannot do anything, they still do something.

Conclusion

As discussed in Chapter 2, there are two causal pathways that result in embattled pauper states choosing not to use diversionary tactics: (1) they prefer an alternative policy to a diversion and can afford to implement it, or (2) they prefer to provoke a diversion, but environmental factors render it impracticable. In each of the cases examined in this chapter, the decision makers likely considered the use of diversionary tactics more attractive than the policy they ultimately implemented but were prevented from pursuing this option (and sometimes other options as well) by constraints in the environment.

A low extractive capacity consistently prevented the leaders from implementing resource-intensive responses to unrest, such as economic reform, widespread repression, and diversionary war, pushing them toward cheaper options, such as reform, foreign intervention, and muddling through. Additional environmental factors also contributed to the governments' final policy choices: the extent of the opposition's demands for political reform; the presence of a low-cost, domestically popular target; the availability of an ally ready and able to provide military assistance; and the international community's willingness to tolerate foreign intervention.

In the decisions of the Argentine junta and/or the U.S. government to stage diversionary spectacles, three of these variables were also necessary conditions: extractive capacity, the extent of reform demands, and the availability of a suitable target. But the remaining variables were only important causes in the cases of nondiversion examined here. The variation across cases regarding the causal importance of these environmental factors underscores the fact that government policy choices are also profoundly shaped by leader preferences. Indeed, whether an environmental factor contributes to a government's decision is determined by how leaders rank the options on the policy menu. For example, in some cases the extent of the opposition's reform demands mattered (France and Peru); in others it was irrelevant (the Habsburg empire). The key is where limited political reform fell on the leader's policy ranking: at or near the top in France and Peru but toward the bottom in Austria. Thus, as the policy substitutability model emphasizes, government policy choices are best explained as a product of environmental factors *and* leader preferences.

Of course, this observation would be less important if leader preferences remained essentially constant—the result would be that the same set of environmental factors generally matter. But these cases make plain that preference rankings are highly variable. For example, muddling through was the French monarchy's highest-ranked option but reviled by the Peruvian president. Therefore, the precise combination of environmental factors that leads a government to select a given response from the menu of alternatives may vary significantly across cases. That said, the benefit of studying the effect of extractive capacity on government decisions is that the practicability of multiple options on the policy menu depends on the state's access to revenue, meaning that this variable will assume causal importance in a large percentage of cases.

When we contrast the instances of nondiversion with Argentina's invasion of the Falkland Islands, we can see why some pauper states miscalculate and stage diversionary spectacles against high-risk targets, while others correctly perceive that a crisis with their adversary is likely to escalate. In each of the cases examined in this chapter, the governments faced a severe domestic threat to the regime and a narrowing of available policy responses, but all avoided the pitfalls of overconfidence. Why? Unlike Argentina, both France and Peru had recently fought bloody conflicts with their main rivals. And even under the best of circumstances, the Habsburgs struggled to pursue a foreign policy that would not aggravate the ethnic and religious tensions within its empire. The bias toward wishful thinking could not overcome these cold facts.

7 Conclusion

What this country needs is a short victorious war to stem the tide of revolution.

—*Russian Interior Minister Vyacheslav Plehve, 1904*[1]

D O UNPOPULAR GOVERNMENTS WAGE DIVERSIONARY WARS and, if so, under what conditions? Are they an effective antidote to a government's domestic ills? This chapter summarizes the book's empirical findings, discusses its contributions to both the study of diversionary war and government decision making, and describes the policy implications for reducing the incidence of diversionary war.

The Causes of Diversionary War

The use of diversionary tactics can be explained with a new decision-making framework—the policy substitutability approach—which proposes that a government's choices result from the interaction between leader preferences and environmental factors. *Leader preferences* refers to how decision makers view the desirability of a full range of potential responses to social unrest and then rank these options, from most to least attractive. *Environmental factors* are those conditions that enable or limit a government's ability to implement these options. Thus, if diversionary war is a leader's preferred response to internal instability and it is practicable, then the state will pursue this policy path. If, however, environmental factors rule out the use of diversionary force, the government is compelled to select an alternative, less palatable, strategy from the menu.

The book proposes that extractive capacity, or the ease with which a state mobilizes societal resources, primarily through the collection of taxes, is an environmental factor that significantly influences how states respond to domestic unrest. Governments with a high extractive capacity, or princely states, have the funds to adopt costly policies, such as diversionary war, economic reform, and repression. Governments with a low extractive capacity, or pauper states, have fewer options from which to choose—only relatively inexpensive policies may be within their reach, such as diversionary spectacles, political reform, requests for foreign intervention, or muddling through. Among princely states, therefore, extractive capacity assumes causal importance when the leader's preferred policy is resource intensive and a high extractive capacity makes it practicable. Among pauper states, extractive capacity influences government decision making when the leader prefers a costly response to unrest but a low extractive capacity renders it impracticable.

Considering only the potential cost of fighting an extended military campaign, one would expect diversionary wars to be most common among princely states. Yet the book makes the opposite prediction: pauper states are more likely than princely states to fight diversionary wars. This is because policy choices, as the substitutability approach emphasizes, are the product of both environmental factors, such as extractive capacity, *and* leader preferences. And most leaders will view diversionary war as an inherently dangerous response to domestic unrest—victory in war is never certain, and a loss on the battlefield will likely lead to a loss of power for an already shaky regime. Instead, leaders who regard the use of diversionary tactics as appealing will prefer to stage lower-risk diversionary spectacles against targets that are unlikely to resist.

If diversionary war is a generally unattractive—and expensive—strategy for managing internal instability, why would cash-strapped pauper states fight full-scale military campaigns? Diversionary wars will be relatively uncommon among princely states because they can afford more-attractive alternatives. But because of their low extractive capacity, pauper states may inadvertently be drawn into costly diversionary wars. The reason is that pauper states are more likely to provoke diversionary spectacles that escalate into major hostilities. Two mutually reinforcing dynamics are responsible for this outcome. First, the countries targeted by pauper states are, on balance, more likely to see their rival as weak and fight back. Second, pauper states are more likely to provoke diversionary spectacles out of desperation—that is, when their preferred policies are too costly. When leaders have limited options from which to choose, they are susceptible to wishful thinking about the likely success of their selected policy. This may mean underestimating the possibility that a diversionary spectacle will escalate into full-scale war. That said, any bias toward overconfidence may be tempered if there is a recent history of violent conflict with potential targets.

The quantitative and qualitative analyses discussed in the preceding chapters provide strong empirical support for the argument that diversionary wars mainly occur when pauper states orchestrate diversionary spectacles that spiral into unwanted wars. The cross-national statistical analysis discussed in Chapter 3 demonstrates that as domestic unrest intensifies, pauper states are generally more likely than princely states to fight interstate wars. Indeed, the results indicated that for resource-poor governments, internal instability significantly increases the probability of interstate war, while for very wealthy governments, unrest has no effect on the likelihood of war.

The cases discussed in chapters 4 through 6 provide evidence of the process by which pauper states are likely to be drawn into full-scale diversionary wars. The first case examined is the Argentine junta's decision to retake the British Falkland Islands in 1982—an example of a diversionary war fought by a pauper state (see Chapter 4). The case followed the predicted causal pathway. Environmental factors, namely a low extractive capacity, prevented Argentina's president, Leopoldo Galtieri, from suppressing widespread opposition to the government's economic austerity measures. Unable to adopt the preferred course of action, the increasingly desperate junta pursued a less-attractive, but also less-expensive, strategy for reducing antipathy toward the state—a diversionary spectacle to reclaim a historical territory, the Falkland Islands. However, Galtieri significantly misjudged London's willingness to defend the islands, and the spectacle spiraled into a costly and undesired war.

The second case, the U.S. expedition to Utah in 1857, is an example of a diversionary spectacle staged by a pauper state that did not escalate (see Chapter 5). Here, the U.S. president, James Buchanan, was able to select his preferred strategy for managing internal tensions over the expansion of slavery into the western territories—limited political reform. But when an opportunity to stage a low-cost diversionary spectacle against the Mormon church arose, he saw a chance to buy his administration time until the political compromise was in place, and seized it. As expected, given that environmental conditions enabled his preferred policy, Buchanan exhibited less overconfidence in assessing the risk of sending federal troops to install a non-Mormon territorial governor in Utah. He downplayed the willingness of the Mormon militia to put up some resistance, but he accurately recognized the Mormon desire to avoid a war with Washington. Thus, while the diversionary spectacle in Utah proved to be costlier than the president had anticipated—indeed, too costly for the U.S. pauper state—it did not become a full-scale war.

Finally, Chapter 6 examines three cases in which pauper states chose not to use diversionary tactics. In each case, environmental factors eliminated the decision makers' preferred responses to domestic unrest. In 1788 France's King Louis XVI would have preferred muddling through to his final policy choice, limited political reform. In 1849 the Habsburg monarchy's minister-president, Prince Felix zu Schwarzenberg, would have preferred repression to requesting Russian intervention in Hungary. And in 1988 Peruvian President Alan García would have preferred a combination of economic and limited political reform to muddling through with a failed policy of decentralized repression. Furthermore, each leader would likely have preferred using diversionary tactics to the policy that was ultimately selected. But despite a narrowing of available options, the respective leaders correctly recognized that a suitable target for a spectacle did not exist. Why were they able to avoid falling into the same trap as the Argentine junta?

In two of the cases—France in 1788 and Peru in 1988—there was a recent history of violent conflict with their chief rivals. France fought a costly war against the British in the American colonies, which ended in 1783, and there was deadly clash between Peruvian and Ecuadoran forces in 1981. In the Habsburg case, the monarchy was unable to find a mission that would rally the Hungarians around the regime without alienating other ethnic and religious groups within the empire. The constant drumbeat of ethnic tensions throughout their territories diminished the likelihood of wishful thinking in Vienna. In contrast, Argentina's long-standing dispute with Britain over the Falkland Islands had never resulted in bloodshed. And in the year before Galtieri came to power, London announced plans to reduce its military presence in the South Atlantic, encouraging Galtieri's misperception that Britain would hand over the islands without a fight.

When considered together, therefore, the case studies suggest that pauper states are likely to be drawn into unwanted diversionary wars if (1) the government stages a diversionary spectacle because environmental factors eliminated preferred responses to unrest, (2) there is no recent history of hostilities with the target to remind the government of the dangers of provoking a diversionary spectacle, and (3) the target is both willing and able to fight back. If any one of these conditions is altered, the chances of an unintended diversionary war will drop dramatically. Because it is unlikely that all of these conditions will be met simultaneously, diversionary wars, even among pauper states, are rare.

State Responses to Domestic Unrest: Leader Preferences and Environmental Factors

Applying the policy substitutability approach to these historical cases illuminates how extractive capacity (along with additional environmental factors) can shape the policy choices of unstable governments. It also reveals noteworthy patterns in how leaders rank the policy alternatives for managing domestic unrest.

Looking first at extractive capacity, we see that, as predicted, a limited ability to mobilize societal resources consistently ruled out costly responses to unrest. In addition to diversionary war, the pauper states were unable to engage in widespread repression or enact expensive economic reforms. Rather surprisingly, in the case of France under Louis XVI, a low extractive capacity also precluded muddling through. The monarchy faced immediate bankruptcy if it could not end the unrest quickly and convince lenders that it was creditworthy.

In the end, extractive capacity played an important causal role in each case. Such a robust finding was not assured because the causal importance of an environmental factor depends on a leader's policy ranking. For example, Buchanan's preferred response to domestic discontent was limited political reform—and a low extractive capacity has no effect on whether a government can implement this option. That said, the feasibility of several options on the policy menu depends on a government's access to resources, meaning that this variable should contribute to a leader's final policy choice in many cases.

The case studies uncover several other environmental factors that can shape how governments respond to unrest. First, whether leaders were able to stage a diversionary spectacle depended on the availability of a suitable target—that is, a low-cost, domestically popular mission. Both Galtieri and Buchanan believed they had found targets that would not resist, but would also generate a rally effect, allowing them to orchestrate a spectacle. For Galtieri, the target was the largely undefended Falkland Islands and, for Buchanan, the heretical Mormon militia in Utah. A spectacle was impracticable in all of the other cases because the leaders expected potential targets to resist and/or because no mission would have been unifying.

It is important to note that whether a suitable target is available is contingent on the government's extractive capacity. The more limited a pauper state's ability to mobilize societal resources, the more difficult it will be to find an adversary where the probability of resistance is sufficiently small. This observation has implications for the claim that a threatening international environment makes it easier for governments to use diversionary tactics. For example, Scott Bennett and Timothy Nordstrom argue that if a country is party to a long-standing rivalry, "diversionary behavior is frequently a plausible policy option" and is more likely.[2] For very impoverished pauper states, however, a rivalry reduces the probability of a diversionary spectacle. Although picking a fight with a rival might generate a sizable rally effect, the adversary is also ready and willing to resist. For example, the expectation that Ecuador, Peru's main rival, would retaliate prevented García from choosing a diversionary spectacle. Thus, unless the adversary is a paper tiger—that is, a very weak rival—it will not be a suitable target for a pauper state. Pauper states are bullies: they have no intention of fighting their equal.

Second, whether a government enacted political reforms depended on the extent of the opposition's demands. Several leaders viewed limited political concessions as a relatively attractive strategy to end the unrest—Louis XVI in 1788, Buchanan in 1857, and García in 1988. But the practicability of this response depended on whether their domestic opponents aimed to topple the government or overturn the political system. While Louis XVI was reluctant to limit his powers, he believed that calling the Estates General would placate the nobility while leaving the monarchy mostly intact. Similarly, Buchanan thought there was a political compromise that would satisfy most of the public while also preserving the political system and ensuring that the Democratic Party remained in power. On the other hand, because Sendero Luminoso sought a Marxist revolution, García could not end the unrest in Peru with limited political reform. His opposition would not have been content with any outcome short of dismantling the country's entire political and economic system.

Third, whether unstable states received foreign military assistance hinged on whether a third party was willing and able to commit troops to quell the unrest—ideally while demanding few concessions in exchange for its help.

A third party is likely to offer aid with few strings attached only if propping up the embattled government is perceived to be in its core national interest.[3] Intervention also depended on whether the international community supported (or at least did not oppose) the military operation. In the case of the Habsburg monarchy in 1849, the Russian tsar feared that a successful rebellion in Hungary would inspire a dangerous revolutionary movement within his own empire and, therefore, was willing to offer the Austrian crown assistance on very favorable terms. Britain, the state most likely to object to Russian intervention, tacitly supported St. Petersburg because it believed that a strong and stable Habsburg empire was necessary to maintain the European balance of power. In the case of Peru, the president likely would have preferred foreign intervention to his final policy choice of muddling through, but no country had the capability and desire to join the fight against Sendero Luminoso. Washington was ready to offer some financial assistance to stem the flow of Peruvian cocaine into the United States but not to provide ground forces for a counterinsurgency campaign.

Finally, the case studies offer some evidence that democratic institutions shape whether unpopular governments are able to use repressive tactics. As discussed in Chapter 2, this is in line with arguments in the diversionary war literature that democratically elected leaders who are drawn to repression are unable to pursue this response to unrest because they fear being voted out of office. Indeed, scholars have speculated that democratic leaders are more likely to use diversionary tactics precisely because repression is impracticable.

Buchanan avoided using repression to end the debate over slavery because he saw himself as a conciliator, meaning that he placed repression at the bottom of his policy ranking. But if repression had been his top-ranked policy, the president would have found it nearly impossible, say, to coerce Republicans into accepting a proslavery outcome in Kansas without guaranteeing that he (and the Democratic Party) would be thrown out of power in the next election. Thus, if the president had a different policy ranking, regime type would almost certainly have assumed causal importance. Further, if a low extractive capacity had not prevented the Argentine junta from using widespread repression and the Habsburg monarchy from ratcheting up its efforts to suppress the Hungarian rebellion, regime type would likely have been part of these causal stories as well. Here, because both governments faced few institutional constraints on their exercise of power, regime type would have functioned as a permissive condition for the use of repression.

But even if autocrats face fewer repercussions from using repression, the case studies demonstrate how they could still wind up employing diversionary tactics. The Argentine junta in 1982 is a prime example. Thus, diversionary wars can occur in both types of political systems. This may explain why the interaction term between democracy and domestic unrest in the statistical model of interstate war was insignificant (see Chapter 3).

Aside from regime type, none of these variables feature in the literature on the causes of diversionary war. Yet, as the case studies demonstrate, they could function as necessary conditions for a government's decision to use diversionary tactics. Some variables were permissive conditions, such as the availability of a suitable target for a diversionary spectacle. Other variables indirectly led to the use of diversionary tactics by eliminating a leader's preferred alternatives—for example, a low extractive capacity and whether opposition groups demanded extreme reforms to the political system.

This list of environmental factors is unlikely to be exhaustive, however. Again, whether an environmental factor assumes causal importance in a particular case depends on a leader's policy ranking. To reveal the full range of environmental factors that can enable or limit a government's ability to pursue options on the policy menu, one must apply the substitutability approach to cases in which the leaders held different preferences.

The cases also offer some insight into how leaders rank the alternative responses to domestic unrest. As expected, there was considerable variation in preferences, reflecting idiosyncrasies specific to each leader. For example, muddling through was Louis XVI's preferred strategy for handing the restive nobility in 1788, but it was near the bottom of the Argentine junta's ranking of policies for dealing with its opposition in 1982.

But there were also a few patterns. Foreign intervention was at or near the bottom of most of the decision makers' policy rankings. This is unsurprising given that leaders might expect to lose much of their country's sovereignty after inviting a third party to intervene—an inherently unpalatable prospect for most governments. Radical political reform was also generally viewed as an unattractive response to unrest, likely because most leaders aim, at a minimum, to stay in power and preserve the political system.

Preferences regarding political reform and repression differed by regime type. The leaders of nondemocracies favored repression over political reform, while the leaders of democracies ranked some degree of political reform above repression. The key decision maker in Argentina, a military dictatorship, and the Habsburg empire, an absolutist monarchy, both harbored a deep-seated aversion to granting the demands of their opponents. At the same time, the presidents of the United States and Peru, both democracies, were both open to a political compromise.[4] The outlier is France's absolutist monarch, Louis XVI, who was taught to believe in the divine right of kings yet was also convinced that a good sovereign does not wage war against his subjects.

This finding suggests that democracy can affect decision making in two ways. As discussed above, democratic institutions may be an external constraint on state behavior, ruling out the use of repression. But democratic norms may also shape leader preferences—politicians who rise to power in democracies are more likely to view political accommodation as an intrinsically attractive response to domestic dissent.

Contributions to the Literature on Policy Substitutability

The book advances the existing research on policy substitution in several ways. First, the policy substitutability approach introduced in Chapter 2 reveals new variables that cause leaders to choose one strategy over another from a menu of options. The framework instructs us to think of decisions as the product of a leader's policy ranking and environmental factors—and the empirics demonstrate that *both* elements shape policy choice.

Second, and related, the new policy substitutability approach produces more-accurate theories of government decision making. Without thinking of policy choices as resulting from an *interaction* between leader preferences and environmental factors, we may arrive at the wrong conclusions about how states are likely to behave and why. For example, if we only consider how a low extractive capacity shapes government responses to domestic unrest, we may conclude that princely states are most likely to fight diversionary wars—they use diversionary force because this policy option is affordable. But this expectation would be incorrect. Instead, we must consider how this environmental factor interacts with leader preferences to understand when and why states fight diversionary wars. In so doing, we discover that such conflicts occur not because they are an inherently palatable response to unrest but rather because governments have few alternative options available to them. And even then, leaders do not set out to fight diversionary wars—they provoke diversionary spectacles that escalate into unwanted wars.

Third, the substitutability approach offers a new method of analysis for the study of individual cases. One first establishes a leader's policy ranking and then searches for variables that either enabled or eliminated each of the options. Using this process, we can identify precisely how preferences and environmental factors together produced the government's final policy choice—in particular, to identify when and why policy substitutions occurred.

This approach is not straightforward. Establishing a leader's preferences is problematic because decision makers may never explicitly rank the available options or even discuss certain options rendered impracticable by constraints in the environment. Neither is it easy to identify the environmental factors that close off options on a policy menu. For example, governments may never discuss how external conditions shape their policy choices, particularly when an environmental factor functions as a permissive condition.

But what is the alternative? Unless one opens up the black box of decision making by performing both of these tasks, however challenging, one cannot accurately determine the causes of a decision in a given case. A variable may appear at first glance to be important, but after identifying a leader's policy ranking, we could discover that it merely ruled out an option that the decision maker perceived as unpalatable and would have avoided in any case. For example, one might conclude that a regime chose not to request foreign intervention because third parties were unwilling to provide assistance—when instead this option fell at the bottom of the leader's policy ranking and would have been selected only if *every* other option on the policy menu was impracticable. Alternatively, a variable may seem unconnected to a government's final policy choice when, in fact, it eliminated the leader's preferred option and, therefore, was a necessary condition for the outcome. For example, prior accounts of the Falklands War had overlooked the fact that it was the Argentina's junta's inability to afford repression that led the government to stage a diversionary spectacle in the Falklands—precisely the kind of "hidden" necessary condition that is so often ignored.

The substitutability approach has very wide applicability, and it can be used to explain decision making in any cases where leaders have multiple options for handling a policy challenge. For example, governments have a range of strategies for encouraging economic development—from autarky to economic liberalism. If a government hoped to encourage development by reducing barriers to trade but faced strong opposition from business elites, the substitutability approach could explain why the leaders instead confiscated the holdings of multinational corporations.

Do Diversionary Wars Work?

The book conducts the first study of the relative utility of diversionary war—that is, whether the use of diversionary force is a better response to domestic unrest than the alternative options on the policy menu. The statistical analysis discussed in Chapter 3 finds that interstate wars are an ineffectual strategy for managing internal instability while conflicts short of war are counterproductive. Therefore, prudent leaders should place this policy option low on their ranking. Instead, unstable democracies and mixed regimes may be better served appeasing their opponents with political reform or increasing government spending. However, autocratic leaders should focus entirely on the economy, either by reducing barriers to international trade or increasing spending. Here, political concessions will only whet the public's appetite for greater change.

There are also some tentative lessons that can be drawn from the case studies regarding the perils of diversionary tactics for pauper states. Neither the Argentine junta's mission to recover the Falkland Islands nor the U.S. government's expedition to Utah was a successful diversion.

The Argentina's invasion of the Falklands initially produced what Richard Ned Lebow has described as an "orgy of nationalism."[5] Immediately following the invasion in April 1982, more than 100,000 Argentines—from Perónists to staunch supporters of the military—gathered in the main square of Buenos Aires to cheer the government's achievement.[6] And every newspaper in the country ran banner headlines celebrating the return of the islands to Argentina.[7] But when the junta suffered a humiliating defeat by the British and was forced to surrender in June, Galtieri was swiftly removed from office, and within a few months, military rule ended.

In its early days, the Utah expedition was also popular. The response of the *New York Daily Times* was typical: "It appears that a cavalry force . . . has been ordered into the Territory of Utah, and the Executive [non-Mormon] authorities about to be appointed for that most unhappy region will be supported in the only proper way, that is by a military force strong enough to compel the obedience of the reckless scoundrels who now control the ignorant masses of the Mormon population."[8] But at no point did the mission divert the public's attention from the debate over the future of slavery in the western territories. Even as federal troops set off for Utah, the nation's gaze remained fixed on events in Kansas.

Together, these cases suggest that pauper states may face a catch-22 when using diversionary tactics. Missions that are sufficiently dramatic to distract the public from the government's failings—such as the Falklands War—are too expensive to conduct and are likely to result in military defeat and wider unrest. Missions that are affordable—such as the diversionary spectacle against the Mormon militia—are insufficiently diverting and have little effect on domestic discontent.

Policy Implications

The substitutability approach may provide policy makers with a wider range of strategies with which to influence the decision making of other governments. The key is in understanding how leaders rank the options on a policy menu and then manipulating which options are practicable in order to direct the leader toward the course of action that one deems desirable. There are essentially two ways of shaping decisions: (1) erecting roadblocks to restrict a government's ability to pursue an undesirable policy path or (2) removing impediments to enable a government to pursue a desired path.

The first strategy could have been deployed to head off the Falklands War. Hoping to avoid a military confrontation with Argentina, the British government studiously avoided issuing any warnings that it would defend the Falkland Islands in the event of Argentine aggression.[9] But this was precisely the opposite strategy from the one Britain should have adopted. London could have thwarted the Argentine junta from staging a diversionary spectacle by strongly signaling its resolve. A clear statement from a high-ranking official that Britain would resist any attempt by Argentina to take the islands by force, plus a continued military presence in the South Atlantic, would likely have been sufficient to convince Buenos Aires that the Falklands was not a low-cost target. The United States could also have helped disabuse Galtieri of the notion that a mission to retake the islands would be cheap by indicating that it would side with Britain in the event of a conflict over the islands.

The second strategy could have been used to channel García away from muddling through with repression. The policy substitutability approach reveals that the Peruvian state's low extractive capacity ruled out the president's preferred strategy of economic reform to co-opt the peasantry and targeted repression of Sendero insurgents. These policies would have been more in line with U.S. interests than the policy the Peruvian president ultimately implemented—the brutal repression of both Senderistas and the peasantry. President Ronald Reagan's primary foreign policy goals in Peru were to combat the export of Peruvian cocaine to the United States and prevent the Marxist insurgents from deposing the government. If Washington had improved García's access to revenues during the first years of his presidency, the Peruvian government would have been able to implement a robust economic reform program, which in turn might have reduced peasant support for Sendero (significantly weakening the insurgency) and made growing coca a less-attractive occupation (reducing Peru's export of cocaine). Furthermore, with additional resources, García's efforts to combat the Senderista guerillas would likely have been more successful. Thus, if the United States had recognized that the Peruvian government's low extractive capacity was partly responsible for its decision to adopt a policy of decentralized repression, it might have been able to push the government toward a more-desirable policy response by increasing its resources.

By using the policy substitutability approach, therefore, policy makers can avoid treating history simply as, in E. H. Carr's words, "a record of what people did, not of what they failed to do" and instead see the full range of options available to decision makers and uncover the often hidden causes that shape their choices.[10]

REFERENCE MATTER

Notes

Chapter 1

1. William Shakespeare, *Henry IV, Part 2*, ed. Barbara A. Mowat and Paul Werstine (New York: Washington Square, 1999), 4.3, 373–375.

2. Christopher Hitchens, "They Bomb Pharmacies, Don't They?" *Salon*, September 23, 1998.

3. John Cochran and Forrest Sawyer, "Strikes Planned Since Last Wednesday," *World News Tonight with Peter Jennings*, August 20, 1998; Sean Hannity and Alan Colmes, "U.S. Bombings of Afghanistan and Sudan," *Fox Hannity & Colmes*, August 20, 1998; Thalia Assuras, "Reaction to President Clinton's Decision to Order U.S. Air Strikes on Terrorist Facilities in Sudan and Afghanistan," *CBS This Morning*, August 21, 1998; Frank Bruni, "U.S. Fury on 2 Continents: Voices; Wagging Tongues in 'Incredibly Cynical Times,'" *New York Times*, August 21, 1998, A12; John F. Harris, "In the Midst of Scandal, Clinton Planned Action," *Washington Post*, August 21, 1998, A1; Bill Hemmer, Andrea Koppel, Daryn Kagan, and Candy Crowley, "America Strikes Back: State Department Issues Warning; Congressional Majority Supports Attacks," *CNN Morning News*, August 21, 1998; "Infinite Reach: Comparison Between Attacks on Terrorists and the Movie 'Wag the Dog,'" *Dateline NBC*, August 21, 1998.

4. Barton Gellman and Dana Priest, "U.S. Strikes Terrorist-Linked Sites in Afghanistan, Factory in Sudan," *Washington Post*, August 21, 1998, A1.

5. Laurie Dhue and Cynthia Tornquist, "'Wag the Dog' Rentals Skyrocket," *CNN Sunday*, August 23, 1998.

6. Brian Knowlton, "Character Rating Sinks, Raising Questions About Ability to Lead Nation: 'I Misled People; I Deeply Regret That,'" *New York Times*, August 19, 1998.

7. Todd Purdum, "U.S. Fury on 2 Continents: Congress; Critics of Clinton Support Attacks," *New York Times*, August 21, 1998, A1.

8. Adam Nagourney and Michael R. Kagay, "High Marks Given to the President But Not the Man," *New York Times*, August 22, 1998, A1.

9. See Ronald Radosh, *Prophets on the Right: Profiles of Conservative Critics of American Globalism* (New York: Simon & Schuster, 1975), 164, note 38. For an argument that Truman exploited, rather than actually escalated, the Berlin crisis for domestic political gain, see Robert A. Divine, "The Cold War and the Election of 1948," *Journal of American History* 59, no. 1 (June 1972): 90–110.

10. Gary A. Donaldson, *Truman Beats Dewey* (Lexington: University of Kentucky Press, 1998), 27; Clark Clifford to Harry S. Truman, November 19, 1947, Memo, Political File, Clifford Papers, 15, accessed March 23, 2010, www.trumanlibrary.org/whistle stop/study_collections/1948campaign/large/docs/documents/pdfs/1-1.pdf

11. Mark Haefele, "John F. Kennedy, USIA, and World Public Opinion," *Diplomatic History* 25, no. 1 (Winter 2001): 65.

12. Thomas G. Paterson and William J. Brophy, "October Missiles and November Elections: The Cuban Missile Crisis and American Politics, 1962," *Journal of American History* 73, no. 1 (June 1986): 87.

13. Ibid., 88.

14. Dominic Johnson and Dominic Tierney, "In the Eye of the Beholder: Victory and Defeat in U.S. Military Operations," in *Understanding Victory and Defeat in Contemporary War*, ed. Jan Angstrom and Isabelle Duyvesteyn (New York: Routledge, 2007), 63.

15. Dominic Tierney, "Prisoner Dilemmas: The American Obsession with POWs and Hostages," *Orbis* 54, no. 1 (Winter 2010): 141.

16. David Patrick Houghton, *U.S. Foreign Policy and the Iran Hostage Crisis* (Cambridge: Cambridge University Press, 2001), 89.

17. Seyom Brown, *The Faces of Power: Constancy and Change in United States Foreign Policy from Truman to Clinton* (New York: Columbia University Press, 1994), 469–470.

18. Steven V. Roberts, "Move in Congress: House Panel, 32–2, Votes to Apply Law Limiting Right to Wage War," *New York Times*, October 28, 1983, A12.

19. Francis X. Clines, "White House Tactics Could Be Costly Next Year," *New York Times*, October 30, 1983, E2. The Reagan administration reacted angrily to these claims. When asked to comment on the report that a presidential staffer believed the operation was intended to divert attention from events in Beirut, White House spokesman, Larry Speakes, exploded: "I tell you what I would do. I'd go back to that source and I'd grab him right by the collar and jerk him up and say, 'You didn't give me the facts.' . . . That is a foolish and incomprehensible deduction." Lesley Stahl, *Reporting Live* (New York: Simon & Schuster, 1999), 180.

20. Jane Kellett Cramer, "'Just Cause' or Just Politics? U.S. Panama Invasion and Standardizing Qualitative Tests for Diversionary War," *Armed Forces & Society* 32, no. 2 (January 2006): 179.

21. Maureen Dowd, "Basking in Power's Glow: Bush's Year as President," *New York Times*, December 31, 1989, 21.

22. Julian E. Zelizer, *The Presidency of George W. Bush: A First Historical Assessment* (Princeton: Princeton University Press, 2010), 104.

23. Todd S. Purdum, "Threats and Responses: The Administration; Bush Officials Say the Time Has Come for Action on Iraq," *New York Times*, September 9, 2002.

24. James Meernik and Peter Waterman, "The Myth of the Diversionary Use of Force by American Presidents," *Political Research Quarterly* 49, no. 3 (September 1996): 573.

25. See Bruce W. Bennett, *Uncertainties in the North Korean Nuclear Threat* (Santa Monica: RAND, 2010), accessed January 3, 2011, www.rand.org/pubs/documented_briefings/2010/RAND_DB589.pdf; Bruce Klingner, "Morning Bell: The Death of Kim Jong-il," *Morning Bell*, December 19, 2011, blog.heritage.org/2011/12/19/morning-bell-the-death-of-kim-jong-il

26. Robert C. Diprizio, *Armed Humanitarians: U.S. Interventions from Northern Iraq to Kosovo* (Baltimore: Johns Hopkins University Press, 2002), 85.

27. Russell Crandall, *Gunboat Diplomacy: U.S. Interventions in the Dominican Republic, Grenada, Panama* (Lanham: Rowman & Littlefield, 2006), 142.

28. Denise M. Bostdorff, *The Presidency and the Rhetoric of Foreign Crisis* (Columbia: University of South Carolina Press, 1994), 175–204.

29. For examples of key works on policy substitutability, see Benjamin A. Most and Harvey Starr, "International Relations Theory, Foreign Policy Substitutability, and 'Nice' Laws," *World Politics* 36, no. 3 (April 1984): 383–406; Benjamin A. Most and Harvey Starr, *Inquiry, Logic, and International Politics* (Columbia: University of South Carolina Press, 1989); Harvey Starr, "Substitutability in Foreign Policy: Theoretically Central, Empirically Elusive," *Journal of Conflict Resolution* 44, no. 1 (February 2000): 128–138.

Chapter 2

1. Charles W. Moores, ed., *Lincoln: Addresses and Letters* (New York: American Book Company, 1914), 159.

2. Ibid.; Jay Monaghan, *Diplomat in Carpet Slippers: Abraham Lincoln Deals with Foreign Affairs* (Indianapolis: Bobbs-Merrill, 1945), 58.

3. Quincy Wright, *A Study of War* (Chicago: University of Chicago Press, 1964), 140.

4. Harvey Starr, "Revolution and War: Rethinking the Linkage Between Internal And External Conflict," *Political Research Quarterly* 47, no. 2 (June 1994): 481.

5. An interstate war is combat between regular armed forces in which each side incurs significant battlefield fatalities.

6. One might wonder here whether identifying cases of diversionary war is particularly challenging because it requires that we uncover a leader's motivation for using force. Establishing a diversionary motive for war is difficult, but no more so

than demonstrating the effect of almost any factor on a leader's decision making—including structural realist variables, such as the international distribution of power.

7. Arno J. Mayer, *Dynamics of Counterrevolution in Europe, 1870–1956: An Analytic Framework* (New York: Harper & Row, 1971), 220–221.

8. Richard N. Rosecrance, *Action and Reaction in World Politics: International Systems in Perspective* (Boston: Little, Brown, 1963), 304–305.

9. Jack S. Levy, "The Diversionary Theory of War: A Critique," in *A Handbook of War Studies*, ed. Manus I. Midlarsky (Ann Arbor: University of Michigan Press, 1989), 262. See also Rudolph J. Rummel, "Dimensions of Conflict Behavior Within and Between Nations," *Yearbook of the Society for General Systems* 8 (1963): 1–50; Raymond Tanter, "Dimensions of Conflict Behavior Within and Between Nations, 1958–1960," *Journal of Conflict Resolution* 10, no. 1 (March 1966): 41–64; Michael Haas, "Social Change and National Aggressiveness, 1900–1960," in *Quantitative International Politics: Insights and Evidence*, ed. J. David Singer (New York: Free Press, 1968); Dinna A. Zinnes and Jonathan Wilkenfeld, "An Analysis of Foreign Conflict Behavior of Nations," in *Comparative Foreign Policy: Theoretical Essays*, ed. W. F. Hanrieder (New York: David McKay, 1971); Jonathan Wilkenfeld, "Models for the Analysis of Foreign Conflict Behavior of States," in *Peace, War, and Numbers*, ed. Bruce M. Russett (Beverly Hills: Sage, 1972).

10. See, for example, T. Clifton Morgan and Kenneth N. Bickers, "Domestic Discontent and the External Use of Force," *Journal of Conflict Resolution* 36, no. 1 (March 1992): 25–52; Ross A. Miller, "Domestic Structures and the Diversionary Use of Force," *American Journal of Political Science* 39, no. 3 (August 1995): 760–785; Karl DeRouen Jr., "The Indirect Link: Politics, the Economy, and the Use of Force," *Journal of Conflict Resolution* 39, no. 4 (December 1995): 671–695; Alastair Smith, "Diversionary Foreign Policy in Democratic Systems," *International Studies Quarterly* 40, no. 1 (March 1996): 133–153; Christopher Gelpi, "Democratic Diversions: Governmental Structure and the Externalization of Domestic Conflict," *Journal of Conflict Resolution* 41, no. 2 (April 1997): 255–282; Benjamin Fordham, "The Politics of Threat Perception and the Use of Force: A Political Economy Model of U.S. Uses of Force, 1949–1994," *International Studies Quarterly* 42, no. 3 (September 1998): 567–590; T. Clifton Morgan and Christopher J. Anderson, "Domestic Support and Diversionary External Conflict in Great Britain, 1950–1992," *Journal of Politics* 61, no. 3 (August 1999): 799–814; Kurt Dassel and Eric Reinhardt, "Domestic Strife and the Initiation of Violence at Home and Abroad," *American Journal of Political Science* 43, no. 1 (January 1999): 56–85; Giacomo Chiozza and Hein E. Goemans, "Peace Through Insecurity: Tenure and International Conflict," *Journal of Conflict Resolution* 47, no. 4 (August 2003): 443–467; Jeffrey Pickering and Emizet F. Kisangani, "Democracy and Diversionary Military Intervention: Reassessing Regime Type and the Diversionary Hypothesis," *International Studies Quarterly* 49, no. 1 (March 2005): 23–43; Emizet F. Kisangani and Jeffrey Pickering, "The Dividends of Diversion: Mature Democracies' Proclivity to Use Diversionary Force and the Rewards They Reap from It," *British Journal of Political Science* 39, no. 3 (July 2009): 483–515.

11. See Brett Ashley Leeds and David Davis, "Domestic Political Vulnerability and International Disputes," *Journal of Conflict Resolution* 41, no. 6 (December 1997): 814–834; D. Scott Bennett and Timothy Nordstrom, "Foreign Policy Substitutability and Internal Economic Problems in Enduring Rivalries," *Journal of Conflict Resolution* 44, no. 1 (February 2000): 33–61; James Meernik, "Domestic Politics and the Political Use of Military Force by the United States," *Political Research Quarterly* 54, no. 4 (December 2001): 889–904; Sara McLaughlin Mitchell and Brandon C. Prins, "Rivalry and Diversionary Uses of Force," *Journal of Conflict Resolution* 48, no. 6 (December 2004): 937–961; Jaroslav Tir, "Territorial Diversion: Diversionary Theory of War and Territorial Conflict," *Journal of Politics* 72, no. 2 (April 2010): 413–425.

12. For examples of studies that find no evidence of a diversionary motivation for war, see James Meernik and Peter Waterman, "The Myth of the Diversionary Use of Force by American Presidents," *Political Research Quarterly* 49, no. 3 (1996): 573–590; Leeds and Davis, "Domestic Political Vulnerability"; Joanne Gowa, "Politics at the Water's Edge: Parties, Votes, and the Use of Force Abroad," *International Organization* 52, no. 2 (Spring 1998): 307–324.

13. Chiozza and Goemans, "Peace Through Insecurity," 446.

14. Gelpi, "Democratic Diversions," 261. See also Graeme A. M. Davies, "Domestic Strife and the Initiation of International Conflicts: A Directed Dyad Analysis, 1950–1992," *Journal of Conflict Resolution* 46, no. 5 (October 2002): 676–692; Pickering and Kisangani, "Democracy and Diversionary Military Intervention"; John R. Oneal and Jaroslav Tir, "Does the Diversionary Use of Force Threaten the Democratic Peace? Assessing the Effect of Economic Growth on Interstate Conflict, 1921–2001," *International Studies Quarterly* 50, no. 4 (December 2006): 755–779.

15. See Edward D. Mansfield and Jack Snyder, "Democratization and the Danger of War," *International Security* 20, no. 1 (Summer 1995): 5–38; Edward D. Mansfield and Jack Snyder, "Democratic Transitions, Institutional Strength, and War," *International Organization* 56, no. 2 (Spring 2002): 297–337; Edward D. Mansfield and Jack Snyder, *Electing to Fight: Why Emerging Democracies Go to War* (Cambridge: MIT Press, 2005).

16. Mansfield and Snyder, *Electing to Fight*, 9; see also 36–37.

17. Miller, "Domestic Structures." See also Zinnes and Wilkenfeld, "An Analysis of Foreign Conflict"; Ross A. Miller, "Regime Type, Strategic Interaction, and the Diversionary Use of Force," *Journal of Conflict Resolution* 43, no. 3 (June 1999): 388–402; Andrew J. Enterline and Kristian S. Gleditsch, "Threats, Opportunity, and Force: Repression and Diversion of Domestic Pressure, 1948–1982," *International Interactions* 26, no. 1 (January 2000): 21–53.

18. See Bennett and Nordstrom, "Foreign Policy Substitutability."

19. Christian Davenport, *State Repression and the Domestic Democratic Peace* (Cambridge: Cambridge University Press, 2007), 35.

20. Opposition groups may often demand greater participation in the political process (i.e., democratization), but not necessarily. For example, Sendero Luminoso in Peru sought a Marxist revolution (see Chapter 6).

21. Gordon Craig, "History as a Humanistic Discipline," in *Historical Literacy: The Case for History in American Education*, ed. Paul A. Gagnon (New York: Macmillan, 1989), 134.

22. Gelpi, "Democratic Diversions," 280.

23. See Bruce M. Russett, "Economic Decline, Electoral Pressure, and the Initiation of Interstate Conflict," in *Prisoners of War? Nation States in the Modern Era*, ed. Charles S. Gochman and Alan Ned Sabrosky (Lexington: Lexington Books, 1990), 123–140; Davies, "Domestic Strife"; Pickering and Kisangani, "Democracy and Diversionary Military Intervention"; David Brulé, "Congressional Opposition, the Economy, and U.S. Dispute Initiation, 1946–2000," *Journal of Conflict Resolution* 50, no. 4 (August 2006): 465; Kisangani and Pickering, "The Dividends of Diversion."

24. Benjamin Fordham, "Strategic Conflict Avoidance and the Diversionary Use of Force," *Journal of Politics* 67, no. 1 (February 2005): 132–153.

25. Another prominent example is Scott Bennett and Timothy Nordstrom's study of whether embattled governments attempt to ameliorate their domestic problems by either initiating a military dispute with a long-standing rival or terminating the enduring rivalry, the assumption being that a decision to seek peace with a rival is evidence that the government has freed up resources to pursue an alternate policy, such as economic reform. The article makes a strong case for building statistical models that allow for substitutability among policy responses. But the main contribution of the article is methodological rather than theoretical. Bennett and Nordstrom do not investigate when or why leaders might substitute specific policies for managing unrest, such as choosing diversionary war over repression. Bennett and Nordstrom, "Foreign Policy Substitutability," 42. See also Leeds and Davis, "Domestic Political Vulnerability"; David H. Clark, "Can Strategic Interaction Divert Diversionary Behavior? A Model of U.S. Conflict Propensity," *Journal of Politics* 65, no. 4 (November 2003): 1013–1039; Mitchell and Prins, "Rivalry and Diversionary Uses of Force"; Emizet F. Kisangani and Jeffrey Pickering, "Diverting with Benevolent Military Force: Reducing Risks and Rising Above Strategic Behavior," *International Studies Quarterly* 51, no. 2 (June 2007): 277–299.

26. Andrew Enterline and Kristian Gleditsch's cross-national study examines whether repression and diversionary war are alternative responses to domestic unrest. They find that because these policies are often implemented simultaneously, they should not be viewed as substitutes but rather as complements. Both repression and diversionary conflict become more likely as unrest intensifies. But there are some grounds for caution about these results. For example, Enterline and Gleditsch consider only whether greater institutional constraints on the chief executive might cause embattled leaders to choose diversionary conflict over repression (they find they do not), overlooking other factors that might lead to policy substitution during periods of internal instability. See "Threats, Opportunity, and Force." David Clark explores the conditions under which U.S. presidents facing high unemployment choose to initiate an economic dispute via the General Agreement on Tariffs and Trade or a militarized dispute. While Clark's study moves the debate forward by showing how the

U.S. policy process can make a diversionary conflict more likely by rendering some responses more difficult, it does not address how the logic of substitutability might shape the decision making of nondemocratic states or even other democracies. See "Trading Butter for Guns: Domestic Imperatives for Foreign Policy Substitution," *Journal of Conflict Resolution* 45, no. 5 (October 2001): 636–660.

27. Kurt Dassel, "Civilians, Soldiers, and Strife: Domestic Sources of International Aggression," *International Security* 23, no. 1 (Summer 1998): 107–140.

28. Glenn Palmer and T. Clifton Morgan, *A Theory of Foreign Policy* (Princeton: Princeton University Press, 2006), 111. See especially Benjamin A. Most and Harvey Starr, "International Relations Theory, Foreign Policy Substitutability, and 'Nice' Laws," *World Politics* 36, no. 3 (April 1984): 383–406; Benjamin A. Most and Harvey Starr, *Inquiry, Logic, and International Politics* (Columbia: University of South Carolina Press, 1989); Harvey Starr, "Substitutability in Foreign Policy: Theoretically Central, Empirically Elusive," *Journal of Conflict Resolution* 44, no. 1 (February 2000): 128–138.

29. Palmer and Morgan, *A Theory of Foreign Policy*, 111.

30. David H. Clark and William Reed, "The Strategic Sources of Foreign Policy Substitution," *American Journal of Political Science* 49, no. 3 (July 2005): 609.

31. See, for example, Benjamin A. Most and Randolph M. Siverson, "Substituting Arms and Alliances, 1870–1914: An Exploration in Comparative Foreign Policy," in *New Directions in the Study of Foreign Policy*, ed. Charles F. Hermann, Charles W. Kegley Jr., and James N. Rosenau (Boston: Allen and Unwin, 1987), 131–160; Will H. Moore, "The Repression of Dissent: A Substitution Model of Government Coercion," *Journal of Conflict Resolution* 44, no. 1 (February 2000): 107–127; Patrick M. Regan, "Substituting Policies During U.S. Interventions in Internal Conflicts: A Little of This, A Little of That," *Journal of Conflict Resolution* 44, no. 1 (February 2000): 90–106; Clark, "Trading Butter for Guns"; Dan G. Cox and A. Cooper Drury, "Democratic Sanctions: Connecting the Democratic Peace and Economic Sanctions," *Journal of Peace Research* 43, no. 6 (November 2006): 709–722; Karl DeRouen Jr. and Shaun Goldfinch, "The Democratic Peace and Substitutability During International Crises: Institutionalized Democracy and Foreign Policy Choices," in *Institutions and Market Economies: The Political Economy of Growth and Development*, ed. William R. Garside (New York: Palgrave Macmillan, 2007), 278–304.

32. Palmer and Morgan, *A Theory of Foreign Policy*, 38.

33. Ibid.

34. For studies that search for complementarity among policy options, see Paul F. Diehl, "Substitutes or Complements? The Effects of Alliances on Military Spending in Major Power Rivalries," *International Interactions* 19, no. 3 (1994): 159–176; Michael D. McGinnis, "Policy Substitutability in Complex Humanitarian Emergencies: A Model of Individual Choice and International Response," *Journal of Conflict Resolution* 44, no. 1 (February 2000): 62–89; T. Clifton Morgan and Glenn Palmer, "A Model of Foreign Policy Substitutability: Selecting the Right Tools for the Job(s)," *Journal of Conflict Resolution* 44, no. 1 (February 2000): 11–32; Clark and Reed, "Strategic Sources of

Foreign Policy Substitution," 609–624; David H. Clark, Timothy Nordstrom, and William Reed, "Substitution Is in the Variance: Resources and Foreign Policy Choice," *American Journal of Political Science* 52, no. 4 (October 2008): 763–773.

35. Palmer and Morgan study the Suez Canal Crisis, arguing that the adoption of one policy (a defensive military alliance) made other policies (especially strategies to change the status quo) more likely—but they do not examine cases of policy substitution. See *A Theory of Foreign Policy*, 161–170.

36. Randolph M. Siverson and Harvey Starr, "Opportunity, Willingness, and the Diffusion of War," *American Political Science Review* 84, no. 1 (March 1990): 48.

37. Siverson and Starr, "Opportunity, Willingness, and the Diffusion of War," 49; Randolph M. Siverson and Harvey Starr, *The Diffusion of War: A Study of Opportunity and Willingness* (Ann Arbor: University of Michigan Press, 1991), 23–25.

38. Benjamin Most and Harvey Starr argue that government decisions are a product of the interaction between opportunity and willingness, and that these factors are "jointly necessary" to explain any policy outcome. Surprisingly, Most and Starr, who also originated the concept of policy substitutability, did not explore how the notions of opportunity and willingness might be used to illuminate the conditions leading to policy substitution. In a discussion of the potential for policy substitutability, they only briefly note that "decision makers will be constrained by the range of available policy options; they will adopt a given policy alternative (such as war) if and only if they have both the 'willingness' and 'opportunity' to do so." More recently, Starr and other scholars in the substitutability research program have suggested that there might be potentially useful connections between opportunity and willingness and policy substitution. See *Inquiry, Logic, and International Politics*, 41, 108. For discussions of the connection between substitutability and opportunity and willingness, see also Harvey Starr, "Revolution and War: Rethinking the Linkage Between Internal and External Conflict," *Political Research Quarterly* 47, no. 2 (June 1994): 491–492; Claudio Cioffi-Revilla and Harvey Starr, "Opportunity, Willingness and Political Uncertainty: Theoretical Foundations of Politics," *Journal of Theoretical Politics* 7, no. 4 (October 1995): 447–476; Gil Friedman and Harvey Starr, *Agency, Structure and International Politics: From Ontology to Empirical Enquiry* (New York: Routledge, 1997), 6–8; Glenn Palmer and Archana Bhandari, "The Investigation of Substitutability in Foreign Policy," *Journal of Conflict Resolution* 44, no. 1 (February 2000): 6–7; Starr, "Substitutability in Foreign Policy," 130–133; Clark and Reed, "The Strategic Sources of Foreign Policy Substitution," 612; Bruce M. Russett, Harvey Starr, and David Kinsella, *World Politics: Menu for Choice*, 9th ed. (Boston: Wadsworth, 2010), 21–24.

39. The literature on policy substitutability rarely uses the concepts of opportunity and willingness. Instead, scholars typically search only for a specific variable, such as regime type, that might cause a policy substitution to occur. One of the problems with this approach is that they tend to select a variable that relates either to opportunity or willingness, thereby overlooking how both dimensions contribute to policy outcomes. As a result, these explanations are almost certainly incomplete.

See, for example, Clark, "Trading Butter for Guns"; Clark and Reed, "The Strategic Sources of Foreign Policy Substitution"; Cox and Drury, "Democratic Sanctions," 709–722; Palmer and Morgan, *A Theory of Foreign Policy*; Clark, Nordstrom, and Reed, "Substitution Is in the Variance." There is one exception. In his study of U.S. military interventions in civil conflicts, Patrick Regan uses the concepts of opportunity and willingness to locate variables that influence government responses to internal conflict. He contends that whether and how Washington chooses to respond to intrastate disputes in foreign countries is shaped by its capabilities (opportunity) and the leader's assessment of risk (willingness). If the president deems a military operation to be too risky or expensive, then he will instead intervene diplomatically or simply do nothing. By identifying variables that shape *both* opportunity and willingness, he produces a better specified model of military intervention—one that incorporates both domestic and international-level influences on decision making that have been overlooked by prior studies. See "Substituting Policies During U.S. Interventions."

40. See, for example, Siverson and Starr, "Opportunity, Willingness, and the Diffusion of War"; Stuart A. Bremer, "Dangerous Dyads: Conditions Affecting the Likelihood of Interstate War, 1816–1965," *Journal of Conflict Resolution* 36, no. 2 (June 1992): 309–341. David Clark and Patrick Regan also examine whether economic interdependence, alliance membership, and shared democratic institutions influence opportunities to engage in conflict. See "Opportunities to Fight: A Statistical Technique for Modeling Unobservable Phenomena," *Journal of Conflict Resolution* 47, no. 1 (February 2003): 94–115.

41. Jeffry A. Frieden, "Actors and Preferences in International Relations," in *Strategic Choice and International Relations*, ed. David A. Lake and Robert Powell (Princeton: Princeton University Press, 1999), 45–56.

42. See, for example, Bruce Bueno de Mesquita, *The War Trap* (New Haven: Yale University Press, 1981); Bueno de Mesquita et al., *The Logic of Political Survival* (Cambridge: MIT Press, 2003).

43. Another influential decision-making model, poliheuristic theory, also assumes that leaders have no preference among policy alternatives. The theory states that leaders initially weigh options on the policy menu using a noncompensatory decision rule—meaning that they first eliminate all alternatives that fail to meet a certain threshold of acceptability on an important dimension (e.g., public approval), even if they perform well on another dimension (e.g., ability to enhance the state's external security). Indeed, Alex Mintz argues that the most important consideration for leaders is whether policies benefit them politically. After ruling out all options that are not viable domestically, the leader then may evaluate the remaining policies in a manner consistent with an expected utility model. Certainly, the acceptability of a policy to the citizenry and/or governing elites is an important environmental factor that will influence whether it is feasible. For example, the practicability of repression may depend on the willingness of the public to accept suppressive measures instituted by the state. That said, poliheuristic theory would lead us to conclude that when an environmental factor, such as public approval, rules out *any* option on the policy

menu, it contributes to the government's final choice. However, the substitutability approach contends that an environmental factor is likely to matter only if it affects the feasibility of options at the top of the leader's policy ranking. See "How Do Leaders Make Decisions? A Poliheuristic Perspective," *Journal of Conflict Resolution* 48, no. 1 (February 2004): 3–13.

44. Davenport, *State Repression*, 42. Emphasis in the original.

45. Christian Davenport, "State Repression and Political Order," *Annual Review of Political Science* 10 (June 2007): 10.

46. See Frederic S. Pearson and Robert A. Baumann, "International Military Intervention, 1946–1988," Inter-University Consortium for Political and Social Research, Data Collection No. 6035 (Ann Arbor: University of Michigan, 1993); Emizet F. Kisangani and Jeffrey Pickering, "International Military Intervention, 1989–2005," Inter-University Consortium for Political and Social Research, Data Collection No. 21282 (Ann Arbor: University of Michigan, 2008).

47. The exception is Ross Miller's study of diversionary war. I discuss his argument and findings below and in Chapter 3. See "Domestic Structures."

48. See Arthur A. Stein, *The Nation at War* (Baltimore: Johns Hopkins University Press, 1980); A. F. K. Organski and Jacek Kugler, *The War Ledger* (Chicago: University of Chicago Press, 1980); Alan C. Lamborn, *The Price of Power: Risk and Foreign Policy in Britain, France, and Germany* (Boston: Unwin Hyman, 1991); Starr, "Revolution and War," 487–491; Thomas Christensen, *Useful Adversaries: Grand Strategy, Domestic Mobilization, and Sino-American Conflict, 1947–1958* (Princeton: Princeton University Press, 1996); Marc V. Simon and Harvey Starr, "Extraction, Allocation, and the Rise and Decline of States: A Simulation Analysis of Two-Level Security Management," *Journal of Conflict Resolution* 40, no. 2 (June 1996): 272–297; Marc V. Simon and Harvey Starr, "A Two-Level Analysis of War and Revolution: A Dynamic Simulation of Response to Threat," in *Decisionmaking on War and Peace: The Cognitive–Rational Debate*, ed. Nehemia Geva and Alex Mintz (Boulder: Lynne Rienner, 1997), 131–162; Fareed Zakaria, *From Wealth to Power: The Unusual Origins of America's World Role* (Princeton: Princeton University Press, 1998); Marc V. Simon and Harvey Starr, "Two-Level Security Management and the Prospects for New Democracies: A Simulation Analysis," *International Studies Quarterly* 44, no. 3 (September 2000): 391–422; James D. Fearon and David D. Laitin, "Ethnicity, Insurgency, and Civil War," *American Political Science Review* 97, no. 1 (February 2003): 75–90.

49. Theda Skocpol, "Bringing the State Back In: Strategies of Analysis in Current Research," in *Bringing the State Back In*, ed. Peter B. Evans, Dietrich Rueschemeyer, and Theda Skocpol (Cambridge: Cambridge University Press, 1985), 17.

50. As Palmer and Morgan put it, "[S]tates with more resources will engage in more foreign policy behaviors, of all types, than states with fewer resources." See *A Theory of Foreign Policy*, 35.

51. The variables of domestic unrest and extractive capacity may be related. For obvious reasons, states facing unrest are more likely to have a low extractive capacity. However, the correlation between these variables is only partial: there are many states

with low extractive capacity and virtually no unrest, such as Paraguay in the 1960s and 1970s. And there also states that have high extractive capacity and experience substantial unrest, such as France during the 1960s. The reason for this is that a large number of factors, in addition to domestic unrest, shape extractive capacity, such as the organization of the bureaucracy and a culture of limited government.

52. Christensen, *Useful Adversaries;* Zakaria, *From Wealth to Power.*

53. One could question whether bracketing countries by their extractive capacity misses the extreme variation in their absolute resources. For example, the United States and Mexico might both classified as pauper states, but because the U.S. economy is so large, Washington has access to far greater resources. In a crisis, however, these actors may find their menu of options similarly constrained. Countries with larger economies, such as the United States, may have more resources, but they also have greater governmental responsibilities that eat up many of these resources. Furthermore, countries with larger economies may also face more unrest simply because the country is bigger. Therefore, governments in countries with small economies that mobilize a low share of resources and governments of countries with large economies that mobilize a low share of resources may respond to crises in comparable ways.

54. Even if there are individual cases where extractive capacity does not contribute to the outcome, we can still make probabilistic predictions about how this variable will shape government decision making in the universe of cases. Imagine a world in which there are three pauper states—1, 2, and 3—all facing domestic unrest, which can choose their response from a menu that includes policies A through E. Country 1's preference ranking is: $A > B > C > D > E$. Country 2's is: $B > C > D > E > A$. And Country 3's is: $C > D > E > A > B$. Now suppose that a low extractive capacity eliminates policies A and B. What is the effect? For Country 3, the elimination of policies A and B has no effect on the government's decision making because it can implement its preferred response. For Countries 1 and 2, extractive capacity is a necessary condition for its final policy choice because this variable eliminates one or more preferred alternatives. While for one country in the universe of cases a low extractive capacity had no effect on the outcome, it did have an effect on the behavior of the other countries. Therefore, we can expect the overall probability of policies C, D, and E to be higher among pauper states.

55. For a discussion of the material costs of repression, see Davenport, *State Repression*, 48.

56. Bueno de Mesquita et al., *The Logic of Political Survival*, 343–344.

57. See, for example, Dipak K. Gupta, Harinder Singh, and Tom Sprague, "Government Coercion of Dissidents: Deterrence or Provocation?" *Journal of Conflict Resolution* 37, no. 2 (June 1993): 301–339.

58. Geoffrey Blainey, *The Causes of War* (New York: Free Press, 1973), 87–88.

59. See Gideon Rose, "Neoclassical Realism and Theories of Foreign Policy," *World Politics* 51, no. 1 (October 1998): 144–172.

60. Zakaria, *From Wealth to Power*, 38.

61. For scholars who argue either implicitly or explicitly that diversionary wars are generally seen as risky responses to unrest and therefore are unlikely to be leaders' preferred response to unrest, see Brulé, "Congressional Opposition"; Gelpi, "Democratic Diversions"; Kisangani and Pickering, "The Dividends of Diversion"; Davies, "Domestic Strife"; Pickering and Kisangani, "Democracy and Diversionary Military Intervention."

62. Winston Churchill, *A Roving Commission: My Early Life* (New York: Charles Scribner's Sons, 1930), 232.

63. Paul Corner and Giovanna Procacci, "The Italian Experience of 'Total' Mobilization, 1915–1920," in *State, Society, and Mobilization in Europe During the First World War,* ed. John Horne (Cambridge: Cambridge University Press, 1997), 231. For an argument that internal cohesion often declines during protracted and costly wars, see Stein, *The Nation at War,* 9–15.

64. In the only study to recognize a potential link between extractive capacity and diversionary war, Miller also suggests, albeit briefly, that when governments have ample revenues or what he terms high "policy resources," they are less likely to resort to a diversion. These regimes, he argues, have the means to "address the *source* of leaders' declining support" and can avoid risking a war that could have "dire consequences." By identifying the importance of extractive capacity for explaining diversionary war, Miller makes an important contribution to the debate on diversionary war, and this book builds on his research in several ways. First, I identify more precisely when extractive capacity influences policy outcomes (i.e., it influences decision making only when a leader's preferred response is resource intensive). Second, I specify the causal mechanism by which extractive capacity leads to a decision to use diversionary tactics in both princely and pauper states. Third, I explain how extractive capacity influences whether embattled leaders consider each of the options on the policy menu, not just diversionary war. See "Domestic Structures," 766. Emphasis in the original.

65. See, for example, Fordham, "Strategic Conflict Avoidance and the Diversionary Use of Force."

66. Richard Ned Lebow, *Between Peace and War: The Nature of International Crisis* (Baltimore: Johns Hopkins University Press, 1981), 114.

67. Jack Snyder, *The Ideology of the Offensive: Military Decision Making and the Disasters of 1914* (Ithaca: Cornell University Press, 1984), 207, 18.

68. Stein, *The Nation at War,* 87.

69. For a description of the negativity bias, see Paul Rozin and Edward B. Royzman, "Negativity Bias, Negativity Dominance, and Contagion," *Personality and Social Psychology Review* 5, no. 4 (November 2001): 296–320.

70. A handful of studies have searched for evidence of a rally effect in countries other than the United States, namely in Israel and the United Kingdom, but the results of this research are inconclusive. Asher Arian and Sigalit Olzaeker find that the 1990 Gulf War crisis increased domestic support for the Israeli government, while Christopher Sprecher and Karl DeRouen conclude that domestic protests have escalated during Israeli military campaigns. In the case of Britain, there is considerable

evidence that the Falklands War contributed to the victory of Margaret Thatcher in the 1983 parliamentary elections. But Brian Lai and Dan Reiter's study of changes in public support for the British government during international crises and wars between 1848 and 2001 finds that there were no rallies after uses of force short of war, or after the Korean, Suez, or Kosovo wars. See Asher Arian and Sigalit Olzaeker, "Political and Economic Interactions with National Security Opinion: The Gulf War Period in Israel," *Journal of Conflict Resolution* 43, no. 1 (February 1999): 58–77; Christopher Sprecher and Karl DeRouen Jr., "Israeli Military Actions and Internalization-Externalization Processes," *Journal of Conflict Resolution* 46, no. 2 (April 2002): 244–259; Brian Lai and Dan Reiter, "Rally 'Round the Union Jack? Public Opinion and the Use of Force in the United Kingdom, 1948–2001," *International Studies Quarterly* 49, no. 2 (June 2005): 255–272.

71. John Mueller's seminal study of presidential popularity found that international events—as long as they directly involved the U.S. president and were dramatic in nature—boosted public support for the government. See *War, Presidents, and Public Opinion* (New York: Wiley, 1973). A number of subsequent studies have also found that international conflicts produce a rally effect contingent on a range of contextual factors, such as the international community's response, the foreign policy objectives of the government, the president's previous popularity, media coverage, content of elite rhetoric (especially among opposition groups and Congress), partisanship, and political awareness. See, for example, Charles W. Ostrom Jr. and Dennis M. Simon, "Promise and Performance: A Dynamic Model of Presidential Popularity," *American Political Science Review* 79, no. 2 (June 1985): 334–358; Robin F. Marra, Charles W. Ostrom Jr., and Dennis M. Simon, "Foreign Policy and Presidential Popularity: Creating Windows of Opportunity in the Perpetual Election," *Journal of Conflict Resolution* 34, no. 4 (December 1990): 588–623; Richard Brody, *Assessing the President: The Media, Elite Opinion, and Public Support* (Stanford: Stanford University Press, 1991); Bruce W. Jentleson, "The Pretty Prudent Public: Post Post-Vietnam American Opinion on the Use of Military Force," *International Studies Quarterly* 36, no. 1 (March 1992): 49–74; Karl DeRouen Jr. and Jeffrey Peake, "The Dynamics of Diversion: The Domestic Implications of Presidential Use of Force," *International Interactions* 28, no. 2 (2002): 191–221; Terrence L. Chapman and Dan Reiter, "The United Nations Security Council and the Rally 'Round the Flag Effect," *Journal of Conflict Resolution* 48, no. 6 (December 2004): 886–909; Jonathan McDonald Ladd, "Predispositions and Public Support for the President During the War on Terrorism," *Public Opinion Quarterly* 71, no. 4 (Winter 2007): 511–538; Tim Groeling and Matthew A. Baum, "Crossing the Water's Edge: Elite Rhetoric, Media Coverage, and the Rally-Round-the-Flag Phenomenon," *Journal of Politics* 70, no. 4 (October 2008): 1065–1085.

72. See, for example, Bradley Lian and John R. Oneal, "Presidents, the Use of Military Force, and Public Opinion," *Journal of Conflict Resolution* 37, no. 2 (June 1993): 277–300; John R. Oneal and Anna Lillian Bryan, "The Rally 'Round the Flag Effect in U.S. Foreign Policy Crises, 1950–1985," *Political Behavior* 17, no. 4 (December 1995): 379–401; Patrick James and Jean-Sébastien Rioux, "International Crises and Linkage

Politics: The Experiences of the United States, 1953–1994," *Political Research Quarterly* 51, no. 3 (September 1998): 781–812; William D. Baker and John R. Oneal, "Patriotism or Opinion Leadership? The Nature and Origins of the 'Rally 'Round the Flag' Effect," *Journal of Conflict Resolution* 45, no. 5 (October 2001): 661–687.

73. See, for example, Mueller, *War, Presidents, and Public Opinion;* Christopher Gelpi, Peter D. Feaver, and Jason Reifler, "Success Matters: Casualty Sensitivity and the War in Iraq," *International Security* 30, no. 3 (Winter 2005/2006): 7–46.

74. In their study of wars between 1823 and 1974, Bruce Bueno de Mesquita and Randolph Siverson find that regardless of regime type, fighting and especially winning an interstate war lengthens leaders' time in office. And in a subsequent study of European, American, and Canadian leaders between 1920 and 1992, Bueno de Mesquita and his coauthors find that low-level conflicts substantially improve a leader's chances of staying in power. However, a battlefield victory benefits democratically elected leaders but does not have a statistically significant effect on the chances that nondemocratic leaders will remain in office. However, Chiozza and Geomans find that leaders are more likely to lose office when a crisis is brewing, but become more secure once troops are mobilized for action. Indeed, as long as they achieve a victory or a draw, all leaders benefit from participating in an international conflict. In a subsequent study, however, they find that war and war outcomes, in particular whether the conflict resulted in a victory or draw, have no effect on leader tenure. See Bruce Bueno de Mesquita and Randolph M. Siverson, "War and the Survival of Political Leaders: A Comparative Study of Regime Types and Political Accountability," *American Political Science Review* 89, no. 4 (December 1995): 841–855; Bruce Bueno de Mesquita et al., "Political Survival and International Conflict," in *War in a Changing World,* ed. Zeev Maoz and Azar Gat (Ann Arbor: University of Michigan Press, 2001); Chiozza and Goemans, "Peace Through Insecurity," 443–467; Giacomo Chiozza and Hein E. Goemans, "International Conflict and the Tenure of Leaders: Is War Still *Ex Post* Inefficient?" *American Journal of Political Science* 48, no. 3 (July 2004): 604–619.

75. Kisangani and Pickering, "The Dividends of Diversion," 496. Although he does not test the argument, Gelpi offers a different logic for why democratic leaders benefit more from diversionary uses of force than do autocratic ones. He argues that diversionary tactics may be less effective in a nondemocracy because the population is less likely to identify with the state and rally around the flag. See "Democratic Diversions," 261.

76. See also Jeffrey Pickering and Emizet F. Kisangani, "Diversionary Despots? Comparing Autocracies' Propensities to Use and to Benefit from Military Force," *American Journal of Political Science* 54, no. 2 (April 2010): 477–493.

77. David A. Baldwin, "Success and Failure in Foreign Policy," *Annual Review of Political Science* 3 (June 2000): 176–177.

78. See, for example, T. David Mason and Dale A. Krane, "The Political Economy of Death Squads: Toward a Theory of the Impact of State-Sanctioned Terror," *International Studies Quarterly* 33, no. 2 (June 1989): 175–198; Karl-Dieter Opp and Wolfgang Roehl, "Repression, Micromobilization, and Political Protest," *Social Forces* 69, no. 2

(December 1990): 521–547; Ronald A. Francisco, "The Relationship Between Coercion and Protest: An Empirical Evaluation in Three Coercive States," *Journal of Conflict Resolution* 39, no. 2 (June 1995): 263–282; Karen Rasler, "Concessions, Repression, and Political Protest in the Iranian Revolution," *American Sociological Review* 61, no. 1 (February 1996): 132–152; Sabine C. Carey, *Protest, Repression and Political Regimes: An Empirical Analysis of Latin America and Sub-Saharan Africa* (London: Routledge, 2009).

79. For example, see Edward N. Muller and Erich Weede, "Cross-National Variation in Political Violence: A Rational Action Approach," *Journal of Conflict Resolution* 34, no. 4 (December 1990): 624–651.

80. Gupta, Singh, and Sprague, "Government Coercion of Dissidents."

81. Jeffrey Dixon, "What Causes Civil Wars? Integrating Quantitative Research Findings," *International Studies Review* 11 (December 2009): 718–719.

82. Rasler, "Concessions, Repression, and Political Protest."

83. Michael Bratton and Nicolas van de Walle, "Popular Protest and Political Reform in Africa," *Comparative Politics* 24, no. 4 (July 1992): 420.

84. For a summary, see Dixon, "What Causes Civil Wars?" 716.

85. Margit Bussmann and Gerald Schneider, "When Globalization Discontent Turns Violent: Foreign Economic Liberalization and Internal War," *International Studies Quarterly* 51, no. 1 (March 2007): 79–97.

86. See Hanne Fjelde and Indra de Soysa, "Coercion, Co-optation, or Cooperation? State Capacity and the Risk of Civil War, 1961–2004," *Conflict Management and Peace Science* 26, no. 1 (February 2009): 9–10; Clayton L. Thyne, "ABC's, 123's, and the Golden Rule: The Pacifying Effect of Education on Civil War, 1980–1999," *International Studies Quarterly* 50, no. 4 (December 2006): 733–754.

87. Thyne, "ABC's, 123's, and the Golden Rule," 734.

88. Dylan Balch-Lindsay and Andrew Enterline, "Killing Time: The World Politics of Civil War Duration, 1820–1992," *International Studies Quarterly* 44, no. 4 (December 2000): 636. Others have found that assisting the government does not have a statistically significant effect on the length of civil wars. See Paul Collier, Anke Hoeffler, and Måns Söderbom, "On the Duration of Civil War," *Journal of Peace Research* 41, no. 3 (May 2004): 253–273; Patrick M. Regan, "Third Party Interventions and the Duration of Intrastate Conflicts," *Journal of Conflict Resolution* 46, no. 1 (February 2002): 55–73.

89. Patrick M. Regan, *Civil Wars and Foreign Powers: Outside Intervention in Intrastate Conflict* (Ann Arbor: University of Michigan Press, 2000).

90. Dylan Balch-Lindsay, Andrew J. Enterline, and Kyle A. Joyce, "Third-Party Intervention and the Civil War Process," *Journal of Peace Research* 45, no. 3 (May 2008): 356.

91. Stephen E. Gent, "Going in When It Counts: Military Intervention and the Outcome of Civil Conflicts," *International Studies Quarterly* 52, no. 4 (December 2008): 713–735.

92. Samuel Huntington, *The Third Wave: Democratization in the Late Twentieth Century* (Norman: University of Oklahoma Press, 1991), 55.

Chapter 3

1. Faten Ghosn, Glenn Palmer, and Stuart Bremer, "The MID3 Data Set, 1993–2001: Procedures, Coding Rules, and Description," *Conflict Management and Peace Science* 21, no. 2 (April 2004): 133–154. If a state became involved in multiple disputes in a given year, I included the dispute with the highest hostility level. For the most part, only great powers became involved in multiple MIDs in a given year, and they represented a small subset of cases in the data set. Thus, while they may have considerable influence in world politics, their behavior is unlikely to have a significant effect on the results.

2. The MID data set codes whether a country initiated a dispute during a given year or was the target of military action by another state. The question then is whether the statistical analysis should include only those low-level conflicts and interstate wars that a state initiated. The theory presented in Chapter 2 predicts that pauper states may provoke low-level spectacles during periods of unrest, but if a war results, it is because the conflict escalated uncontrollably into a major military campaign. In the analysis of low-level spectacles, therefore, we certainly should include all conflicts where the state was first to act. But we also need to include disputes in which the adversary was coded as the first mover. According to MID, the initiator of a dispute is simply the first state to engage in an action that is codable. Importantly, codable actions overlap only partially with what my theory defines as a diversionary spectacle. There will be some episodes that will be captured by MID and will represent diversionary spectacles. But there may be others that my theory would see as diversionary spectacles but that would not be coded as the initiation of a dispute according to MID. For example, if the Argentine junta's first attempt to provoke a spectacle in 1982 was, say, to announce that it would use force to defend the Falkland Islands if Britain challenged its historical right to the territory, this move would not be coded by MID because the threat was not sufficiently specific. But if London responded by threatening to send troops if Argentina occupied the islands, this act would be codable—and the United Kingdom would be the initiator of the dispute. Thus, we cannot rely on the initiator of a dispute to determine who caused the conflict. Turning to the analysis of interstate war, MID identifies only which country took the first codable action in the low-level spectacle dispute that resulted in war. This does not tell us which state was responsible for provoking the dispute or escalating hostilities, meaning that all wars should be included the analysis. For a discussion of how MID codes dispute initiation, see Ghosn, Palmer, and Bremer, "The MID3 Data Set, 1993–2001," 138–139.

3. See A. F. K. Organski and Jacek Kugler, *The War Ledger* (Chicago: University of Chicago Press, 1980); Jacek Kugler and Marina Arbetman, "Relative Political Capacity: Political Extraction and Political Reach," in *Political Capacity and Economic Behavior,* ed. Marina Arbetman and Jacek Kugler (Boulder: Westview, 1997).

4. Kugler and Arbetman, "Relative Political Capacity," 18.

5. Yi Feng, Jacek Kugler, and Paul J. Zak, "The Politics of Fertility and Economic Development," *International Studies Quarterly* 44, no. 4 (December 2000): 690–691.

6. Charles Lewis Taylor and David A. Jodice, *World Handbook of Political and Social Indicators III: 1948–1982*, 2nd ed. (Ann Arbor: Inter-university Consortium for Political and Social Research, 1986). Instead, I could have used unrest data from the Arthur Banks Cross-National Times Series Data Archive. See Arthur S. Banks, *Cross-National Time-Series Data Archive, 1815–2003* (Binghamton: Databanks International, 2005). I prefer the World Handbook measure of unrest for several reasons. First, Taylor and Jodice are transparent regarding their coding procedures, whereas the Banks data set does not report the criteria used to identify incidents of unrest. Taylor and Jodice also use multiple sources to catalog events, which is important for regions like Africa, where it is often difficult to get good estimates of internal instability. Finally, there are several key articles that use the World Handbook data set, making it especially useful to employ the same measure. For examples of studies of diversionary war that use this measure of unrest, see Ross A. Miller, "Domestic Structures and the Diversionary Use of Force," *American Journal of Political Science* 39, no. 3 (August 1995): 760–785; Christopher Gelpi, "Democratic Diversions: Governmental Structure and the Externalization of Domestic Conflict," *Journal of Conflict Resolution* 41, no. 2 (April 1997): 255–282; Ross A. Miller, "Regime Type, Strategic Interaction, and the Diversionary Use of Force," *Journal of Conflict Resolution* 43, no. 3 (June 1999): 388–402; Graeme A. M. Davies, "Domestic Strife and the Initiation of International Conflicts: A Directed Dyad Analysis, 1950–1992," *Journal of Conflict Resolution* 46, no. 5 (October 2002): 676–692.

7. Many studies in the diversionary war literature focus on electoral threats to regimes. But using this convention has a major and obvious downside: it limits the analysis to democracies. This research examines the potential for diversionary war in all types of political systems. The issue then is finding the best indicator of an internal threat to the government across regime types. One option is a measure of a country's economic health. But this is a flawed proxy. The public may withdraw its support for the government for many reasons that have little or nothing to do with the economy. Thus, a government could worry about its survival even when the economy is growing. The other option is domestic unrest. Domestic unrest, while imperfect, is the best measure we have. Governments are likely to be sensitive to internal strife, whatever its cause. And data on unrest are widely available. Unsurprisingly, many cross-national studies of diversionary war rely on domestic unrest data to identify threats to regime survival.

8. The drawback with this approach is that the gap in time between the episodes of unrest and an interstate war or spectacle could be as little as one day or as distant as two years. To address this concern, I removed the lags from the measure of unrest and reran the regressions. The substantive results were nearly identical.

9. Failing to reject the null hypothesis—which is that the effect of domestic unrest on the likelihood of a low-level spectacle does not vary with a state's extractive capacity—does not necessarily mean that the null itself is true. Rather, it indicates that the main hypothesis is not supported by the evidence. That said, an insignificant finding is consistent with my argument. And the case studies increase our confidence

that extractive capacity shapes the decisions of unstable states to engage in diversionary spectacles as predicted. For a discussion of what we can learn from a statistically insignificant result, see Jeff Gill, "The Insignificance of Null Hypothesis Significance Testing," *Political Research Quarterly* 52, no. 3 (September 1999): 660–661.

10.   To control for time dependence, I generated variables for peace years, peace years squared, and peace years cubed. A Wald test indicated that these variables should be included in the model of low-level spectacles but not interstate war. David Carter and Curtis Signorino argue that cubic polynomials are easier to create and interpret than cubic splines, another common technique for dealing with time dependence. However, I also ran the models with cubic splines, and the results were identical. See "Back to the Future: Modeling Time Dependence in Binary Data," *Political Analysis* 18, no. 3 (Summer 2010): 271–292. For a discussion of cubic splines, see Nathaniel Beck, Jonathan N. Katz, and Richard Tucker, "Taking Time Seriously: Time-Series–Cross-Section Analysis with a Binary Dependent Variable," *American Journal of Political Science* 42, no. 4 (October 1998): 1260–1288.

11.   Monty G. Marshall and Keith Jaggers, *Polity IV Project: Political Regime Characteristics and Transitions, 1800–2002* (College Park: Center for International Development and Conflict Management, University of Maryland, 2002).

12.   J. David Singer, Stuart Bremer, and John Stuckey, "Capability Distribution, Uncertainty, and Major Power War, 1820–1965," in *Peace, War, and Numbers*, ed. Bruce M. Russett (Beverly Hills: Sage, 1972), 19–48.

13.   Sonali Singh and Christopher R. Way, "The Correlates of Nuclear Proliferation: A Quantitative Test," *Journal of Conflict Resolution* 48, no. 6 (December 2004): 869.

14.   James Klein, Gary Goertz, and Paul F. Diehl, "The New Rivalry Dataset: Procedures and Patterns," *Journal of Peace Research* 43, no. 3 (May 2006): 331–348.

15.   See, for example, Benjamin Fordham, "Strategic Conflict Avoidance and the Diversionary Use of Force," *Journal of Politics* 67, no. 1 (February 2005): 132–153.

16.   Because *extractive capacity$_{t-1}$, democracy$_{t-1}$, enduring rivalry$_{t-1}$,* and *disputes$_{t-1}$* are each interacted with *domestic unrest$_{t-1}$,* there is the potential for a high degree of multicollinearity among these variables. The rule of thumb is that collinearity may be a problem for estimation if the largest variance inflation factor (VIF) is higher than 10 and the mean VIF is higher than 1.0. As expected, the VIF for *domestic unrest$_{t-1}$* is 11.31, and the mean VIF is 4.76. Extreme collinearity between the interaction terms and the constitutive terms can either make it impossible to estimate the model parameters or increase the standard error of the interaction terms. However, the models do converge, and several of the interaction terms achieve significance. And dropping the interaction terms could introduce omitted variable bias, which outweighs the dangers from collinearity. See Samprit Chatterjee, Bertram Price, and Ali S. Hadi, *Regression Analysis by Example*, 3rd ed. (New York: Wiley, 1999); Thomas Brambor, William Roberts Clark, and Matt Golder, "Understanding Interaction Models: Improving Empirical Analyses," *Political Analysis* 14, no. 1 (Winter 2006): 70–71.

17. When analyzing cross-sectional time series data, there is the potential for unobserved heterogeneity across the units. That is, the likelihood of a low-level spectacle or interstate war may be explained by factors unique to each country in the analysis—factors that are not completely captured by the independent variables included in the models. A failure to account for unobserved heterogeneity can produce biased results. One strategy for addressing this problem is a fixed-effects approach. However, a fixed-effects model does not work well when we wish to analyze variables that change very slowly, because they will be highly correlated with the country fixed effects and thus will have large standard errors. Such is the case with several causal factors in this analysis. In such situations, we instead can use a random-effects model. I estimated the models of interstate war and low-level spectacles using random-effects probit. The results for interstate war were nearly identical to those produced by the standard pooled probit model. Further, the correlation coefficient (ρ) in the random-effects model was not significant, indicating that it is correct to use a pooled probit model. The random-effects and pooled probit models of low-level spectacles also produced similar results. But here, the correlation coefficient in the random-effects model was statistically significant, although very small ($\rho=0.006$). This suggests that very little of the total variance of the error term is accounted for by unobserved heterogeneity. Consequently, the results of the pooled probit analyses are presented in this chapter. However, there are important differences between the rare-events logit model and the pooled probit model of interstate war (see Table 3.2).

18. See Gary King and Langche Zeng, "Logistic Regression in Rare Events Data," *Political Analysis* 9, no. 2 (Spring 2001): 137–163.

19. To ensure the robustness of the results, I ran dozens of models, with various combinations of the control variables. *Domestic unrest*$_{t-1}$ $\times$ *extractive capacity*$_{t-1}$ achieves statistical significance at the 95-percent level of confidence only if all of the other interaction terms and one or more control variables are omitted. These results are available in an online appendix: http://wmpeople.wm.edu/site/page/acoake

20. Brambor, Clarke, and Golder, "Understanding Interaction Models," 74.

21. Bennet A. Zelner, "Using Simulation to Interpret Results from Logit, Probit, and Other Nonlinear Models," *Strategic Management Journal* 30, no. 12 (December 2009): 1337.

22. I computed changes in the probability of interstate war when *domestic unrest*$_{t-1}$ increases from 0 to 77 annual incidents of unrest (the 95th percentile) at values of extractive capacity between 0.1 and 2.5. Ninety-nine percent of cases have an extractive capacity within this range. *Regime transition* and *national capabilities*$_{t-1}$ were held at their means. *Democracy*$_{t-1}$ was set at its mode, which is 0. I also assumed that there were opportunities for using diversionary force in the international system: *enduring rivalry*$_{t-1}$ was set at 1, and *disputes*$_{t-1}$ was set at its median, which is 0.2. To calculate the differences in predicted probabilities, I used Clarify. See Gary King, Michael Tomz, and Jason Wittenberg, "Making the Most of Statistical Analyses: Improving Interpretation and Presentation," *American Journal of Political Science* 44, no. 2 (2000): 347–361;

Michael Tomz, Jason Wittenberg, and Gary King, *CLARIFY: Software for Interpreting and Presenting Statistical Results,* Version 2.1 (Cambridge: Harvard University, 2003).

23. I computed the change in the probability of a low-level spectacle when *domestic unrest*$_{t-1}$ increases from 0 to 77 annual incidents of unrest (the 95th percentile) for states with enduring rivals and those without. *Regime transition* and *national capabilities*$_{t-1}$ were held at their means. *Democracy*$_{t-1}$ was set at its mode, which is 0. *Disputes*$_{t-1}$ was set at its median, which is 0.2. I again used Clarify to calculate the changes in probabilities. When all of the insignificant interaction terms are excluded from the model, *domestic unrest*$_{t-1}$ × *extractive capacity*$_{t-1}$ is significant at the 95-percent level of confidence. The conditional effect of domestic unrest on the probability of a low-level spectacle is positive and significant at the 95-percent confidence level for states without a rival (+0.023, 0.002 to 0.045) and insignificant for states with a rival (−0.004, −0.018 to 0.010).

24. I computed the change in probability of an interstate war when *domestic unrest*$_{t-1}$ increases from 0 to 77 annual incidents of unrest (the 95th percentile) for states with enduring rivals and those without. *Extractive capacity*$_{t-1}$, *regime transition*, and *national capabilities*$_{t-1}$ were held at their means. *Democracy*$_{t-1}$ was set at its mode, which is 0. *Disputes*$_{t-1}$ was set at its median, which is 0.2. Again, I used Clarify to calculate the changes in probabilities.

25. Brambor, Clark, and Golder, "Understanding Interaction Models," 72–73.

26. Taylor and Jodice, *World Handbook of Political and Social Indicators III.*

27. Ghosn, Palmer, and Bremer, "The MID3 Data Set, 1993–2001."

28. Taylor and Jodice, *World Handbook of Political and Social Indicators III.* This measure of repression has been used in a number of studies of repression. See, for example, Christian Davenport, "The Weight of the Past: Exploring Lagged Determinants of Political Repression," *Political Research Quarterly* 49, no. 2 (June 1996): 389–390.

29. Taylor and Jodice, *World Handbook of Political and Social Indicators III.* Because *repression*$_{t-1}$ counts instances in which the state imposes "negative sanctions" and *political reform*$_{t-1}$ counts instances in which the state eliminates "negative sanctions," one might wonder whether repression and political reform are simply mirror images of each other and, if they are, whether they are highly correlated. In practice, these variables do not move in lockstep. For example, in a given year, a government may impose, say, three restrictive measures while adopting two completely unrelated reforms. And Pearson's r reveals that these variables are not highly correlated ($r=0.41$).

30. Although this proxy includes all expenditures, not just money allocated to social programs, it is the best measure available for the time period covered in this analysis.

31. Banks, *Cross-National Time-Series Data Archive, 1815–2003.*

32. See Singh and Way, "The Correlates of Nuclear Proliferation," 867–868.

33. Frederic S. Pearson and Robert A. Baumann, "International Military Intervention, 1946-1988," Inter-University Consortium for Political and Social Research, Data Collection No. 6035 (Ann Arbor: University of Michigan, 1993).

34. Marshall and Jaggers, *Polity IV Project.*

35. For an excellent survey of these findings, see Jeffrey Dixon, "What Causes Civil Wars? Integrating Quantitative Research Findings," *International Studies Review* 11, no. 4 (December 2009): 709.

36. Patrick M. Regan and Daniel Norton, "Greed, Grievance, and Mobilization in Civil Wars," *Journal of Conflict Resolution* 49, no. 3 (June 2005): 329.

37. Banks, *Cross-National Time-Series Data Archive, 1815–2003.*

38. Dixon, "What Causes Civil Wars?" 715.

39. Banks, *Cross-National Time-Series Data Archive, 1815–2003.*

40. See, for example, James D. Fearon and David D. Laitin, "Ethnicity, Insurgency, and Civil War," *American Political Science Review* 97, no. 1 (February 2003): 78.

41. See Karen Rasler, "Concessions, Repression, and Political Protest in the Iranian Revolution," *American Sociological Review* 61, no. 1 (February 1996): 134–135; Sabine C. Carey, "The Dynamic Relationship Between Protest and Repression," *Political Research Quarterly* 59, no. 1 (March 2006): 4.

42. For a similar approach to managing temporal dependence in count models, see Jeffrey Pickering, "War-Weariness and Cumulative Effects: Victors, Vanquished, and Subsequent Interstate Intervention," *Journal of Peace Research* 39, no. 3 (May 2002): 327.

43. A likelihood ratio test indicates that these data exhibit overdispersion and, therefore, that this variation on the Poisson count model is appropriate. See Gary King, "Event Count Models for International Relations: Generalizations and Applications," *International Studies Quarterly* 33, no. 2 (1989): 123–147; J. Scott Long and Jeremy Freese, *Regression Models for Categorical Dependent Variables Using Stata*, 2nd ed. (College Station: Stata Press, 2006), 372–377.

44. *Foreign intervention*$_{t-1}$ achieves its highest level of statistical significance if one estimates a model for both democratic states and mixed regimes.

45. To estimate the predicted counts for each of the policy options, the variables were set at the following values: *low-level spectacle*$_{t-1}$=1, *interstate war*$_{t-1}$=1, *political reform*$_{t-1}$=7 (95th percentile), *repression*$_{t-1}$=34 (95th percentile), *government expenditures*$_{t-1}$=24 (95th percentile), *economic liberalization*=24 (95th percentile), and *foreign intervention*$_{t-1}$=1. Population, economic growth$_{t-1}$, and ethnic fractionalization were set at their means, and *domestic unrest*$_{t-1}$ was set at its median, which is 2 annual incidents of unrest.

46. It is important that the cases exhibit the full range of outcomes. Without ensuring variation on the dependent variable, we could conclude the presence of a given factor leads to a particular outcome, when it is actually also present in cases where the outcome is different. See Barbara Geddes, "How the Cases You Choose Affect the Answers You Get: Selection Bias in Comparative Politics," *Political Analysis* 2, no. 1 (1990): 131–150.

47. See Alexander L. George, "Case Studies and Theory Development: The Method of Structured, Focused Comparison," in *Diplomacy: New Approaches in History, Theory, and Policy*, ed. Paul Gordon Lauren (New York: Free Press, 1979), 43–68.

48. For each of the cases, I evaluated the extractive capacity of the state by an-swering the following question: how readily could the state raise revenues from soci-ety? When available, Kugler and Arbetman's measure of relative political extraction was used to gauge the extractive capacity of the states examined in the case studies. I also used primary and secondary sources either to supplement Kugler and Arbet-man's measure or, when their data were not available, to evaluate the state's ability to mobilize resources. I examined historians' accounts, records of the government's finances, and public statements of key policy makers to ascertain the ease with which the state was able to extract resources from the national economy. If, for example, (1) experts on the period state that the government struggled to collect taxes, (2) the government's financial accounts indicate a decline in revenues (often despite a growing economy), and (3) prominent members of the government bemoaned the state's in-ability to improve its finances, then I conclude that the government was a pauper state.

A state's extractive capacity may be a function of a number of factors, including the efficiency of the government's bureaucracy, the strength of the executive relative to the legislature, the popularity of the regime, the presence of powerful opposition groups, and domestic norms regarding the proper size and role of the state. Although an exhaustive discussion of the variables that shape a state's ability to raise revenues is outside the domain of this analysis, I note in each of the case studies those factors that influenced the extractive capacity of the state. The purpose of this is to confront head-on the concern that the degree of domestic unrest within the country accounts entirely for the state's ability to extract resources from society. If so, one could con-clude that domestic unrest and extractive capacity measure the same phenomenon: support for the government. In each of the cases, factors other than domestic unrest or dissatisfaction with the regime's policy were at least partly responsible for the dif-ficulties the state faced in raising resources. I was also careful to distinguish between situations in which the government was impoverished because of the state's inability to raise revenues and those in which the lack of government revenue was because of a declining national economy—that is, when there were simply no societal resources available for leaders to extract.

49. John Gerring, *Social Science Methodology: A Criterial Framework* (Cambridge: Cambridge University Press, 2001), 219.

50. I do not conduct separate studies of pauper states that attempted to implement economic reforms or engage in widespread repression, but there are points in these three cases when the governments seriously contemplated or made some limited at-tempts at executing these policies—and found them to be too expensive.

Chapter 4

1. In Argentina, the islands are known as Islas Malvinas.

2. Earl Aaron Reitan, *The Thatcher Revolution: Margaret Thatcher, John Major, Tony Blair, and the Transformation of Modern Britain, 1979–2001* (Lanham: Rowman & Littlefield, 2003), 46.

3. Paul H. Lewis, *Guerrillas and Generals: The "Dirty War" in Argentina* (Westport: Praeger, 2002), 181.

4. Luis Alberto Romero, *A History of Argentina in the Twentieth Century* (University Park: Pennsylvania State University Press, 2002), 240.

5. For discussions of how the unrest differed from previous periods of instability, see Arthur Gavshon and Desmond Rice, *The Sinking of the Belgrano* (London: Secker and Warburg, 1984), 18; Aldo C. Vacs, "Authoritarian Breakdown and Redemocratization in Argentina," in *Authoritarians and Democrats: Regime Transition in Latin America,* ed. James M. Malloy and Mitchell A. Seligson (Pittsburgh: University of Pittsburgh Press, 1987), 27; Gerardo Luis Munck, *Authoritarianism and Democratization: Soldiers and Workers in Argentina, 1976–1983* (University Park: Pennsylvania State University Press, 1998), 134–135.

6. Juan E. Corradi, *The Fitful Republic: Economy, Society, and Politics in Argentina* (Boulder: Westview, 1985), 136–137.

7. Gary W. Wynia, *Argentina: Illusions and Realities,* 2nd ed. (New York: Holmes and Meier, 1992), 12; David R. Mares, *Violent Peace: Militarized Interstate Bargaining in Latin America* (New York: Columbia University Press, 2001), 152.

8. "President Galtieri Gives Inaugural Speech," *Buenos Aires Domestic Service,* December 24, 1981.

9. In order to weigh the relative causal importance of extractive capacity (and other variables) for explaining the leader's decision making in each case, I employ the logic of necessary and sufficient conditions. A few words about using these concepts are needed here. It is important to emphasize that the language of necessary and sufficient is used to identify the cause(s) of a particular leader's decision at a particular moment in time. For example, in regard to the Argentine junta's decision to invade the Falkland Islands, the goal is to identify the necessary or sufficient conditions of the government's plan to use force against this particular target in 1982. Of course, in each case one can conceive of a number of rival causal schemes that could have resulted in the same policy choice. In a broader sense, no variable is ever truly "necessary" for something to happen because the introduction of fantastical new variables can always provide a causal pathway in the absence of the supposedly necessary variable. Furthermore, one can imagine alternate scenarios in which, for example, the state's extractive capacity was high or there was no domestic unrest, and the same policy was nevertheless chosen. Because other conditions could have produced the same or a similar outcome, one identifies a cause as necessary or sufficient knowing that it was not in any ultimate sense either necessary or sufficient. Yet this predicament can be escaped. One can reasonably claim that a cause was necessary or sufficient as long as one fully specifies the background factors that form the context in which the event occurred. Put differently, a condition can be necessary or sufficient in a particular context. If, for example, the escalating domestic unrest in Argentina and the state's low extractive capacity were necessary or sufficient for the junta to send troops to the Falklands, we must describe, as much as possible, the background against which these factors assumed causal importance. This is not only required in order to produce a

204   Notes to Page 81

complete explanation of each individual case but also to identify which necessary conditions may be generalizable to other cases. It will enable one to distinguish, as much as possible, between those conditions that were necessary given the context in which each government acted and those that might be necessary conditions for any government to adopt a given policy in almost any place and at almost any time. For further discussion, see John Gerring, *Social Science Methodology: A Criterial Framework* (Cambridge: Cambridge University Press, 2001), 149–151; Gary Goertz and Harvey Starr, "Introduction: Necessary Condition Logics, Research Design, and Theory," in *Necessary Conditions: Theory, Methodology, and Applications,* ed. Gary Goertz and Harvey Starr (Lanham: Rowman & Littlefield, 2003), 3–12; Gary Goertz, "The Substantive Importance of Necessary Condition Hypotheses," in *Necessary Conditions: Theory, Methodology, and Applications,* ed. Gary Goertz and Harvey Starr (Lanham: Rowman & Littlefield, 2003), 65–94.

10. Craig L. Arceneaux, *Bounded Missions: Military Regimes and Democratization in the Southern Cone and Brazil* (University Park: Pennsylvania State University Press, 2001), 128.

11. Munck, *Authoritarianism and Democratization,* 127.

12. Romero, *A History of Argentina,* 241.

13. David Pion-Berlin, "The Fall of Military Rule in Argentina: 1976–1983," *Journal of Interamerican Studies and World Affairs* 27, no. 2 (Summer 1985): 67; Malloy and Seligson, *Authoritarians and Democrats,* 27.

14. Virginia Gamba, *The Falklands/Malvinas War: A Model for North–South Crisis Prevention* (Boston: Allen & Unwin, 1987), 75.

15. Pion-Berlin, "The Fall of Military Rule in Argentina," 67. Perhaps most revealing is a notorious episode earlier in his career, when Galtieri was commander of the Second Army Corps. During a visit to a secret detention center in which suspected dissidents were tortured and executed, Galtieri allowed a female prisoner to escape death because she shared a name with his daughter: "If I say you live, you live; if I say you die, you die. As it happens you have the same Christian name as my daughter, and so you live." James S. Henry, *The Blood Bankers: Tales from the Global Underground Economy* (New York: Basic, 2005), 230.

16. Antonius C. G. M. Robben, *Political Violence and Trauma in Argentina* (Philadelphia: University of Pennsylvania Press, 2005), 188.

17. Edward Mansfield and Jack Snyder argue that as the public became more politically active and the prospect of a complete transition to democracy grew, the Galtieri-led junta desperately sought to win the support of the citizenry at the ballot box. Therefore, the invasion of the Falklands was a stratagem to bolster public support for the regime in impending multiparty elections. However, most accounts suggest that the president's aim was to forestall democratization, not to improve his chances of winning office in a democratic Argentina. That is, a transition to civilian rule was increasingly feared, but it was not seen as inevitable. See *Electing to Fight: Why Emerging Democracies Go to War* (Cambridge: MIT Press, 2005), 219–220.

18. Daniel K. Gibran, *The Falklands War: Britain Versus the Past in the South Atlantic* (Jefferson: McFarland, 1998), 64.

19. See Mares, *Violent Peace*, 152; Munck, *Authoritarianism and Democratization*, 140–141; James W. McGuire, *Peronism Without Perón: Unions, Parties, and Democracy in Argentina* (Stanford: Stanford University Press, 1999), 177.

20. See Martin Honeywell and Jenny Pearce, *Falklands/Malvinas: Whose Crisis?* (London: Latin America Bureau, 1982), 76; James W. McGuire, "Interim Government and Democratic Consolidation: Argentina in Comparative Perspective," in *Between States: Interim Governments and Democratic Transitions*, ed. Yossi Shain and Juan J. Linz (Cambridge: Cambridge University Press, 1995), 187; Romero, *A History of Argentina*, 241; Lewis, *Guerrillas and Generals*, 183. Some even argue that Galtieri "favored continuing the military's rule indefinitely." Gretchen Helmke, *Courts Under Constraints: Judges, Generals, and Presidents in Argentina* (Cambridge: Cambridge University Press, 2005), 73. See also Jonathan Kirshner, *Appeasing Bankers: Financial Caution on the Road to War* (Princeton: Princeton University Press, 2007), 176.

21. Gibran, *The Falklands War*, 64.

22. Pion-Berlin, "The Fall of Military Rule in Argentina," 65.

23. Edward E. Azar, *The Management of Protracted Social Conflict: Theory and Cases* (Brookfield: Gower, 1990), 85.

24. Miguel Angel Centeno, *Blood and Debt, War and the Nation-State in Latin America* (University Park: Pennsylvania State University Press, 2002), 88.

25. If the junta had preferred a war with Britain, environmental factors would have made this course of action extremely dangerous. The main obstacle was a balance of capabilities—from the number and quality of troops to communications technology and firepower—that favored London. On the one hand, London was not guaranteed a victory, especially given that 8,800 miles separated the Falkland Islands from Great Britain. Even as a pauper state, Argentina proved to be a tough adversary. After the hostilities began in April 1982, Argentine aircraft were able inflict significant damage on the British task force sent to protect the islands. If the junta had acquired additional Exocet antiship missiles—something Argentina as a princely state might have accomplished more easily—the damage would have been even greater. On the other hand, war with Britain would still have been high risk. The balance of capabilities would not have been easily or swiftly redressed, even if Argentina had a higher extractive capacity. See "Argentina Sticks to Its Guns But Pins Hopes on Diplomacy," *Latin America Weekly Report*, April 23, 1982; Gavshon and Rice, *The Sinking of the Belgrano*, 30–31.

26. Pion-Berlin, "The Fall of Military Rule in Argentina," 69; Juan Carlos Torre and Liliana de Riz, "Argentina Since 1946," in *Argentina Since Independence*, ed. Leslie Bethell (Cambridge: Cambridge University Press, 1993), 337.

27. William C. Smith, "Reflections on the Political Economy of Authoritarian Rule and Capitalist Reorganization in Contemporary Argentina," in *Generals in Retreat: The Crisis of Military Rule in Latin America*, ed. Philip O'Brien and Paul Cammack (Manchester: Manchester University Press, 1985), 60.

28. Ibid., 60. See also Torre and de Riz, "Argentina Since 1946," 337–338.

29. T. V. Paul, *Asymmetric Conflicts: War Initiation by Weaker Powers* (Cambridge: Cambridge University Press, 1994), 160.

30. Edward Schumacher, "Minister Acts Strongly on Argentine Economy," *New York Times*, February 16, 1982, D1.

31. "Argentina: An Odd Alliance," *Economist*, January 30, 1982, 47.

32. Mónica Peralta-Ramos, *The Political–Economy of Argentina: Power and Class Since 1930* (Boulder: Westview, 1992), 87.

33. World Bank, *Argentina: Economic Memorandum*, vol. 1 (Washington, DC: World Bank, 1985), 96, 99.

34. As discussed in Chapter 3, Jacek Kugler and Marina Arbetman estimate the level of tax revenues that each government could collect based on the country's total economic resources. If a government extracts revenues equal to the expected amount based on the size of its economy, a state receives a score of 1.0. Scores less than 1.0 indicate that the government did worse than expected relative to the size of its national economy. Kugler and Arbetman give Argentina an extractive capacity score of 0.56 in 1981 and 0.52 in 1982. See "Relative Political Capacity: Political Extraction and Political Reach," in *Political Capacity and Economic Behavior*, ed. Marina Arbetman and Jacek Kugler (Boulder: Westview, 1997), 11–45.

35. William C. Smith, *Authoritarianism and the Crisis of the Argentine Political Economy* (Stanford: Stanford University Press, 1989), 245.

36. Ibid., 246.

37. World Bank, *Argentina*, xxvii.

38. Ibid., 19.

39. Romero, *A History of Argentina*, 256.

40. "Galtieri Speaks in La Pampa on Government Goals," *La Nación*, February 13, 1982, 1, 12.

41. Diana Taylor, *Disappearing Acts: Spectacles of Gender and Nationalism in Argentina's "Dirty War"* (Durham: Duke University Press, 1997), 60.

42. Wynia, *Argentina*, 12.

43. Oscar Raul Cardoso, Ricardo Kirschbaum, and Eduardo van der Kooy, *Falklands: The Secret Plot*, trans. Bernard Ethel (Surrey: Preston, 1987), 87. The impracticability of sustained repression is supported by the fact that when the junta faced widespread popular unrest following Argentina's defeat in the Falklands, it set a date for elections instead of attempting to restore order through internal policing.

44. Helmke, *Courts Under Constraints*, 73.

45. Helmut Norpoth, *Confidence Regained: Economics, Mrs. Thatcher, and the British Voter* (Ann Arbor: University of Michigan Press, 1992), 148. See also Rubén O. Moro, *The History of the South Atlantic Conflict: The War for the Malvinas* (New York: Praeger, 1989), 30; Paul Eddy and Magnus Linklater, *The Falklands War* (London: André Deutsch, 1982), 133; Max Hastings and Simon Jenkins, *The Battle for the Falklands* (London: Michael Joseph, 1983), 75; Gavshon and Rice, *The Sinking of the Belgrano*, 46; Alexander M. Haig Jr., *Caveat: Realism, Reagan, and Foreign Policy* (New York:

Macmillan, 1984), 276; Cardoso, Kirschbaum, and van der Kooy, *Falklands,* 102; Wynia, *Argentina,* 16.

46. Juan Carlos Murguizur, "The South Atlantic Conflict: An Argentinian Point of View," *International Defense Review* 16, no. 2 (1983): 135.

47. David Rock, *Authoritarian Argentina: The Nationalist Movement, Its History and Its Impact* (Berkeley: University of California Press, 1993), 232.

48. Gavshon and Rice, *The Sinking of the Belgrano,* 46.

49. Richard C. Thornton, *The Falklands Sting: Reagan, Thatcher, and Argentina's Bomb* (Washington, DC: Brassey's, 1998), 147. See also Lawrence D. Freedman, "Reconsiderations: The War of the Falkland Islands," *Foreign Affairs* 61, no. 1 (Fall 1982): 199; Nicanor Costa Méndez, "Beyond Deterrence: The Malvinas–Falklands Case," *Journal of Social Issues* 43, no. 4 (Winter 1987): 120; Lawrence D. Freedman and Virginia Gamba-Stonehouse, *Signals of War: The Falklands Conflict of 1982* (Boston: Faber and Faber, 1990), 142; Romero, *A History of Argentina,* 243.

50. Wynia, *Argentina,* 8.

51. See Hastings and Jenkins, *The Battle for the Falklands,* 47; John Nott, *Here Today, Gone Tomorrow: Recollections of an Errant Politician* (London: Politico's, 2002), 254–256.

52. See Hastings and Jenkins, *The Battle for the Falklands,* 47; Nora Kinzer Stewart, *South Atlantic Conflict of 1982: A Case Study in Military Cohesion* (Alexandria: U.S. Army Research Institute for the Behavioral and Social Sciences, 1988), 60.

53. Admittedly, the junta did not intend to invade the islands in April. The junta was compelled to move up its plan for invasion by several months after Argentine workers landed on South Georgia, refused to request formal authorization for their presence, and hoisted an Argentine flag. Therefore, one could argue that the military might have been better prepared for an invasion had it taken place in July or October as originally anticipated. That said, the abbreviated timetable cannot account for the absence of a plan to defend the islands against a British reprisal.

54. See Gavshon and Rice, *The Sinking of the Belgrano,* 30–31; Stewart, *South Atlantic Conflict of 1982,* 59–60; Freedman and Gamba-Stonehouse, *Signals of War,* 142; Thornton, *The Falklands Sting,* 106.

55. Gavshon and Rice, *The Sinking of the Belgrano,* 31.

56. Dov S. Zakheim, "The South Atlantic Conflict: Strategic, Military, and Technological Lessons," in *The Falklands War: Lessons for Strategy, Diplomacy, and International Law,* ed. Alberto R. Coll and Anthony C. Arend (Boston: Allen & Unwin, 1985), 160.

57. Cardoso, Kirschbaum, and van der Kooy, *Falklands,* 97.

58. Lord Franks, "Falkland Islands Review: Report of a Committee of Privy Counsellors," London: Her Majesty's Stationery Office, January 1983, 76–77.

59. Martin Mullins, *In the Shadow of the Generals: Foreign Policy Making in Argentina, Brazil and Chile* (Burlington: Ashgate, 2006), 56.

60. Galtieri, who was then commander of the army and a member of the military government, also made a very favorable impression on many officials in the Reagan

administration. After one visit, he was described as "Argentina's General Patton" and said to possess a "majestic personality." See Thornton, *The Falklands Sting*, 70; Cardoso, Kirschbaum, and van der Kooy, *Falklands*, 15.

61. David Lewis Feldman, "The United States Role in the Malvinas Crisis, 1982: Misguidance and Misperception in Argentina's Decision to Go to War," *Journal of Interamerican Studies and World Affairs* 27, no. 2 (Summer 1985): 6. The belief that the United States would remain strictly neutral or even side with Argentina instead of Britain, its historical ally, was a product of wishful thinking and miscommunication. A conversation between Argentina's foreign minister, Nicanor Costa Méndez, and the U.S. assistant secretary of state for Latin American affairs, Thomas Enders, is thought to have been particularly influential in shaping the junta's perception of the likely U.S. stance on a conflict between Argentina and the United Kingdom. After politely listening to a lengthy presentation on the legality of Argentina's Falkland Islands claims, Enders told Costa Méndez that U.S. policy toward the dispute was "hands off." Enders later insisted that he had not given Argentina a green light to invade. "What I said to him was that we were 'hands off' *on the basic dispute*, but that we hoped they would get on with the discussions with the British." Michael Charlton, *The Little Platoon: Diplomacy and the Falklands Dispute* (London: Blackwell, 1989), 165. Emphasis in the original. See also Richard Ned Lebow, "Miscalculation in the South Atlantic: The Origins of the Falklands War," in *Psychology & Deterrence*, ed. Robert Jervis, Richard Ned Lebow, and Janice Gross Stein (Baltimore: Johns Hopkins University Press, 1985), 112; Honeywell and Pearce, *Falklands/Malvinas*, 81–82; Hastings and Jenkins, *The Battle for the Falklands*, 70; Cardoso, Kirschbaum, and van der Kooy, *Falklands*, 120; Smith, *Authoritarianism*, 256; Wynia, *Argentina*, 14.

62. J. Iglesias Rouco, "The Foreign Offensive," *La Prensa*, January 24, 1982.

63. Lebow, "Miscalculation in the South Atlantic," 113.

64. In the end, American assistance, although limited, helped Britain win the war. See Lawrence D. Freedman, *Britain and the Falklands War* (London: Basil Blackwell, 1988), 72.

65. James McGuire and Jonathan Kirshner both argue that the junta sought to provoke a diversionary conflict in the Falklands to buy time for economic reforms to take effect, though neither considers why the government did not attempt repression. See McGuire, "Interim Government and Democratic Consolidation, 187; Kirshner, *Appeasing Bankers*, 177.

66. See Guillermo A. Makin, "Argentine Approaches to the Falklands/Malvinas: Was the Resort to Violence Foreseeable?" *International Affairs* 59, no. 3 (Summer 1982): 398–401; Cardoso, Kirschbaum, and van der Kooy, *Falklands*, 27–28; John Arquilla and María Moyano Rasmussen, "The Origins of the South Atlantic War," *Journal of Latin American Studies* 33, no. 4 (November 2001): 748; Lawrence D. Freedman, *The Origins of the Falklands War*, vol. 1 of *The Official History of the Falklands Campaign* (New York: Routledge, 2005), 132–133. There is some evidence that in early December 1981, Galtieri agreed to reclaim the Falklands in exchange for Admiral Jorge Anaya's support in his bid to replace Viola as president. If such a backroom deal was

made, Galtieri likely did not require much convincing. As Iain Guest writes, the general "readily agreed" to Anaya's conditions because the junta "desperately needed a boost, and the Malvinas was the one issue that united all shades of opinion in Argentina." *Behind the Disappearances: Argentina's Dirty War Against Human Rights and the United Nations* (Philadelphia: University of Pennsylvania Press, 1990), 338. For a discussion of Anaya's interest in the Falklands and his role in bringing Galtieri to power, see David A. Welch, *Justice and the Genesis of War* (New York: Cambridge University Press, 1995), 166.

67. The junta proposed creating a commission that would meet monthly to negotiate the transfer of the Falkland Islands to Argentina and warned that an agreement had to be reached "without further delays or dilatory arguments." Although Britain agreed to hold monthly meetings on the Falklands issue, it refused to recognize Argentina's claim to the islands. London's perceived intransigence prompted the Argentine Ministry of Foreign Affairs to issue a veiled threat regarding its willingness to use force in the Falklands: "The new system constitutes an effective step for the early solution of the dispute. However, should this not occur, Argentina reserves [the right] to terminate the working of this mechanism and to choose freely the procedure which best accords with her interests." Welch, *Justice and the Genesis of War*, 161–162.

68. On January 5, 1982, the junta established a Joint Armed forces study group that was authorized to begin planning for an invasion should the February negotiations be unsuccessful. William Ben Hunt, *Getting to War: Predicting International Conflict with Mass Media Indicators* (Ann Arbor: University of Michigan Press, 1997), 20.

69. See, for example, Eddy and Linklater, *The Falklands War*, 29–30, 62; Hastings and Jenkins, *The Battle for the Falklands*, 48; Alejandro Dabat and Luis Lorenzano, *Argentina: The Malvinas and the End of Military Rule*, trans. Ralph Johnstone (London: Verso, 1984), 72, 76–77; Haig, *Caveat*, 263, 296; Corradi, *The Fitful Republic*, 136–137; Cardoso, Kirschbaum, and van der Kooy, *Falklands*, 21, 35; Jimmy Burns, *The Land That Lost Its Heroes: The Falklands, the Post-War, and Alfonsin* (London: Bloomsbury, 1987), 30; Azar, *The Management of Protracted Social Conflict*, 85; Wynia, *Argentina*, 12–13; Gibran, *The Falklands War*, 70; Munck, *Authoritarianism and Democratization*, 141–142; Hunt, *Getting to War*, 20; Romero, *A History of Argentina*, 242. A small number of scholars argue that domestic instability was one of several factors that contributed to the decision to invade. See Gamba, *The Falklands/Malvinas War*, 131–132; Douglas Kinney, *National Interest/National Honor: The Diplomacy of the Falklands Crisis* (New York: Praeger, 1989), 61; Smith, *Authoritarianism*, 256; Freedman and Gamba-Stonehouse, *Signals of War*, 4.

70 "Islands Used as Vote Catchers," *Latin America Weekly Report*, March 12, 1982, 5. See also "Stroke of Genius or Fatal Gamble," *Latin America Weekly Report*, April 9, 1982, 11; Edward Schumacher, "Argentina Sped Past the Point of No Return," *New York Times*, April 11, 1982; "Argentina: Nationalists All," *Economist*, April 17, 1982, 25; "Forces That Galtieri Unleashed," *Latin America Weekly Review*, April 30, 1982, 9.

71. Eddy and Linklater, *The Falklands War*, 28.

72. Cardoso, Kirschbaum, and van der Kooy, *Falklands*, 21.

73. Gavshon and Rice, *The Sinking of the Belgrano,* 58.

74. Haig, *Caveat,* 263.

75. See Gibran, *The Falklands War,* 65–66; Eddy and Linklater, *The Falklands War,* 29.

76. Gibran, *The Falklands War,* 66.

77. Dabat and Lorenzano, *Argentina,* 79; Arie Marcelo Kacowicz, *Peaceful Territorial Change* (Columbia: University of South Carolina Press, 1994), 165.

78. Freedman and Gamba-Stonehouse, *Signals of War,* 11. Britain's decision to lift sanctions against and sell arms to the Chilean government appeared to confirm the junta's suspicions.

79. See Eddy and Linklater, *The Falklands War,* 28.

80. A few weeks after coming to power, Galtieri indicated that he was prepared to repudiate a 1972 treaty with Chile, which stated that any border disputes would be submitted to the International Court of Justice. See Honeywell and Pearce, *Falklands/ Malvinas,* 80–81; Hastings and Jenkins, *The Battle for the Falklands,* 47.

81. Franks, "Falkland Islands Review," 43.

82. Gamba, *The Falklands/Malvinas War,* 105.

83. Lebow, "Miscalculation in the South Atlantic," 119.

84. Ibid., 108.

85. Cardoso, Kirschbaum, and van der Kooy, *Falklands,* 144.

86. There is some debate about when the junta committed to invading the Falklands. Taylor Fravel argues "no decision to invade" was made in January 1982. See "The Limits of Diversion: Rethinking Internal and External Conflict," *Security Studies* 19, no. 2 (May 2010): 319. It is true that no precise date for an invasion was set in January, as the junta was waiting on the outcome of the February talks to determine whether taking the Falklands by force would be necessary. However, many scholars believe that junta did commit to a limited military intervention, should negotiations fail, in January 1982. See Makin, "Argentine Approaches to the Falklands/Malvinas," 398–401; Cardoso, Kirschbaum, and van der Kooy, *Falklands,* 27–28; Hunt, *Getting to War,* 20; Arquilla and Rasmussen, "The Origins of the South Atlantic War," 748; Freedman, *The Origins of the Falklands War,* 132–133. Indeed, several scholars make the stronger argument that Galtieri decided to reclaim the islands, by force if necessary, in early December. See Eddy and Linklater, *The Falklands War,* 30, 62; Guest, *Behind the Disappearances,* 338; Welch, *Justice and the Genesis of War,* 166; Mares, *Violent Peace,* 152; Klaus Friedrich Veigel, *Dictatorship, Democracy, and Globalization: Argentina and the Cost of Paralysis, 1973–2001* (University Park: Pennsylvania State University Press, 2009), 94.

87. Fravel, "The Limits of Diversion," 311.

88. Fravel further notes that Roberto Viola, Galtieri's immediate predecessor, faced the same domestic challenges during his short presidency but chose not to provoke a diversionary conflict. Therefore, Fravel concludes, the failed February talks were the real cause of the Falklands invasion. However, Viola's decision not to use diversionary tactics is better explained by the fact that, as a "soft-liner," one of his

preferred responses to the unrest was limited political reform, a policy that was practicable for a pauper state. There was no need to divert public attention from internal problems if his intent was to accede to the public's demands. For a discussion of Viola's political views, see Munck, *Authoritarianism and Democratization*, 119–129.

89. Fravel, "The Limits of Diversion," 318.

90. Jack S. Levy and Lily I. Vakili, "Diversionary Action by Authoritarian Regimes: Argentina in the Falklands/Malvinas Case," in *The Internationalization of Communal Strife*, ed. Manus Midlarsky (New York: Routledge, 1992), 127.

91. Ibid., 123.

92. Lewis, *Guerrillas and Generals*, 179.

93. David Pion-Berlin, *Through Corridors of Power: Institutions and Civil–Military Relations in Argentina* (University Park: Pennsylvania State University Press, 1997), 62. See also Pion-Berlin, "The Fall of Military Rule in Argentina," 70.

94. Honeywell and Pearce, *Falklands/Malvinas*, 79; Eddy and Linklater, *The Falklands War*, 62.

95. It is noteworthy that the junta chose as its unifying mission virtually the only policy that also promised to increase public approval of the government.

96. At most, there was an interaction between the internal instability and the conflict among the elite. After the domestic unrest began to escalate and the junta fragmented, the infighting among the military elite opened the door for the public to express its dissatisfaction with the government's performance.

97. Levy and Vakili, "Diversionary Action by Authoritarian Regimes," 122.

Chapter 5

1. Will Bagley, *Blood of the Prophets: Brigham Young and the Massacre at Mountain Meadows* (Norman: University of Oklahoma Press, 2002), 23.

2. Richard Lyman Bushman and Jed Woodworth, *Joseph Smith: Rough Stone Rolling* (New York: Vintage, 2007), 355.

3. Bagley, *Blood of the Prophets*, 22.

4. Kenneth M. Stampp, *America in 1857: A Nation on the Brink* (Oxford: Oxford University Press, 1990), 197.

5. William P. MacKinnon, ed., *At Sword's Point, Part I: A Documentary History of the Utah War to 1858* (Norman: Arthur H. Clark, 2008), 481–483.

6. Richard D. Poll and Ralph W. Hansen, "'Buchanan's Blunder': The Utah War, 1857–1858," *Military Affairs* 25, no. 3 (Autumn 1961): 122.

7. Roy Franklin Nichols, *The Disruption of American Democracy* (New York: Collier, 1962), 108.

8. Philip S. Klein, *President James Buchanan: A Biography* (University Park: Pennsylvania State University Press, 1962), 261. Emphasis in the original.

9. Jean H. Baker, *James Buchanan* (New York: Times Books, 2004), 68. See also Norman F. Furniss, *The Mormon Conflict, 1850–1859* (New Haven: Yale University Press, 1960), vii.

10. James Buchanan, *The Works of James Buchanan: Comprising His Speeches, State Papers, and Private Correspondence, 1856–1860*, vol. 10, ed. John Bassett Moore (Philadelphia: Lippincott, 1910), 92.

11. Thomas Goodrich, *War to the Knife: Bleeding Kansas, 1854–1861* (Mechanicsburg: Stackpole, 1998), 111–118.

12. Nicole Etcheson, *Bleeding Kansas: Contested Liberty in the Civil War Era* (Lawrence: University of Kansas Press, 2004), 113.

13. Historians have documented only 38 actual political killings in 1856, with most deaths resulting from property disputes and personal quarrels. Dale E. Watts, "How Bloody Was Bleeding Kansas? Political Killings in Kansas Territory, 1854–1861," *Kansas History* 18, no. 2 (Summer 1995): 123; Douglas Brinkley, *American Heritage History of the United States* (New York: Viking, 1998), 191.

14. Etcheson, *Bleeding Kansas*, 138.

15. See Michael F. Holt, *The Political Crisis of the 1850s* (New York: Wiley, 1978), 189–194. For example, four-fifths of the first national Republican Party platform dealt with slavery, and specifically the need to prevent the encroachment of slavery into the West. See James M. McPherson, *Battle Cry of Freedom: The Civil War Era* (Oxford: Oxford University Press, 1988), 154.

16. Allan Nevins, *A House Dividing, 1852–1857*, vol. 2 of *Ordeal of the Union* (New York: Charles Scribner's Sons, 1947), 449; Holt, *The Political Crisis of the 1850s*, 194–197; Stampp, *America in 1857*, 143.

17. Roger L. Ransom, *Conflict and Compromise: The Political Economy of Slavery, Emancipation, and the American Civil War* (New York: Cambridge University Press, 1989), 121–122, 127. See also Etcheson, *Bleeding Kansas*, 3–4.

18. Stampp, *America in 1857*, 120–121.

19. McPherson, *Battle Cry of Freedom*, 149.

20. Douglas W. Jaenicke, "The Rupture of the Antebellum Democratic Party: Prelude to Southern Secession from the Union," *Party Politics* 1, no. 3 (July 1995): 354.

21. Ransom, *Conflict and Compromise*, 123. See also James A. Rawley, *Race & Politics: "Bleeding Kansas" and the Coming of the Civil War* (Lincoln: University of Nebraska Press, 1979), 143; Jaenicke, "The Rupture of the Antebellum Democratic Party," 351.

22. Klein, *President James Buchanan*, 289.

23. David E. Meerse, "James Buchanan, The Patronage and the Northern Democratic Party, 1857–1858" (Ph.D. diss., University of Illinois, 1969), 262.

24. Stampp, *America in 1857*, 168–169.

25. McPherson, *Battle Cry of Freedom*, 163.

26. Rawley, *Race & Politics*, 179.

27. Stampp, *America in 1857*, 121.

28. William J. Cooper Jr. and Thomas E. Terrill, *The American South: A History*, vol. 1, 4th ed. (Lanham: Rowman & Littlefield, 2009), 340.

29. William W. Freehling, *Secessionists Triumphant, 1854–1861*, vol. 2 of *The Road to Disunion* (Oxford: Oxford University Press, 2007), 104.

30. Baker, *James Buchanan*, 71. During the 1856 campaign, Buchanan "believed with all his heart that Republican victory would mean immediate and inevitable secession—and he more than half indicated that he thought it might be justified." Nevins, *A House Dividing, 1852–1857*, 502.

31. Stampp, *America in 1857*, 68.

32. Ibid., 68. William MacKinnon notes that there is essentially one surviving letter written by Buchanan discussing events in Utah. See *At Sword's Point*, 122, n. 43.

33. Baker, *James Buchanan*, 76.

34. Ibid.

35. Elbert B. Smith, *The Presidency of James Buchanan* (Lawrence: University of Kansas Press, 1975), 31; Michael J. Birkner, "Introduction: Getting to Know James Buchanan, Again," in *James Buchanan and the Political Crisis of the 1850s*, ed. Michael J. Birkner (Selinsgrove: Susquehanna University Press, 1996), 25.

36. Smith, *The Presidency of James Buchanan*, 17.

37. McPherson, *Battle Cry of Freedom*, 157–158.

38. Robert E. Terrill, "James Buchanan: Romancing the Union," in *Before the Rhetorical Presidency*, ed. Martin J. Medhurst (College Station: Texas A&M University Press, 2008), 165.

39. Holt, *The Political Crisis of the 1850s*, 187; Ransom, *Conflict and Compromise*, 158.

40. Stampp, *America in 1857*, 48.

41. See Allan Nevins, *Douglas, Buchanan, and Party Chaos, 1857–1859*, vol. 1 of *The Emergence of Lincoln* (New York: Charles Scribner's Sons, 1950), 168, 240, 255; Baker, *James Buchanan*, 55, 69, 74, 150.

42. Smith, *The Presidency of James Buchanan*, 6.

43. Ibid.; Elizabeth R. Varon, *Disunion!: The Coming of the American Civil War, 1789–1859* (Chapel Hill: University of North Carolina Press, 2008), 10.

44. Historians have offered a range of explanations for Buchanan's decision to support the Lecompton constitution in the fall of 1857, variously highlighting his weak character and poor judgment, the fear of southern secession, the influence of proslavery friends and his Cabinet, and his own pro-southern convictions—or some combination of these factors. See George Fort Milton, *Eve of Conflict: Stephen A. Douglas and the Needless War* (Boston: Houghton Mifflin, 1934), 271; Nevins, *Douglas, Buchanan, and Party Chaos;* James P. Shenton, *Robert John Walker: A Politician from Jackson to Lincoln* (New York: Columbia University Press, 1961), 174; Klein, *President James Buchanan*, 303; Smith, *The Presidency of James Buchanan*, 38, 40; Holt, *The Political Crisis of the 1850s*, 204; Stampp, *America in 1857*, 284–285; Baker, *James Buchanan*, 147–150; Etcheson, *Bleeding Kansas*, 158–159.

45. Klein, *President James Buchanan*, 262. Emphasis added. See also Nevins, *Douglas, Buchanan, and Party Chaos*, 169; Stampp, *America in 1857*, 4.

46. Buchanan, *The Works of James Buchanan*, 107.

47. From his inauguration until November 1857, Buchanan consistently resisted pressure from southern Democrats to adopt the proslavery position on Kansas. See

George D. Harmon, "President James Buchanan's Betrayal of Governor Robert J. Walker of Kansas," *Pennsylvania Magazine of History and Biography* 53, no. 1 (1929), 90; Milton, *Eve of Conflict*, 262; Shenton, *Robert John Walker*, 163–164; Klein, *President James Buchanan*, 290–295; David M. Potter, *The Impending Crisis, 1848–1961* (New York: Harper & Row, 1976), 298, 303–304; Holt, *The Political Crisis of the 1850s*, 203; Stampp, *America in 1857*, 159–160, 176–177, 281; Etcheson, *Bleeding Kansas*, 143–147.

48. MacKinnon, *At Sword's Point*, 123.

49. Walter A. MacDougall, *Throes of Democracy: The American Civil War Era, 1829–1877* (New York: HarperCollins, 2008), 365. See also William P. MacKinnon, "125 Years of Conspiracy Theories: Origins of the Utah Expedition of 1857–58," *Utah Historical Quarterly* 52, no. 3 (Summer 1984): 228.

50. Leonard J. Arrington and Davis Bitton, *The Mormon Experience: A History of the Latter-Day Saints* (Urbana: University of Illinois Press, 1992), 166.

51. Furniss, *The Mormon Conflict*, 78.

52. Todd M. Kerstetter, *God's Country, Uncle Sam's Land: Faith and Conflict in the American West* (Urbana: University of Illinois Press, 2008), 60.

53. Robert W. Coakley, *The Role of the Federal Military Forces in Domestic Disorders, 1789–1878* (Washington, DC: Center of Military History, United States Army, 1988), 178.

54. Buchanan once remarked, for example: "But this I believe: Providence has given to the American people a great and glorious mission to perform, even that of extending the blessings of Christianity and of civil and religious liberty over the whole North American continent." Frederick Moore Binder, *James Buchanan and the American Empire* (Selinsgrove: Susquehanna University Press, 1994), 51.

55. Russell McClintock, *Lincoln and the Decision for War: The Northern Response to Secession* (Chapel Hill: University of North Carolina Press, 2008), 68.

56. Nevins, *Douglas, Buchanan, and Party Chaos*, 169; Klein, *President James Buchanan*, 288–90; Meerse, *James Buchanan*, 256–257, 265–268; Holt, *The Political Crisis of the 1850s*, 203; Stampp, *America in 1857*, 9–14, 144–168.

57. Buchanan also used his power of appointment to distribute other territorial positions among proslavery and free-soil settlers with the hope of creating "a territorial Democratic party that transcended sectional issues." To win over the free-soilers, the president allocated several important posts to northerners, including ones on the notoriously proslavery Kansas Supreme Court. Buchanan also allocated several key offices to southerners to reassure proslavery settlers that they would have a voice in the new Democratic Party of Kansas. Meerse, *James Buchanan*, 266; see also 263–265.

58. For a discussion of Walker's reputation among Democrats and Republicans and how news of his appointment was initially received, see Stampp, *America in 1857*, 160–161.

59. Klein, *President James Buchanan*, 292.

60. Nichols, *The Disruption of American Democracy*, 107.

61. Stampp, *America in 1857*, 159.

62. Richard Franklin Bensel, *Yankee Leviathan: The Origins of Central State Authority in America, 1859–1877* (Cambridge: Cambridge University Press, 1990), ix.

63. See Ibid., 2–3, 36, 85; Stampp, *America in 1857*, 30; James M. Gallman, *The North Fights the Civil War: The Home Front* (Chicago: I. R. Dee, 1994), 181; Fareed Zakaria, *From Wealth to Power: The Unusual Origins of America's World Role* (Princeton: Princeton University Press, 1998), 55; Baker, *President James Buchanan*, 90; Mark R. Wilson, *The Business of Civil War: Military Mobilization and the State, 1861–1865* (Baltimore: Johns Hopkins University Press, 2006), 36.

64. John Joseph Wallis, "American Government Finance in the Long Run: 1790 to 1990," *Journal of Economic Perspectives* 14, no. 1 (Winter 2000): 65. See also John Joseph Wallis, "The National Era," in *Government and the American Economy: A New History*, ed. Price V. Fishback et al. (Chicago: University of Chicago Press, 2007), 148–187.

65. Peter J. Parish, *The North and the Nation in the Era of the Civil War*, ed. Adam I. P. Smith, and Susan-Mary Grant (New York: Fordham University Press, 2003), 73.

66. W. Elliot Brownlee, *Federal Taxation in America: A Short History* (Washington, DC: Woodrow Wilson Center, 1996), 10–23.

67. Nevins, *Douglas, Buchanan, and Party Chaos*, 220.

68. James L. Huston, *The Panic of 1857 and the Coming of the Civil War* (Baton Rouge: Louisiana State University Press, 1987), 12.

69. See, for example, John Ashworth, *The Coming of the Civil War, 1850–1861*, vol. 2 of *Slavery, Capitalism, and Politics in the Antebellum Republic* (Cambridge: Cambridge University Press, 2008), 369, 371–384.

70. George Ticknor Curtis, *Life of James Buchanan: Fifteenth President of the United States*, vol. 2 (New York: Harper, 1883), 191.

71. Wilson, *The Business of Civil War*, 52.

72. Ibid., 38.

73. Arrington and Bitton, *The Mormon Experience*, 166; Francis Paul Prucha, *The Great Father: The United States Government and the American Indians* (Lincoln: University of Nebraska Press, 1984), 128.

74. Hubert Howe Bancroft, *History of Utah, 1540–1886* (San Francisco: History Company, 1890), 509.

75. Furniss, *The Mormon Conflict*, 98–99.

76. Wilson, *The Business of Civil War*, 52.

77. Richard D. Poll and William P. MacKinnon, "Causes of the Utah War Reconsidered," *Journal of Mormon History* 20, no. 2 (Fall 1994): 18; Wilson, *The Business of Civil War*, 55.

78. Furniss, *The Mormon Conflict*, 175.

79. MacKinnon, *At Sword's Point*, 485.

80. Nichols, *The Disruption of American Democracy*, 183.

81. Furniss, *The Mormon Conflict*, 171. See also Coakley, *The Role of the Federal Military Forces*, 205–209.

82. Republicans worried that the troops could be used against the free-staters in Kansas, and Democrats feared that they could be used against the southern states if a Republican won the 1860 presidential election.

83. Wilson, *The Business of Civil War*, 54.

84. Ibid.

85. Nichols, *The Disruption of American Democracy*, 184; Clifford L. Scott, *Search for Sanctuary: Brigham Young and the White Mountain Expedition* (Salt Lake City: University of Utah Press, 1984), 195.

86. Furniss, *The Mormon Conflict*, 89. See also Scott, *Search for Sanctuary*, 24.

87. Ibid., 84.

88. Robert Bruce Flanders, *Nauvoo: Kingdom on the Mississippi* (Urbana: University of Illinois Press, 1975), 278–305.

89. Bagley, *Blood of the Prophets*, 52.

90. David Bigler and Will Bagley, eds., *Innocent Blood: Essential Narratives of the Mountain Meadows Massacre* (Norman: Arthur H. Clark, 2008), 26.

91. Stampp, *America in 1857*, 199.

92. Thomas Bender, *A Nation Among Nations: America's Place in World History* (New York: Hill and Wang, 2006), 161. As a result, an additional benefit of military action in Utah was that it would silence the Republican Party elite, who sometimes argued that support for slavery implied support for polygamy. See Andrew L. Neff, *History of Utah, 1847 to 1869* (Salt Lake City: Deseret News Press, 1940), 457–460; Richard D. Poll, "The Mormon Question Enters National Politics 1850–1856," *Utah Historical Quarterly* 25 (April 1957): 128–130; Furniss, *The Mormon Conflict*, 75; Scott, *The Search for Sanctuary*, 24; Leonard J. Arrington, *Brigham Young: American Moses* (Urbana: University of Illinois Press, 1986), 251.

93. Stampp, *America in 1857*, 200.

94. Robert Walter Johannsen, *The Frontier, the Union, and Stephen A. Douglas* (Urbana: University of Illinois Press, 1989), 116.

95. See Furniss, *The Mormon Conflict*, 68; Coakley, *The Role of the Federal Military Forces*, 201; Michael L. Tate, *The Frontier Army in the Settlement of the West* (Norman: University of Oklahoma Press, 1999), 85; George Rollie Adams, *General William S. Harney: Prince of Dragoons* (Lincoln: University of Nebraska Press, 2006), 165; MacKinnon, *At Sword's Point*, 416.

96. U.S. War Department, *Annual Report of the Secretary of War*, vol. 2, part IV (Washington, DC: U.S. Government Printing Office, 1858), 8.

97. James Buchanan, *Mr. Buchanan's Administration on the Eve of the Rebellion* (New York: Appleton-Century, 1866), 233.

98. Furniss, *The Mormon Conflict*, 68. See also Donald R. Moorman and Gene A. Sessions, *Camp Floyd and the Mormons: The Utah War* (Salt Lake City: University of Utah Press, 1992), 182; MacKinnon, *At Sword's Point*, 117.

99. "Latest Intelligence by Telegraph to the New-York Daily Times," *New York Daily Times*, June 9, 1857, 4.

100. Coakley, *The Role of the Federal Military Forces*, 198.

101. MacKinnon, *At Sword's Point*, 102.

102. Le Roy Reuben Hafen and Ann Woodbury Hafen, *Mormon Resistance: A Documentary Account of the Utah Expedition, 1857–1858* (Lincoln: University of Nebraska Press, 2005), 366.

103. MacKinnon, *At Sword's Point*, 71.

104. See Furniss, *The Mormon Conflict*, 96; Thomas W. Cutrer, *Ben McCulloch and the Frontier Military Tradition* (Chapel Hill: University of North Carolina Press, 1993), 151.

105. MacKinnon, *At Sword's Point*, 116, 122, 128.

106. The precise date of Buchanan's final decision to green-light the military expedition is unknown, but most historians speculate that it occurred sometime in May. See, for example, Furniss, *The Mormon Conflict*, 126; Coakley, *The Role of the Federal Military Forces*, 196; Bagley, *Blood of the Prophets*, 79. In *At Sword's Point*, MacKinnon suggests that planning for the Utah expedition may have begun as early as April 15, with the decision to send General Harney to Kansas (p. 140). Although Harney would eventually lead the Utah expedition, at this time, as MacKinnon elsewhere acknowledges, his "reassignment was almost certainly a function not of a move on Utah, but rather on the administration's higher priority need for the regular army to maintain order in Kansas" (p. 128). The only other evidence is a letter, dated April 15, from a lieutenant stationed in Kansas to his father reporting that he was to be deployed to "the Plains." The lieutenant speculated that he was to be sent to Utah (pp. 126–127).

107. MacKinnon, *At Sword's Point*, 133.

108. Harmon, "President James Buchanan's Betrayal," 86. See also MacKinnon, *At Sword's Point*, 123.

109. Lyon Gardiner Tyler, *The Letters and Times of the Tylers*, vol. 2 (c. 1884–1886; repr., New York: Da Capo, 1970), 516.

110. David A. Williams, "President Buchanan Receives a Proposal for an Anti-Mormon Crusade, 1857," *Brigham Young University Studies* 14, no. 1 (Autumn 1973): 103.

111. Stampp, *America in 1857*, 82.

112. Tyler, *The Letters and Times of the Tylers*, 645–646; Elizabeth Tyler Coleman, *Priscilla Cooper Tyler and the American Scene, 1816–1889* (Tuscaloosa: University of Alabama Press, 2006), 131.

113. Harmon, "President James Buchanan's Betrayal," 85–88; Nevins, *Douglas, Buchanan, and Party Chaos*, 242.

114. Williams, "President Buchanan Receives a Proposal," 104–105. Emphasis in the original.

115. In the aftermath of the Utah expedition, observers conjectured that Buchanan's motivation for sending troops was primarily diversionary. A year after the conflict ended, for example, Albert Browne published the first monograph on the campaign in the *Atlantic Monthly*. Browne, an abolitionist and correspondent for the *New York Tribune* during the expedition, theorized that Buchanan's "paramount idea was to gag the North and induce her to forget that she had been robbed of her birthright, by forcing on the attention of the country other questions of absorbing interest. One of the most obvious of these was supplied by the condition of affairs in Utah." Albert G. Browne Jr., "The Utah Expedition," *Atlantic Monthly* 3, no. 17 (March 1859): 364. See also William P. MacKinnon, "Albert Gallatin Browne Jr.: Brief Life of an Early War Correspondent: 1832–1891," *Harvard Magazine* 111 (November/December 2008): 48.

116. Bagley, *Blood of the Prophets*, 79.

117. James M. McCaffrey, *The Army in Transformation, 1790–1860* (Westport: Greenwood, 2006), 17. Upon learning of the expedition, Brigham Young himself complained that the "Government has not condescended to cause an investigation committee . . . to inquire into and ascertain the truth, as is customary in such cases." Poll and MacKinnon, "The Causes of the Utah War Reconsidered," 22.

118. Furniss, *The Mormon Conflict*, 62. See also Klein, *President James Buchanan*, 316.

119. See, for example, Howard Roberts Lamar, *The Far Southwest, 1846–1912: A Territorial History* (New Haven: Yale University Press, 1966), 294; Sarah Barringer Gordon, *The Mormon Question: Polygamy and Constitutional Conflict in Nineteenth-Century America* (Chapel Hill: University of North Carolina Press, 2002), 60–61; Sally Zanjani, *Devils Will Reign: How Nevada Began* (Reno: University of Nevada Press, 2006), 76; MacDougall, *Throes of Democracy*, 374; Matthew J. Grow, *"Liberty to the Downtrodden": Thomas L. Kane, Romantic Reformer* (New Haven: Yale University Press, 2009), 150. Some historians suggest that Buchanan may have harbored diversionary motives but avoid asserting that the expedition was solely intended to distract from events in Kansas: MacKinnon, "125 Years of Conspiracy Theories," 226, 228; Arrington and Bitton, *The Mormon Experience*, 166; Poll and MacKinnon, "The Causes of the Utah War Reconsidered," 29, 31; Terryl L. Givens, *The Viper on the Hearth: Mormons, Myths, and the Construction of Heresy* (Oxford: Oxford University Press, 1997), 38; Kerstetter, *God's Country, Uncle Sam's Land*, 48.

120. Bagley, *Blood of the Prophets*, 62.

121. Baker, *James Buchanan*, 92.

122. Stampp, *America in 1857*, 200. See also Nevins, *Douglas, Buchanan, and Party Chaos*, 318; Furniss, *The Mormon Conflict*, vii, 77–78.

123. See David L. Bigler, *Forgotten Kingdom: The Mormon Theocracy in the American West, 1847–1896* (Logan: Utah State University Press, 1998); Bagley, *Blood of the Prophets*, 38–54; Stephen Cresswell, *Mormons and Cowboys, Moonshiners and Klansmen: Federal Law Enforcement in the South and West, 1870–1893* (Tuscaloosa: University of Alabama Press, 2002), 79–132; John Kincaid, "Extinguishing the Twin Relics of Barbaric Multiculturalism—Slavery and Polygamy—from American Federalism," *Publius* 33, no. 1 (Winter 2003): 75–92.

124. MacKinnon, *At Sword's Point*, 46.

125. Furniss, *The Mormon Conflict*, 30.

126. Historian Norman Furniss notes that this dispute included all of the "general accusations that caused Americans in 1857 to demand the use of force against the Mormons." Yet it did not result in a military expedition. Furniss attributes the peaceful conclusion of the 1851 crisis largely to the successful public relations efforts of the Mormon church, as well as the poor reputations of the federal officials reporting back to Washington. This explanation is unsatisfying. First, Judge Drummond, whose letters touched off the crisis of 1857, was also known to be a scoundrel—yet this mattered little to Buchanan. Second and more importantly, Furniss does not explain why, in

this incident, the White House was willing to ignore the public's demands for military intervention and patiently wait to receive all the facts. See *The Mormon Conflict*, 28.

127. Klein, *President James Buchanan*, 316.

128. Bagley, *Blood of the Prophets*, 90.

129. Furniss, *The Mormon Conflict*, 123.

130. Bagley, *Blood of the Prophets*, 206.

Chapter 6

1. The term *prerevolution* was first used by Jean Egret in his classic history of the period. See *The French Prerevolution, 1787–1788*, trans. Wesley D. Camp (Chicago: University of Chicago Press, 1977).

2. Pierre Goubert, *The Ancien Régime: French Society, 1600–1750*, trans. Steve Cox (New York: Harper Torchbooks, 1969), 17.

3. Lucius Hudson Holt and Alexander Wheeler Chilton, *A Brief History of Europe from 1789–1815* (New York: Macmillan, 1919), 56.

4. William Doyle, *Origins of the French Revolution*, 3rd ed. (Oxford: Oxford University Press, 1999), 92.

5. John Jeter Hurt, *Louis XIV and the Parlements: The Assertion of Royal Authority* (Manchester: Manchester University Press, 2002), 2.

6. Of course, in an absolutist monarchy, the parlements "might raise barricades but never barriers." To overcome parlementary resistance, for example, the king could command obedience in a *lit de justice*, a ceremony in which the monarch appeared in front of the magistrates and declared a law registered. William Doyle, *Officers, Nobles and Revolutionaries: Essays on Eighteenth-Century France* (London: Hambledon, 1995), 39.

7. Kathryn Norberg, "The French Fiscal Crisis of 1788 and the Financial Origins of the Revolution of 1789," in *Fiscal Crises, Liberty, and Representative Government 1450–1789*, ed. Philip T. Hoffman and Kathryn Norberg (Stanford: Stanford University Press, 1994), 292. See also Roland E. Mousnier, *The Organs of State and Society*, vol. 2 of *The Institutions of France Under the Absolute Monarchy, 1598–1789*, trans. Arthur Goldhammer (Chicago: University of Chicago Press, 1984), 654–656; Eugene Nelson White, "The French Revolution and the Politics of Government Finance, 1770–1815," *Journal of Economic History* 55, no. 2 (June 1995): 229, 233; Munro Price, *The Road from Versailles: Louis XVI, Marie Antoinette, and the Fall of the French Monarchy* (New York: St. Martin's, 2002), 23.

8. Bailey Stone, *The Genesis of the French Revolution: A Global–Historical Interpretation* (Cambridge: Cambridge University Press, 1994), 158.

9. P. M. Jones, *Reform and Revolution in France: The Politics of Transition, 1774–1791* (Cambridge: Cambridge University Press, 1995), 115. Calonne also believed that calling the Assembly of Notables would increase investor confidence in the state and improve the monarchy's credit. By granting the Notables oversight of the government's fiscal policy, the monarchy would reassure foreign and domestic creditors that future loans

would be repaid. See Bernard Faÿ, *Louis XVI: Or The End of a World*, trans. Patrick O'Brien (Chicago: Henry Regnery, 1967), 302; Doyle, *Origins of the French Revolution*, 92.

10. James B. Collins, *The State in Early Modern France* (Cambridge: Cambridge University Press, 1995), 258.

11. Price, *The Road from Versailles*, 27.

12. R. R. Palmer, *The Challenge*, vol. 1 of *The Age of the Democratic Revolution: A Political History of Europe and America, 1760–1800* (Princeton: Princeton University Press, 1959), 458.

13. Collins, *The State in Early Modern France*, 264.

14. Egret, *The French Prerevolution*, 151.

15. Norberg, "The French Fiscal Crisis of 1788," 296. See also Mitchell B. Garrett, *The Estates General of 1789: The Problems of Composition and Organization* (New York: Appleton-Century, 1935), 16.

16. Egret, *The French Prerevolution*, 171.

17. See Mousnier, *The Organs of State and Society*, 666; John Hardman, *Louis XVI* (New Haven: Yale University Press, 1993), 135; Doyle, *Origins of the French Revolution*, 106–107; Munro Price, "Politics: Louis XVI," in *Old Regime France, 1648–1788*, ed. William Doyle (Oxford: Oxford University Press, 2001), 247.

18. Alfred Cobban, *A History of Modern France* (New York: George Braziller, 1965), 105. See also J. M. Roberts, *The French Revolution* (Oxford: Oxford University Press, 1978), 8; Michel Vovelle, *The Fall of the French Monarchy, 1787–1792*, trans. Susan Burke (Cambridge: Cambridge University Press, 1984), 83; Collins, *The State in Early Modern France*, 238.

19. Caroline Weber, *Queen of Fashion: What Marie Antoinette Wore to the Revolution* (New York: Macmillan, 2006), 195.

20. T. C. W. Blanning, *The Culture of Power and the Power of Culture: Old Regime Europe, 1660–1789* (Oxford: Oxford University Press, 2002), 422.

21. Hardman, *Louis XVI*, 128–129. Italics in the original.

22. Jones, *Reform and Revolution in France*, 109.

23. John Hardman, *Louis XVI: The Silent King* (London: Arnold, 2000), 21, 93; Price, *The Road from Versailles*, 5–6.

24. Joël Felix and Frank Tallett, "The French Experience, 1661–1815," in *The Fiscal-Military State in Eighteenth-Century Europe: Essays in Honour of P. G. M. Dickson*, ed. Christopher Storrs (Burlington: Ashgate, 2009), 162.

25. Doyle, *Origins of the French Revolution*, 99.

26. Ibid., 101.

27. Faÿ, *Louis XVI*, 293–294.

28. Hardman, *Louis XVI*, 171.

29. Some scholars assert that Louis XVI intended to undo earlier reforms and forcibly subdue Paris in July of 1789. For example, Stephen Walt argues that the monarchy intended to repress the uprising in Paris but that this plan was interrupted by the storming of the Bastille. This telling is apparently confirmed by the fact that the

king was gathering thousands of troops around the outskirts of the city. However, recent archival evidence has not revealed "a shred of evidence" for this argument. Instead, most historians now contend that the purpose of these forces was purely to defend the royal family and key government buildings and not to suppress a popular uprising in the city. See Stephen Walt, *Revolution and War* (Ithaca: Cornell University Press, 1996), 53; Samuel F. Scott, *The Response of the Royal Army to the French Revolution: The Role and Development of the Line Army, 1787–93* (Oxford: Clarendon, 1978), 52–56.

30. Hardman, *Louis XVI,* 155.

31. Price, *The Road from Versailles,* 113.

32. Hardman, *Louis XVI: The Silent King,* 120.

33. Orville T. Murphy, *The Diplomatic Retreat of France and Public Opinion on the Eve of the French Revolution, 1783–1789* (Washington, DC: Catholic University of America Press, 1998), 16.

34. Alexis de Tocqueville, *The Old Regime and the Revolution,* trans. John Bonner (New York: Harper, 1876), 129.

35. Jack A. Goldstone, *Revolution and Rebellion in the Early Modern World* (Berkeley: University of California Press, 1991), 202.

36. Jeremy J. Whiteman, *Reform, Revolution and French Global Policy, 1787–1791* (Burlington: Ashgate, 2002), 45–46.

37. Whiteman, *Reform, Revolution and French Global Policy,* 46.

38. See Cobban, *A History of Modern France,* 131; Theda Skocpol, *States and Social Revolutions: A Comparative Analysis of France, Russia, and China* (Cambridge: Cambridge University Press, 1979), 60–61; Norberg, "The French Fiscal Crisis of 1788," 293–294; Murphy, *The Diplomatic Retreat of France,* Chapter 2.

39. Thomas J. Sargent and François R. Velde, "Macroeconomic Features of the French Revolution," *Journal of Political Economy* 103, no. 3 (June 1995): 488.

40. Whiteman, *Reform, Revolution and French Global Policy,* 59. See also Blanning, *The Culture of Power and the Power of Culture,* 422.

41. Bailey Stone, *Reinterpreting the French Revolution: A Global–Historical Interpretation* (Cambridge: Cambridge University Press, 2002), 52.

42. Murphy, *The Diplomatic Retreat of France,* 35.

43. Interestingly, although a diversionary war was second on the king's policy ranking, it would probably never have been chosen. A higher extractive capacity might have enabled the government to wage a diversionary war, but it also would have allowed the king to muddle through, and this preferred alternative would have been selected.

44. Murphy, *The Diplomatic Retreat of France,* 166.

45. Ibid.

46. Paul Kennedy, *The Rise and Fall of the Great Powers: Economic Change and Military Conflict from 1500 to 2000* (New York: Random House, 1987), 121.

47. Hardman, *Louis XVI,* 100.

48. Collins, *The State in Early Modern France,* 260.

49. Egret, *The French Prerevolution*, 181. See also Doyle, *Origins of the French Revolution*, 106.

50. Ibid.

51. Collins, *The State in Early Modern France*, 259. See also Vovelle, *The Fall of the French Monarchy*, 83.

52. Hardman, *Louis XVI*, 144.

53. David M. Goldfrank, *The Origins of the Crimean War* (London: Longman, 1994), 59.

54. R. J. W. Evans, "1848–1849 in the Habsburg Monarchy," in *The Revolutions in Europe, 1848–1849: From Reform to Reaction*, ed. R. J. W. Evans and Hartmut Pogge Von Strandmann (Oxford: Oxford University Press, 2000), 183.

55. C. A. Macartney, *The Habsburg Empire, 1790–1918* (London: Weidenfeld and Nicolson, 1968), 323.

56. Jean-Paul Bled, *Franz Joseph* (Oxford: Blackwell, 1992), 44; Macartney, *The Habsburg Empire*, 362.

57. Alan Sked, *The Decline and Fall of the Habsburg Empire, 1815–1918*, 2nd ed. (London: Longman, 2001), 93; F. R. Bridge, *The Habsburg Monarchy Among the Great Powers, 1815–1918* (Oxford: Berg, 1990), 40; Paul Ginsborg, *Daniele Manin and the Venetian Revolution of 1848–49* (Cambridge: Cambridge University Press, 1979), 2.

58. Sked, *The Decline and Fall of the Habsburg Empire*, 93–94.

59. Macartney, *The Habsburg Empire*, 377.

60. For an argument that the conservatives within the court were often at odds in their efforts to preserve the monarchy, see Sked, *The Decline and Fall of the Habsburg Empire*, 127–136.

61. Mike Rapport, *1848: Year of Revolution* (New York: Basic, 2009), 313.

62. Bled, *Franz Joseph*, 70; Steven Beller, *Francis Joseph* (London: Longman, 1996), 49. See also Joseph Redlich, *Emperor Francis Joseph of Austria: A Biography* (London: Macmillan, 1929), 47; Bridge, *The Habsburg Monarchy Among the Great Powers*, 8, 13; Andràs Gerö, *Emperor Francis Joseph, King of the Hungarians* (Boulder: Eastern European Monographs, 2001), 51.

63. Schwarzenberg and Francis Joseph may have disagreed about whether the empire should become a constitutional monarchy, as many liberals in Vienna demanded. While Francis Joseph believed that a constitution was "an infringement on the ruler's God-given duties to rule as his conscience saw fit," the "evidence suggests that Schwarzenberg was by no means a convinced absolutist and might well have been prepared to work with an elected parliament." However, they were in perfect agreement regarding imperial policy toward Hungary. Beller, *Francis Joseph*, 54; Sked, *The Decline and Fall of the Habsburg Empire*, 144. For discussions of Francis Joseph's absolutism, see Bled, *Franz Joseph*, 38–40, 51; Beller, *Francis Joseph*, 2; Gerö, *Emperor Francis Joseph, King of the Hungarians*, 17; John Van der Kiste, *Emperor Francis Joseph: Life, Death and the Fall of the Habsburg Empire* (Phoenix Mill: Sutton, 2005), 22. For the debate on Schwarzenberg's attitude toward constitutionalism, see Adolf Schwarzenberg, *Prince Felix zu Schwarzenberg: Prime Minister of Austria, 1848–1852* (New York: Columbia University

Press, 1946), 36; Sked, *The Decline and Fall of the Habsburg Empire*, 144–152; Bled, *Franz Joseph*, 47, 54; James J. Sheehan, *German History, 1770–1866* (Oxford: Oxford University Press, 1993), 701; J. A. S. Grenville, *Europe Reshaped, 1848–1878*, 2nd ed. (Oxford: Wiley-Blackwell, 2000), 130–131.

64. Bled, *Franz Joseph*, 46; Kenneth W. Rock, "Felix Schwarzenberg: Military Diplomat," *Austrian History Yearbook* 11 (1975): 94. See also Schwarzenberg, *Prince Felix zu Schwarzenberg*, 30, 33; Kenneth W. Rock, "Reply," *Austrian History Yearbook* 11 (1975): 106; Gunther E. Rothenberg, *The Army of Francis Joseph* (West Lafayette: Purdue University Press, 1976), 31; Sked, *The Decline and Fall of the Habsburg Empire*, 142–143; Bridge, *The Habsburg Monarchy Among the Great Powers*, 43; Sheehan, *German History*, 701; Roger Price, "'The Holy Struggle Against Anarchy': The Development of Counter-revolution in 1848," in *Europe in 1848: Revolution and Reform*, ed. Dieter Dowe et al., trans. David Higgins (New York: Berghahn, 2001), 45; Gerö, *Emperor Francis Joseph, King of the Hungarians*, 62; Robert Bideleux and Ian Jeffries, *A History of Eastern Europe: Crisis and Change*, 2nd ed. (New York: Routledge, 2007), 234.

65. Rothenberg, *The Army of Francis Joseph*, 33. See also Redlich, *Emperor Francis Joseph of Austria*, 54; Anatol Murad, *Franz Joseph I of Austria and His Empire* (New York: Twayne, 1968), 37; Rock, "Felix Schwarzenberg," 88.

66. Schwarzenberg, *Prince Felix zu Schwarzenberg*, 26.

67. Ibid., 59.

68. Kenneth W. Rock, "Schwarzenberg Versus Nicholas I, Round One: The Negotiation of the Habsburg–Romanov Alliance Against Hungary in 1849,"*Austrian History Yearbook* 6 (1970): 115.

69. Schwarzenberg, *Prince Felix zu Schwarzenberg*, 25.

70. Rock, "Schwarzenberg Versus Nicholas I," 117.

71. Ibid.

72. Bled, *Franz Joseph*, 57.

73. Geoffrey Wawro, "The Habsburg Flucht nach vorne in 1866: Domestic Political Origins of the Austro–Prussian War," *International History Review* 17, no. 2 (May 1995): 222.

74. Ibid., 242.

75. Beller, *Francis Joseph*, 35.

76. Ibid.

77. Macartney, *The Habsburg Empire*, 257; Ginsborg, *Daniele Manin and the Venetian Revolution of 1848–49*, 3. The primary problem was not the empire's overall resources; the problem was the state's inability to access to those resources. Although it lagged far behind the other great powers, namely Britain, the Habsburg empire experienced slow but steady economic growth in the three decades before the Hungarian revolution. Sked, *The Decline and Fall of the Habsburg Empire*, 68–69.

78. Macartney, *The Habsburg Empire*, 203.

79. Beller, *Francis Joseph*, 35. See also David Laven, *Venice and Venetia Under the Habsburgs, 1815–1835* (Oxford: Oxford University Press, 2002), 222.

80. Macartney, *The Habsburg Empire*, 258; Sked, *The Decline and Fall of the Habsburg Empire*, 74.

81. Sked, *The Decline and Fall of the Habsburg Empire*, 75.

82. Ian W. Roberts, *Nicolas I and the Russian Intervention in Hungary* (New York: St. Martin's, 1991), 77–110.

83. Rock, "Schwarzenberg Versus Nicholas I," 137.

84. Roberts, *Nicolas I and the Russian Intervention in Hungary*, 135.

85. Ibid.

86. Laven, *Venice and Venetia Under the Habsburgs*, 223; Bled, *Franz Joseph*, 35.

87. Bled, *Franz Joseph*, 59.

88. Robert A. Kann, *A History of the Habsburg Empire, 1526–1918* (Berkeley: University of California Press, 1974), 251. The Habsburg offensive in Hungary was also impeded by several strategic blunders made by Windischgrätz in January and February 1849. These errors in judgment were neither necessary nor sufficient for Schwarzenberg's subsequent decision to request foreign intervention. The monarchy's lack of resources, combined with the wider unrest, would have made success against the Hungarians difficult for any commander. Indeed, generals fighting in Transylvania, Croatia, and Galicia all suffered losses to the honvédség during the same period.

89. Dominic Lieven, *Empire: The Russian Empire and Its Rivals* (New Haven: Yale University Press, 2002), 165.

90. Alan Palmer, *Twilight of the Habsburgs: The Life and Times of Emperor Francis Joseph* (New York: Grove, 1994), 58.

91. Bled, *Franz Joseph*, 22–23.

92. Bridge, *The Habsburg Monarchy Among the Great Powers*, 20.

93. Murad, *Franz Joseph I of Austria and His Empire*, 37.

94. Bridge, *The Habsburg Monarchy Among the Great Powers*, 45.

95. Rock, "Felix Schwarzenberg," 92, note 35. Schwarzenberg adeptly played upon Nicholas's worries. He wrote to the tsar's foreign minister, for example: the Hungarians are "adventurers without honor and without country, the scum of all nations, [who] have made their rendezvous in order to establish the triumph of a detestable cause. Opposition to such a triumph is at this time a project worthy of the solicitude of all enlightened governments." He also warned the tsar that thousands of volunteers from Russian-controlled Poland were flooding into Hungary to aid the revolutionaries. Rock, "Felix Schwarzenberg," 91, note 32.

96. Goldfrank, *The Origins of the Crimean War*, 66.

97. Grenville, *Europe Reshaped*, 72–75.

98. Róbert Hermann, "The Summer Campaign," in *The Hungarian Revolution and War of Independence, 1848–1849: A Military History*, ed. Gábor Bona, trans. Nóra Arató (Boulder: Social Science Monographs, 1999), 378.

99. Redlich, *Emperor Francis Joseph of Austria*, 57.

100. Rock, "Schwarzenberg Versus Nicholas I," 136.

101. Redlich, *Emperor Francis Joseph of Austria*, 56–57.

102. Rock, "Schwarzenberg Versus Nicholas I," 139, 114.

103. William H. Stiles, *Austria in 1848–49: Being a History of the Late Political Movements in Vienna, Milan, Venice, and Prague*, vol. 2 (1852; repr., New York: Arno, 1971), 276.

104. *Sendero Luminoso* translates as "The Peruvian Communist Party of the Shining Path of Mariátegui" or simply "Shining Path."

105. Philip Mauceri, "Military Politics and Counter-Insurgency in Peru," *Journal of Interamerican Studies and World Affairs* 33, no. 4 (Winter 1991): 90; Gustavo Gorriti, *The Shining Path: A History of the Millenarian War in Peru*, trans. Robin Kirk (Chapel Hill: University of North Carolina Press, 1999), 78.

106. William A. Hazleton and Sandra Woy-Hazleton, "Terrorism and the Marxist Left: Peru's Struggle Against Sendero Luminoso," *Terrorism* 11 (1988): 480.

107. Deborah Poole and Gerardo Rénique, *Peru: Time of Fear* (London: Latin American Bureau, 1992), 5.

108. A state of emergency was declared in Ayachuco and the neighboring provinces of Apurimac and Huancavelica, and political–military commands were installed in each emergency zone to coordinate and implement military policy.

109. Mauceri, "Military Politics and Counter-Insurgency in Peru," 91.

110. Raúl P. Saba, *Political Development and Democracy in Peru: Continuity in Change and Crisis* (Boulder: Westview, 1987), 75.

111. Peter F. Klarén, *Peru: Society and Nationhood in the Andes* (Oxford: Oxford University Press, 2000), 382.

112. Francisco Durand, *Business and Politics in Peru: The State and the National Bourgeoisie* (Boulder: Westview, 1994), 114.

113. David Scott Palmer, "The Changing Political Economy of Peru Under Military and Civilian Rule," *Inter-American Economic Affairs* 37, no. 4 (Spring 1984): 57.

114. Mauceri, "Military Politics and Counter-Insurgency in Peru," 103.

115. Carol Graham, *Peru's APRA: Parties, Politics, and the Elusive Quest for Democracy* (Boulder: Lynne Rienner, 1992), 156.

116. Hazleton and Woy-Hazleton, "Terrorism and the Marxist Left," 485.

117. Mauceri, "Military Politics and Counter-Insurgency in Peru," 97.

118. John Crabtree, *Peru Under García: An Opportunity Lost* (Pittsburgh: Pittsburgh University Press, 1992), 111.

119. Maxwell A. Cameron, *Democracy and Authoritarianism in Peru: Political Coalitions and Social Change* (New York: St. Martin's, 1994), 44.

120. James F. Rochlin, *Vanguard Revolutionaries in Latin America: Peru, Colombia, Mexico* (Boulder: Lynne Rienner, 2003), 39. Of course, many peasants refused to aid the government because they feared Sendero retribution. The Senderistas were known to execute as imperialist collaborators peasants suspected of cooperating with the state. Ton De Wit and Vera Gianotten, "The Center's Multiple Failures," in *The Shining Path of Peru*, ed. David Scott Palmer, 2nd ed. (New York: St. Martin's, 1994), 67.

121. See Riordan Roett, "Peru: The Message from García," *Foreign Affairs* 64, no. 2 (Winter 1985): 277–279.

122. Graham, *Peru's APRA*, 210.

123. Carol Graham, "Peru's APRA Party in Power: Impossible Revolution, Relinquished Reform," *Journal of Interamerican Studies and World Affairs* 32, no. 3 (Autumn 1990): 110. Italics in the original.

124. Ibid., 106.

125. Enrique Obando, "Civil–Military Relations in Peru, 1980–1996: How to Control and Coopt the Military (and the Consequences of Doing So)," in *Shining and Other Paths: War and Society in Peru, 1980–1995*, ed. Steve J. Stern (Durham: Duke University Press, 1998), 389.

126. See Roett, "Peru: The Message from García," 282.

127. Daniel M. Masterson, *Militarism and Politics in Latin America: Peru from Sánchez Cerro to Sendero Luminoso* (Westport: Greenwood, 1991), 270.

128. Stefanie Mann, *Peru's Relations with Pacific Asia: Democracy and Foreign Policy Under Alan García, Alberto Fujimori, and Alejandro Toledo* (Berlin: Lit Verlag, 2006), 119.

129. Rubén Berríos, "Peru: Managing Foreign Policy Amid Political and Economic Crisis," in *Latin American and Caribbean Foreign Policy,* ed. Frank O. Mora and Jeanne A. K. Hey (Lanham: Rowman & Littlefield, 2003), 212.

130. Cynthia McClintock and Fabián Vallas, *The United States and Peru: Cooperation at a Cost* (London: Routledge, 2003), 34.

131. Ronald Bruce St. John, *The Foreign Policy of Peru* (Boulder: Lynne Rienner, 1992), 211.

132. John Sheahan, *Searching for a Better Society: The Peruvian Economy from 1950* (University Park: Pennsylvania State University Press, 1999), 140–141.

133. Philip Mauceri, *State Under Siege: Development and Policy Making in Peru* (Boulder: Westview, 1996), 70.

134. Klarén, *Peru,* 385, 389.

135. Crabtree, *Peru Under García,* 62. For example, Mauceri writes that under García, it "was common knowledge among Lima businessmen that no one had ever been sent to prison for tax evasion and while the state had a right to shut down businesses for tax evasion, no major businesses had ever been affected." See *State Under Siege,* 70.

136. Crabtree, *Peru Under García,* 8.

137. See Graham, *Peru's APRA,* 105; Klarén, *Peru,* 385–386.

138. Crabtree, *Peru Under García,* 61.

139. Ibid., 32–33.

140. Crabtree, *Peru Under García,* 61. See also Mauceri, "Military Politics and Counter-Insurgency in Peru," 95; David T. Mason, *Caught in the Crossfire: Revolution, Repression and the Rational Peasant* (Lanham: Rowman & Littlefield, 2004), 254–255.

141. Crabtree, *Peru Under García,* 213.

142. Poole and Rénique, *Peru,* 8.

143. Mauceri, *State Under Siege,* 139.

144. Crabtree, *Peru Under García,* 205.

145. Sewall H. Menzel, *Fire in the Andes: U.S. Foreign Policy and Cocaine Politics in Bolivia and Peru* (Lanham: University Press of America, 1996), 125.

146. Crabtree, *Peru Under García*, 198. It is revealing to note that some improvement in the state's extractive capacity under García's successor, Alberto Fujimori, enhanced the government's ability to combat Sendero. Tax reform was at the top of Fujimori's policy agenda when he assumed the presidency; it was his intention to "resurrect and reconstruct the extractive capabilities of the state," which he did with some success. By increasing the state's resources, Fujimori hoped to enable the government to "eliminate the threat of SL [Sendero Luminoso] guerillas and the narcotraffickers at will." Thus, after ensuring the state's access to revenues, Fujimori focused on improving the military's preparedness and equipping the paramilitaries with the materiel to fight Sendero, making them a more-potent force—indeed key players—in the counterinsurgency. Carol Wise, "State Policy and Social Conflict in Peru," in *The Peruvian Labyrinth: Polity, Society, Economy*, ed. Maxwell A. Cameron and Philip Mauceri (University Park: Pennsylvania State University Press, 1997), 98–99; Menzel, *Fire in the Andes*, 208. See also Mauceri, *State Under Siege*, 145.

147. Klarén, *Peru*, 386.

148. Mauceri, "Military Politics and Counter-Insurgency in Peru," 100. See also Klarén, *Peru*, 407.

149. Mauceri, *State Under Siege*, 139.

150. Mauceri, "Military Politics and Counter-Insurgency in Peru," 103. Italics in the original.

151. Miguel Angel Centeno, *Blood and Debt: War and the Nation-State in Latin America* (University Park: Pennsylvania State University Press, 2002), 85.

152. David R. Mares, "Deterrence Bargaining in the Ecuador–Peru Enduring Rivalry: Designing Strategies Around Military Weakness," *Security Studies* 6, no. 2 (Winter 1996/1997): 104.

153. David R. Mares, *Violent Peace: Militarized Interstate Bargaining in Latin America* (New York: Columbia University Press, 2001), 174.

154. A low extractive capacity was partly responsible for this decline. During his presidency, García also sought to rein in defense spending in an effort to assert civilian control over the military. See James D. Rudolph, *Peru: The Evolution of a Crisis* (New York: Praeger, 1992), 118–120.

155. Mason, *Caught in the Crossfire*, 232.

156. Rochlin, *Vanguard Revolutionaries*, 56.

157. Crabtree, *Peru Under García*, 99.

158. After all, "Not One Step Back" would become its national slogan regarding the dispute. Mares, "Deterrence Bargaining," 118. Mares points out that Ecuador did not choose to dispute until 1991 a Peruvian outpost that was built in contested territory in 1987, suggesting that it was only in the early 1990s that it saw itself as having the advantage in a conflict with Peru. However, it is hard to imagine that Ecuador would have failed to capitalize on war earlier if Peru was the aggressor and international opinion was in its favor.

159. Brazil and Argentina were the only two countries in Latin America that had greater military capabilities than Peru's. See Centeno, *Blood and Debt*, 95. In 1986

Bolivia suspected that Sendero guerrillas might have been infiltrating from Peru. In response, it moved troops to the border and engaged in counterinsurgency exercises with the United States in order to prepare for possible action against Senderistas in Bolivia. However, there is no evidence that Bolivia ever considered offering or even could have provided aid to Peru. See "Bolivian Minister on Threat from Peruvian Guerrillas," *BBC Monitoring Service,* January 15, 1987; "US and Bolivian Troops Hold Joint Exercises," *Christian Science Monitor,* May 13, 1987, 2.

160. St. John, *The Foreign Policy of Peru,* 207.

161. Furthermore, Argentina would have jeopardized efforts to improve its relationship with Brazil and Chile. In 1985, for example, Argentina and Peru signed a pact settling the Beagle Channel dispute.

162. Kenneth Roberts and Mark Peceny, "Human Rights and United States Policy Toward Peru," in *The Peruvian Labyrinth: Polity, Society, Economy,* ed. Maxwell A. Cameron and Philip Mauceri, 179–192 (College Park: Pennsylvania State University Press, 1997), 213.

163. Mauceri, "Military Politics and Counter-Insurgency in Peru," 104.

164. Roberts and Peceny, "Human Rights and United States Policy Toward Peru," 213.

165. Mauceri, *State Under Siege,* 144.

166. Cynthia McClintock, "The Decimation of Peru's Sendero Luminoso," in *Comparative Peace Processes in Latin America,* ed. Cynthia J. Arnson (Stanford: Stanford University Press, 1999), 236.

167. Mauceri, "Military Politics and Counter-Insurgency in Peru," 102.

168. Crabtree, *Peru Under García,* 205.

169. Ibid., 185.

Chapter 7

1. Robert I. Rotberg and Theodore K. Rabb, *The Origin and Prevention of Major Wars* (Cambridge: Cambridge University Press, 1988), 94. Historians question the authenticity of Plehv's remark, which reportedly was made during the first months of the Russo–Japanese war. Geoffrey Blainey notes that this comment was recorded only in the diary of Plehv's political rival, who sought to blame the interior minister for the outbreak of the war. That said, Sidney Harcave notes that other members of the government also wrote of Plehv's belief that the war would distract the public and lessen its desire for political reform. See Geoffrey Blainey, *The Causes of War* (New York: Free Press, 1973), 76; Sidney Harcave, *Count Sergei Witte and the Twilight of Imperial Russia: A Biography* (Armonk: M. E. Sharpe, 2004), 109.

2. D. Scott Bennett and Timothy Nordstrom, "Foreign Policy Substitutability and Internal Economic Problems in Enduring Rivalries," *Journal of Conflict Resolution* 44, no. 1 (February 2000): 38, note 4. Ahmer Tarar likewise argues that "when diversionary behavior is about demonstrating competence rather than creating a short-term 'rally round the flag' effect, a leader has incentives to use force against a challenging

target." While this may be true of princely states, a spectacle against a "challenging target" is not an option for pauper states. "Diversionary Incentives and the Bargaining Approach to War," *International Studies Quarterly* 50, no. 1 (March 2006): 169.

3. Many governments may view turmoil in a neighboring country as an opportunity to exploit, choosing to demand substantial recompense for aiding the government. Indeed, nearby countries may be dangerous rivals rather than good neighbors; they may launch what Geoffrey Blainey calls a "death-watch war," aggravating an internal struggle to weaken a neighboring state before invading. See *The Causes of War*, 68–86.

4. The 21-point Polity scale of regime type is often converted to a three-part categorization of "nondemocracies" (–10 to –7), "mixed or transitional regimes" (–6 to 6), and "democracies" (7 to 10). Austria had a Polity score of –7 in 1849, the United States had a score of 8 in 1857, Argentina had a score of –8 in 1982, and Peru had a score of 7 in 1988. Polity data do not cover the French prerevolutionary period. See Monty G. Marshall and Keith Jaggers, *Polity IV Project: Political Regime Characteristics and Transitions, 1800–2002* (College Park: Center for International Development and Conflict Management, 2002).

5. Richard Ned Lebow, "Miscalculation in the South Atlantic: The Origins of the Falklands War," in *Psychology & Deterrence*, ed. Robert Jervis, Richard Ned Lebow, and Janice Gross Stein (Baltimore: Johns Hopkins University Press, 1985), 114.

6. "Argentina: Nationalists All," *Economist*, April 17, 1982, 25.

7. Lebow, "Miscalculation in the South Atlantic," 114.

8. "The President and Mormons," *New York Daily Times*, June 4, 1857, 4.

9. Lebow, "Miscalculation in the South Atlantic," 101.

10. Edward H. Carr, *What Is History?* (New York: Random House, 1961), 167.

Bibliography

Adams, George Rollie. *General William S. Harney: Prince of Dragoons*. Lincoln: University of Nebraska Press, 2006.

Arceneaux, Craig L. *Bounded Missions: Military Regimes and Democratization in the Southern Cone and Brazil*. University Park: Pennsylvania State University Press, 2001.

"Argentina: An Odd Alliance." *Economist*, January 30, 1982.

"Argentina: Nationalists All." *Economist*, April 17, 1982.

"Argentina Sticks to Its Guns But Pins Hopes on Diplomacy." *Latin America Weekly Report*, April 23, 1982.

Arian, Asher, and Sigalit Olzaeker. "Political and Economic Interactions with National Security Opinion: The Gulf War Period in Israel." *Journal of Conflict Resolution* 43, no. 1 (February 1999): 58–77.

Arquilla, John, and María Moyano Rasmussen. "The Origins of the South Atlantic War." *Journal of Latin American Studies* 33, no. 4 (November 2001): 739–775.

Arrington, Leonard J. *Brigham Young: American Moses*. Urbana: University of Illinois Press, 1986.

Arrington, Leonard J., and Davis Bitton. *The Mormon Experience: A History of the Latter-Day Saints*. Urbana: University of Illinois Press, 1992.

Ashworth, John. *The Coming of the Civil War, 1850–1861*. Vol. 2 of *Slavery, Capitalism, and Politics in the Antebellum Republic*. Cambridge: Cambridge University Press, 2008.

Assuras, Thalia. "Reaction to President Clinton's Decision to Order U.S. Air Strikes on Terrorist Facilities in Sudan and Afghanistan." *CBS This Morning*, August 21, 1998.

Azar, Edward E. *The Management of Protracted Social Conflict: Theory and Cases.* Brookfield: Gower, 1990.

Bagley, Will. *Blood of the Prophets: Brigham Young and the Massacre at Mountain Meadows.* Norman: University of Oklahoma Press, 2002.

Baker, Jean H. *James Buchanan.* New York: Times Books, 2004.

Baker, William D., and John R. Oneal. "Patriotism or Opinion Leadership? The Nature and Origins of the 'Rally 'Round the Flag' Effect." *Journal of Conflict Resolution* 45, no. 5 (October 2001): 661–687.

Balch-Lindsay, Dylan, and Andrew J. Enterline. "Killing Time: The World Politics of Civil War Duration, 1820–1992." *International Studies Quarterly* 44, no. 4 (December 2000): 615–642.

Balch-Lindsay, Dylan, Andrew J. Enterline, and Kyle A. Joyce. "Third-Party Intervention and the Civil War Process." *Journal of Peace Research* 45, no. 3 (May 2008): 345–363.

Baldwin, David A. "Success and Failure in Foreign Policy." *Annual Review of Political Science* 3 (June 2000): 167–182.

Bancroft, Hubert Howe. *History of Utah, 1540–1886.* San Francisco: History Company, 1890.

Banks, Arthur S. *Cross-National Time-Series Data Archive, 1815–2003.* Binghamton: Databanks International, 2005.

Beck, Nathaniel, Jonathan N. Katz, and Richard Tucker. "Taking Time Seriously: Time-Series–Cross-Section Analysis with a Binary Dependent Variable." *American Journal of Political Science* 42, no. 4 (October 1998): 1260–1288.

Beller, Steven. *Francis Joseph.* London: Longman, 1996.

Bender, Thomas. *A Nation Among Nations: America's Place in World History.* New York: Hill and Wang, 2006.

Bennett, Bruce W. *Uncertainties in the North Korean Nuclear Threat.* Santa Monica: RAND, 2010. Accessed January 3, 2011. www.rand.org/pubs/documented_brief ings/2010/RAND_DB589.pdf.

Bennett, D. Scott, and Timothy Nordstrom. "Foreign Policy Substitutability and Internal Economic Problems in Enduring Rivalries." *Journal of Conflict Resolution* 44, no. 1 (February 2000): 33–61.

Bensel, Richard Franklin. *Yankee Leviathan: The Origins of Central State Authority in America, 1859–1877.* Cambridge: Cambridge University Press, 1990.

Berríos, Rubén. "Peru: Managing Foreign Policy Amid Political and Economic Crisis." In *Latin American and Caribbean Foreign Policy,* edited by Frank O. Mora and Jeanne A. K. Hey, 206–227. Lanham: Rowman & Littlefield, 2003.

Bideleux, Robert, and Ian Jeffries. *A History of Eastern Europe: Crisis and Change.* 2nd ed. New York: Routledge, 2007.

Bigler, David L. *Forgotten Kingdom: The Mormon Theocracy in the American West, 1847–1896.* Logan: Utah State University Press, 1998.

Bigler, David L., and Will Bagley, eds. *Innocent Blood: Essential Narratives of the Mountain Meadows Massacre.* Norman: Arthur H. Clark, 2008.

Binder, Frederick Moore. *James Buchanan and the American Empire*. Selinsgrove: Susquehanna University Press, 1994.

Birkner, Michael J. "Introduction: Getting to Know James Buchanan, Again." In *James Buchanan and the Political Crisis of the 1850s*, edited by Michael J. Birkner, 17–36. Selinsgrove: Susquehanna University Press, 1996.

Blainey, Geoffrey. *The Causes of War*. New York: Free Press, 1973.

Blanning, T. C. W. *The Culture of Power and the Power of Culture: Old Regime Europe, 1660–1789*. Oxford: Oxford University Press, 2002.

Bled, Jean-Paul. *Franz Joseph*. Oxford: Blackwell, 1992.

"Bolivian Minister on Threat from Peruvian Guerrillas." *BBC Monitoring Service*, January 15, 1987.

Bostdorff, Denise M. *The Presidency and the Rhetoric of Foreign Crisis*. Columbia: University of South Carolina Press, 1994.

Brambor, Thomas, William Roberts Clark, and Matt Golder. "Understanding Interaction Models: Improving Empirical Analyses." *Political Analysis* 14, no. 1 (Winter 2006): 63–82.

Bratton, Michael, and Nicolas Van de Walle. "Popular Protest and Political Reform in Africa." *Comparative Politics* 24, no. 4 (July 1992): 419–442.

Bremer, Stuart A. "Dangerous Dyads: Conditions Affecting the Likelihood of Interstate War, 1816–1965." *Journal of Conflict Resolution* 36, no. 2 (June 1992): 309–341.

Bridge, F. R. *The Habsburg Monarchy Among the Great Powers, 1815–1918*. Oxford: Berg, 1990.

Brinkley, Douglas. *American Heritage History of the United States*. New York: Viking, 1998.

Brody, Richard. *Assessing the President: The Media, Elite Opinion, and Public Support*. Stanford: Stanford University Press, 1991.

Brown, Seyom. *The Faces of Power: Constancy and Change in United States Foreign Policy from Truman to Clinton*. New York: Columbia University Press, 1994.

Browne, Albert G., Jr. "The Utah Expedition." *Atlantic Monthly* 3, no. 17 (March 1859): 361–375.

Brownlee, W. Elliot. *Federal Taxation in America: A Short History*. Washington, DC: Woodrow Wilson Center, 1996.

Brulé, David. "Congressional Opposition, the Economy, and U.S. Dispute Initiation, 1946–2000." *Journal of Conflict Resolution* 50, no. 4 (August 2006): 463–483.

Bruni, Frank. "U.S. Fury on 2 Continents: Voices; Wagging Tongues in 'Incredibly Cynical Times.'" *New York Times*, August 21, 1998.

Buchanan, James. *Mr. Buchanan's Administration on the Eve of the Rebellion*. New York: Appleton-Century, 1866.

———. *The Works of James Buchanan: Comprising His Speeches, State Papers, and Private Correspondence, 1856–1860*. Vol. 10. Edited by John Bassett Moore. Philadelphia: Lippincott, 1910.

Bueno de Mesquita, Bruce. *The War Trap*. New Haven: Yale University Press, 1981.

Bueno de Mesquita, Bruce, James D. Morrow, Randolph M. Siverson, and Alastair
   Smith. "Political Survival and International Conflict." In *War in a Changing
   World*, edited by Zeev Maoz and Azar Gat, 183–207. Ann Arbor: University of
   Michigan Press, 2001.

Bueno de Mesquita, Bruce, and Randolph M. Siverson. "War and the Survival of
   Political Leaders: A Comparative Study of Regime Types and Political Accountability." *American Political Science Review* 89, no. 4 (December 1995): 841–855.

Bueno de Mesquita, Bruce, Alastair Smith, Randolph M. Siverson, and James D.
   Morrow. *The Logic of Political Survival.* Cambridge: MIT Press, 2003.

Burns, Jimmy. *The Land That Lost Its Heroes: The Falklands, the Post-War, and Alfonsin.* London: Bloomsbury, 1987.

Bushman, Richard Lyman, and Jed Woodworth. *Joseph Smith: Rough Stone Rolling.*
   New York: Vintage, 2007.

Bussmann, Margit, and Gerald Schneider. "When Globalization Discontent Turns
   Violent: Foreign Economic Liberalization and Internal War." *International Studies Quarterly* 51, no. 1 (March 2007): 79–97.

Cameron, Maxwell A. *Democracy and Authoritarianism in Peru: Political Coalitions
   and Social Change.* New York: St. Martin's, 1994.

Cardoso, Oscar Raul, Ricardo Kirschbaum, and Eduardo van der Kooy. *Falklands:
   The Secret Plot.* Translated by Bernard Ethel. Surrey: Preston Editions, 1987.

Carey, Sabine C. "The Dynamic Relationship Between Protest and Repression." *Political Research Quarterly* 59, no. 1 (March 2006): 1–11.

———. *Protest, Repression and Political Regimes: An Empirical Analysis of Latin America and Sub-Saharan Africa.* London: Routledge, 2009.

Carr, Edward H. *What Is History?* New York: Random House, 1961.

Carter, David B., and Curtis S. Signorino. "Back to the Future: Modeling Time
   Dependence in Binary Data." *Political Analysis* 18, no. 3 (Summer 2010): 271–292.

Centeno, Miguel Angel. *Blood and Debt: War and the Nation-State in Latin America.*
   University Park: Pennsylvania State University Press, 2002.

Chapman, Terrence L., and Dan Reiter. "The United Nations Security Council and
   the Rally 'Round the Flag Effect." *Journal of Conflict Resolution* 48, no. 6 (December 2004): 886–909.

Charlton, Michael. *The Little Platoon: Diplomacy and the Falklands Dispute.* London:
   Blackwell, 1989.

Chatterjee, Samprit, Bertram Price, and Ali S. Hadi. *Regression Analysis by Example.*
   3rd ed. New York: Wiley, 1999.

Chiozza, Giacomo, and Hein E. Goemans. "International Conflict and the Tenure of
   Leaders: Is War Still *Ex Post* Inefficient?" *American Journal of Political Science* 48,
   no. 3 (July 2004): 604–619.

———. "Peace Through Insecurity: Tenure and International Conflict." *Journal of
   Conflict Resolution* 47, no. 4 (August 2003): 443–467.

Christensen, Thomas. *Useful Adversaries: Grand Strategy, Domestic Mobilization, and
   Sino-American Conflict, 1947–1958.* Princeton: Princeton University Press, 1996.

Churchill, Winston. *A Roving Commission: My Early Life*. New York: Charles Scribner's Sons, 1930.

Cioffi-Revilla, Claudio, and Harvey Starr. "Opportunity, Willingness and Political Uncertainty: Theoretical Foundations of Politics." *Journal of Theoretical Politics* 7, no. 4 (October 1995): 447–476.

Clark, David H. "Can Strategic Interaction Divert Diversionary Behavior? A Model of U.S. Conflict Propensity." *Journal of Politics* 65, no. 4 (November 2003): 1013–1039.

———. "Trading Butter for Guns: Domestic Imperatives for Foreign Policy Substitution." *Journal of Conflict Resolution* 45, no. 5 (October 2001): 636–660.

Clark, David H., Timothy Nordstrom, and William Reed. "Substitution Is in the Variance: Resources and Foreign Policy Choice." *American Journal of Political Science* 52, no. 4 (October 2008) 763–773.

Clark, David H., and William Reed. "The Strategic Sources of Foreign Policy Substitution." *American Journal of Political Science* 49, no. 3 (July 2005): 609–624.

Clark, David H., and Patrick M. Regan. "Opportunities to Fight: A Statistical Technique for Modeling Unobservable Phenomena." *Journal of Conflict Resolution* 47, no. 1 (February 2003): 94–115.

Clifford, Clark. Clifford Papers. Accessed on March 23, 2010. www.trumanlibrary.org/hstpaper/clifford.htm.

Clines, Francis X. "White House Tactics Could Be Costly Next Year." *New York Times*, October 30, 1983.

Coakley, Robert W. *The Role of the Federal Military Forces in Domestic Disorders, 1789–1878*. Washington, DC: Center of Military History, United States Army, 1988.

Cobban, Alfred. *A History of Modern France*. New York: George Braziller, 1965.

Cochran, John, and Forrest Sawyer. "Strikes Planned Since Last Wednesday." *World News Tonight with Peter Jennings*, August 20, 1998.

Coleman, Elizabeth Tyler. *Priscilla Cooper Tyler and the American Scene, 1816–1889*. Tuscaloosa: University of Alabama Press, 2006.

Collier, Paul, Anke Hoeffler, and Måns Söderbom. "On the Duration of Civil War." *Journal of Peace Research* 41, no. 3 (May 2004): 253–273.

Collins, James B. *The State in Early Modern France*. Cambridge: Cambridge University Press, 1995.

Cooper, William J., Jr., and Thomas E. Terrill. *The American South: A History*. Vol. 1. 4th ed. Lanham: Rowman & Littlefield, 2009.

Corner, Paul, and Giovanna Procacci. "The Italian Experience of 'Total' Mobilization, 1915–1920." In *State, Society, and Mobilization in Europe During the First World War*, edited by John Horne, 223–241. Cambridge: Cambridge University Press, 1997.

Corradi, Juan E. *The Fitful Republic: Economy, Society, and Politics in Argentina*. Boulder: Westview, 1985.

Costa Méndez, Nicanor. "Beyond Deterrence: The Malvinas–Falklands Case." *Journal of Social Issues* 43, no. 4 (Winter 1987): 119–122.

Cox, Dan G., and A. Cooper Drury. "Democratic Sanctions: Connecting the Democratic Peace and Economic Sanctions." *Journal of Peace Research* 43, no. 6 (November 2006): 709–722.

Crabtree, John. *Peru Under García: An Opportunity Lost.* Pittsburgh: University of Pittsburgh Press, 1992.

Craig, Gordon. "History as a Humanistic Discipline." In *Historical Literacy: The Case for History in American Education,* edited by Paul A. Gagnon, 119–137. New York: Macmillan, 1989.

Cramer, Jane Kellett. "'Just Cause' or Just Politics? U.S. Panama Invasion and Standardizing Qualitative Tests for Diversionary War." *Armed Forces & Society* 32, no. 2 (January 2006): 178–201.

Crandall, Russell. *Gunboat Diplomacy: U.S. Interventions in the Dominican Republic, Grenada, Panama.* Lanham: Rowman & Littlefield, 2006.

Cresswell, Stephen. *Mormons and Cowboys, Moonshiners and Klansmen: Federal Law Enforcement in the South and West, 1870–1893.* Tuscaloosa: University of Alabama Press, 2002.

Curtis, George Ticknor. *Life of James Buchanan: Fifteenth President of the United States.* Vol. 2. New York: Harper, 1883.

Cutrer, Thomas W. *Ben McCulloch and the Frontier Military Tradition.* Chapel Hill: University of North Carolina Press, 1993.

Dabat, Alejandro, and Luis Lorenzano. *Argentina: The Malvinas and the End of Military Rule.* Translated by Ralph Johnstone. London: Verso, 1984.

Dassel, Kurt. "Civilians, Soldiers, and Strife: Domestic Sources of International Aggression." *International Security* 23, no. 1 (Summer 1998): 107–140.

Dassel, Kurt, and Eric Reinhardt. "Domestic Strife and the Initiation of Violence at Home and Abroad." *American Journal of Political Science* 43, no. 1 (January 1999): 56–85.

Davenport, Christian. *State Repression and the Domestic Democratic Peace.* Cambridge: Cambridge University Press, 2007.

———. "State Repression and Political Order." *Annual Review of Political Science* 10 (June 2007): 1–23.

———. "The Weight of the Past: Exploring Lagged Determinants of Political Repression." *Political Research Quarterly* 49, no. 2 (June 1996): 377–403.

Davies, Graeme A. M. "Domestic Strife and the Initiation of International Conflicts: A Directed Dyad Analysis, 1950–1992." *Journal of Conflict Resolution* 46, no. 5 (October 2002): 676–692.

DeRouen, Karl, Jr. "The Indirect Link: Politics, the Economy, and the Use of Force." *Journal of Conflict Resolution* 39, no. 4 (December 1995): 671–695.

DeRouen, Karl, Jr., and Shaun Goldfinch. "The Democratic Peace and Substitutability During International Crises: Institutionalized Democracy and Foreign Policy Choices." In *Institutions and Market Economies: The Political Economy of Growth and Development,* edited by William R. Garside, 278–304. New York: Palgrave Macmillan, 2007.

DeRouen, Karl, Jr., and Jeffrey Peake. "The Dynamics of Diversion: The Domestic Implications of Presidential Use of Force." *International Interactions* 28, no. 2 (2002): 191–221.

de Tocqueville, Alexis. *The Old Regime and the Revolution.* Translated by John Bonner. New York: Harper, 1876.

de Wit, Ton, and Vera Gianotten. "The Center's Multiple Failures." In *The Shining Path of Peru,* edited by David Scott Palmer, 63–75. 2nd ed. New York: St. Martin's, 1994.

Dhue, Laurie, and Cynthia Tornquist. "'Wag the Dog' Rentals Skyrocket." *CNN Sunday,* August 23, 1998.

Diehl, Paul F. "Substitutes or Complements? The Effects of Alliances on Military Spending in Major Power Rivalries." *International Interactions* 19, no. 3 (1994): 159–176.

Diprizio, Robert C. *Armed Humanitarians: U.S. Interventions from Northern Iraq to Kosovo.* Baltimore: Johns Hopkins University Press, 2002.

Divine, Robert A. "The Cold War and the Election of 1948." *Journal of American History* 59, no. 1 (June 1972): 90–110.

Dixon, Jeffrey. "What Causes Civil Wars? Integrating Quantitative Research Findings." *International Studies Review* 11, no. 4 (December 2009): 707–735.

Donaldson, Gary A. *Truman Beats Dewey.* Lexington: University of Kentucky Press, 1998.

Dowd, Maureen. "Basking in Power's Glow: Bush's Year as President." *New York Times,* December 31, 1989.

Doyle, William. *Officers, Nobles and Revolutionaries: Essays on Eighteenth-Century France.* London: Hambledon, 1995.

———. *Origins of the French Revolution.* 3rd ed. Oxford: Oxford University Press, 1999.

Durand, Francisco. *Business and Politics in Peru: The State and the National Bourgeoisie.* Boulder: Westview, 1994.

Eddy, Paul, and Magnus Linklater. *The Falklands War.* London: André Deutsch, 1982.

Egret, Jean. *The French Prerevolution, 1787–1788.* Translated by Wesley D. Camp. Chicago: University of Chicago Press, 1977.

Enterline, Andrew J., and Kristian S. Gleditsch. "Threats, Opportunity, and Force: Repression and Diversion of Domestic Pressure, 1948–1982." *International Interactions* 26, no. 1 (January 2000): 21–53.

Etcheson, Nicole. *Bleeding Kansas: Contested Liberty in the Civil War Era.* Lawrence: University of Kansas Press, 2004.

Evans, R. J. W. "1848–1849 in the Habsburg Monarchy." In *The Revolutions in Europe, 1848–1849: From Reform to Reaction,* edited by R. J. W. Evans and Hartmut Pogge Von Strandmann, 181–206. Oxford: Oxford University Press, 2000.

Faÿ, Bernard. *Louis XVI: Or the End of a World.* Translated by Patrick O'Brien. Chicago: Henry Regnery, 1967.

Fearon, James D., and David D. Laitin. "Ethnicity, Insurgency, and Civil War." *American Political Science Review* 97, no. 1 (February 2003): 75–90.

Feldman, David Lewis. "The United States Role in the Malvinas Crisis, 1982: Misguidance and Misperception in Argentina's Decision to Go to War." *Journal of Interamerican Studies and World Affairs* 27, no. 2 (Summer 1985): 1–22.

Felix, Joël, and Frank Tallett. "The French Experience, 1661–1815." In *The Fiscal-Military State in Eighteenth-Century Europe: Essays in Honour of P. G. M. Dickson,* edited by Christopher Storrs, 147–166. Burlington: Ashgate, 2009.

Feng, Yi, Jacek Kugler, and Paul J. Zak. "The Politics of Fertility and Economic Development." *International Studies Quarterly* 44, no. 4 (December 2000): 667–693.

Fjelde, Hanne, and Indra de Soysa. "Coercion, Co-optation, or Cooperation? State Capacity and the Risk of Civil War, 1961–2004." *Conflict Management and Peace Science* 26, no. 1 (February 2009): 5–25.

Flanders, Robert Bruce. *Nauvoo: Kingdom on the Mississippi.* Urbana: University of Illinois Press, 1975.

"Forces That Galtieri Unleashed." *Latin America Weekly Review,* April 30, 1982.

Fordham, Benjamin. "The Politics of Threat Perception and the Use of Force: A Political Economy Model of U.S. Uses of Force, 1949–1994." *International Studies Quarterly* 42, no. 3 (September 1998): 567–590.

———. "Strategic Conflict Avoidance and the Diversionary Use of Force." *Journal of Politics* 67, no. 1 (February 2005): 132–153.

Francisco, Ronald A. "The Relationship Between Coercion and Protest: An Empirical Evaluation in Three Coercive States." *Journal of Conflict Resolution* 39, no. 2 (June 1995): 263–282.

Franks, Lord. "Falkland Islands Review: Report of a Committee of Privy Counsellors." London: Her Majesty's Stationery Office, January, 1983.

Fravel, Taylor. "The Limits of Diversion: Rethinking Internal and External Conflict." *Security Studies* 19, no. 2 (May 2010): 307–341.

Freedman, Lawrence D. *Britain and the Falklands War.* London: Basil Blackwell, 1988.

———. *The Origins of the Falklands War.* Vol. 1 of *The Official History of the Falklands Campaign.* New York: Routledge, 2005.

———. "Reconsiderations: The War of the Falkland Islands." *Foreign Affairs* 61, no. 1 (Fall 1982): 196–210.

Freedman, Lawrence D., and Virginia Gamba-Stonehouse. *Signals of War: The Falklands Conflict of 1982.* Boston: Faber and Faber, 1990.

Freehling, William W. *Secessionists Triumphant, 1854–1861.* Vol. 2 of *The Road to Disunion.* Oxford: Oxford University Press, 2007.

Frieden, Jeffry A. "Actors and Preferences in International Relations." In *Strategic Choice and International Relations,* edited by David A. Lake and Robert Powell, 39–76. Princeton: Princeton University Press, 1999.

Friedman, Gil, and Harvey Starr. *Agency, Structure and International Politics: From Ontology to Empirical Enquiry.* New York: Routledge, 1997.

Furniss, Norman F. *The Mormon Conflict, 1850–1859.* New Haven: Yale University Press, 1960.

Gallman, James M. *The North Fights the Civil War: The Home Front.* Chicago: I. R. Dee, 1994.

"Galtieri Speaks in La Pampa on Government Goals." *La Nación*, February 13, 1982.

Gamba, Virginia. *The Falklands/Malvinas War: A Model for North–South Crisis Prevention.* Boston: Allen & Unwin, 1987.

Garrett, Mitchell B. *The Estates General of 1789: The Problems of Composition and Organization.* New York: Appleton-Century, 1935.

Gavshon, Arthur, and Desmond Rice. *The Sinking of the Belgrano.* London: Secker and Warburg, 1984.

Geddes, Barbara. "How the Cases You Choose Affect the Answers You Get: Selection Bias in Comparative Politics." *Political Analysis* 2, no. 1 (1990): 131–150.

Gellman, Barton, and Dana Priest. "U.S. Strikes Terrorist-Linked Sites in Afghanistan, Factory in Sudan." *Washington Post*, August 21, 1998.

Gelpi, Christopher. "Democratic Diversions: Governmental Structure and the Externalization of Domestic Conflict." *Journal of Conflict Resolution* 41, no. 2 (April 1997): 255–282.

Gelpi, Christopher, Peter D. Feaver, and Jason Reifler. "Success Matters: Casualty Sensitivity and the War in Iraq." *International Security* 30, no. 3 (Winter 2005/2006): 7–46.

Gent, Stephen E. "Going in When It Counts: Military Intervention and the Outcome of Civil Conflicts." *International Studies Quarterly* 52, no. 4 (December 2008): 713–735.

George, Alexander L. "Case Studies and Theory Development: The Method of Structured, Focused Comparison." In *Diplomacy: New Approaches in History, Theory, and Policy*, edited by Paul Gordon Lauren, 43–68. New York: Free Press, 1979.

Gerö, András. *Emperor Francis Joseph, King of the Hungarians.* Boulder: Eastern European Monographs, 2001.

Gerring, John. *Social Science Methodology: A Criterial Framework.* Cambridge: Cambridge University Press, 2001.

Ghosn, Faten, Glenn Palmer, and Stuart A. Bremer. "The MID3 Data Set, 1993–2001: Procedures, Coding Rules, and Description." *Conflict Management and Peace Science* 21, no. 2 (April 2004): 133–154.

Gibran, Daniel K. *The Falklands War: Britain Versus the Past in the South Atlantic.* Jefferson: McFarland, 1998.

Gill, Jeff. "The Insignificance of Null Hypothesis Significance Testing." *Political Research Quarterly* 52, no. 3 (September 1999): 647–674.

Ginsborg, Paul. *Daniele Manin and the Venetian Revolution of 1848–49.* Cambridge: Cambridge University Press, 1979.

Givens, Terryl L. *The Viper on the Hearth: Mormons, Myths, and the Construction of Heresy.* Oxford: Oxford University Press, 1997.

Goertz, Gary. "The Substantive Importance of Necessary Condition Hypotheses." In *Necessary Conditions: Theory, Methodology, and Applications*, edited by Gary Goertz and Harvey Starr, 65–94. Lanham: Rowman & Littlefield, 2003.

Goertz, Gary, and Harvey Starr. "Introduction: Necessary Condition Logics, Research Design, and Theory." In *Necessary Conditions: Theory, Methodology, and Applications,* edited by Gary Goertz and Harvey Starr, 1–23. Lanham: Rowman & Littlefield, 2003.

Goldfrank, David M. *The Origins of the Crimean War.* London: Longman, 1994.

Goldstone, Jack A. *Revolution and Rebellion in the Early Modern World.* Berkeley: University of California Press, 1991.

Goodrich, Thomas. *War to the Knife: Bleeding Kansas, 1854–1861.* Mechanicsburg: Stackpole, 1998.

Gordon, Sarah Barringer. *The Mormon Question: Polygamy and Constitutional Conflict in Nineteenth-Century America.* Chapel Hill: University of North Carolina Press, 2002.

Gorriti, Gustavo. *The Shining Path: A History of the Millenarian War in Peru.* Translated by Robin Kirk. Chapel Hill: University of North Carolina Press, 1999.

Goubert, Pierre. *The Ancien Régime: French Society, 1600–1750.* Translated by Steve Cox. New York: Harper Torchbooks, 1969.

Gowa, Joanne. "Politics at the Water's Edge: Parties, Votes, and the Use of Force Abroad." *International Organization* 52, no. 2 (Spring 1998): 307–324.

Graham, Carol. *Peru's APRA: Parties, Politics, and the Elusive Quest for Democracy.* Boulder: Lynne Rienner, 1992.

———. "Peru's APRA Party in Power: Impossible Revolution, Relinquished Reform." *Journal of Interamerican Studies and World Affairs* 32, no. 3 (Autumn 1990): 75–115.

Grenville, J. A. S. *Europe Reshaped, 1848–1878.* 2nd ed. Oxford: Wiley-Blackwell, 2000.

Groeling, Tim, and Matthew A. Baum. "Crossing the Water's Edge: Elite Rhetoric, Media Coverage, and the Rally-Round-the-Flag Phenomenon." *Journal of Politics* 70, no. 4 (October 2008): 1065–1085.

Grow, Matthew J. *"Liberty to the Downtrodden": Thomas L. Kane, Romantic Reformer.* New Haven: Yale University Press, 2009.

Guest, Iain. *Behind the Disappearances: Argentina's Dirty War Against Human Rights and the United Nations.* Philadelphia: University of Pennsylvania Press, 1990.

Gupta, Dipak K., Harinder Singh, and Tom Sprague. "Government Coercion of Dissidents: Deterrence or Provocation?" *Journal of Conflict Resolution* 37, no. 2 (June 1993): 301–339.

Haas, Michael. "Social Change and National Aggressiveness, 1900–1960." In *Quantitative International Politics: Insights and Evidence,* edited by J. David Singer, 215–244. New York: Free Press, 1968.

Haefele, Mark. "John F. Kennedy, USIA, and World Public Opinion." *Diplomatic History* 25, no. 1 (Winter 2001): 63–84.

Hafen, Le Roy Reuben, and Ann Woodbury Hafen. *Mormon Resistance: A Documentary Account of the Utah Expedition, 1857–1858.* Lincoln: University of Nebraska Press, 2005.

Haig, Alexander M., Jr. *Caveat: Realism, Reagan, and Foreign Policy.* New York: Macmillan, 1984.

Hannity, Sean, and Alan Colmes. "U.S. Bombings of Afghanistan and Sudan." *Fox Hannity & Colmes,* August 20, 1998.

Harcave, Sidney. *Count Sergei Witte and the Twilight of Imperial Russia: A Biography.* Armonk: M. E. Sharpe, 2004.

Hardman, John. *Louis XVI.* New Haven: Yale University Press, 1993.

———. *Louis XVI: The Silent King.* London: Arnold, 2000.

Harmon, George D. "President James Buchanan's Betrayal of Governor Robert J. Walker of Kansas." *Pennsylvania Magazine of History and Biography* 53, no. 1 (1929): 51–91.

Harris, John F. "In the Midst of Scandal, Clinton Planned Action." *Washington Post,* August 21, 1998.

Hastings, Max, and Simon Jenkins. *The Battle for the Falklands.* London: Michael Joseph, 1983.

Hazleton, William A., and Sandra Woy-Hazleton. "Terrorism and the Marxist Left: Peru's Struggle Against Sendero Luminoso." *Terrorism* 11 (1988): 471–490.

Helmke, Gretchen. *Courts Under Constraints: Judges, Generals, and Presidents in Argentina.* Cambridge: Cambridge University Press, 2005.

Hemmer, Bill, Andrea Koppel, Daryn Kagan, and Candy Crowley. "America Strikes Back: State Department Issues Warning: Congressional Majority Supports Attacks." *CNN Morning News,* August 21, 1998.

Henry, James S. *The Blood Bankers: Tales from the Global Underground Economy.* New York: Basic, 2005.

Hermann, Róbert. "The Summer Campaign." In *The Hungarian Revolution and War of Independence, 1848–1849: A Military History,* edited by Gábor Bóna, 377–429. Translated by Nóra Arató. Boulder: Social Science Monographs, 1999.

Hitchens, Christopher. "They Bomb Pharmacies, Don't They?" *Salon,* September 23, 1998.

Holt, Lucius Hudson, and Alexander Wheeler Chilton. *A Brief History of Europe from 1789–1815.* New York: Macmillan, 1919.

Holt, Michael F. *The Political Crisis of the 1850s.* New York: Wiley, 1978.

Honeywell, Martin, and Jenny Pearce. *Falklands/Malvinas: Whose Crisis?* London: Latin America Bureau, 1982.

Houghton, David Patrick. *U.S. Foreign Policy and the Iran Hostage Crisis.* Cambridge: Cambridge University Press, 2001.

Hunt, William Ben. *Getting to War: Predicting International Conflict with Mass Media Indicators.* Ann Arbor: University of Michigan Press, 1997.

Huntington, Samuel. *The Third Wave: Democratization in the Late Twentieth Century.* Norman: University of Oklahoma Press, 1991.

Hurt, John Jeter. *Louis XIV and the Parlements: The Assertion of Royal Authority.* Manchester: Manchester University Press, 2002.

Huston, James L. *The Panic of 1857 and the Coming of the Civil War.* Baton Rouge: Louisiana State University Press, 1987.

"Infinite Reach: Comparison Between Attacks on Terrorists and the Movie 'Wag the Dog.'" *Dateline NBC,* August, 21, 1998.

"Islands Used as Vote Catchers." *Latin America Weekly Report,* March 12, 1982.

Jaenicke, Douglas W. "The Rupture of the Antebellum Democratic Party: Prelude to Southern Secession from the Union." *Party Politics* 1, no. 3 (July 1995): 347–367.

James, Patrick, and Jean-Sébastien Rioux. "International Crises and Linkage Politics: The Experiences of the United States, 1953–1994." *Political Research Quarterly* 51, no. 3 (September 1998): 781–812.

Jentleson, Bruce W. "The Pretty Prudent Public: Post Post-Vietnam American Opinion on the Use of Military Force." *International Studies Quarterly* 36, no. 1 (March 1992): 49–74.

Johannsen, Robert Walter. *The Frontier, the Union, and Stephen A. Douglas.* Urbana: University of Illinois Press, 1989.

Johnson, Dominic, and Dominic Tierney. "In the Eye of the Beholder: Victory and Defeat in U.S. Military Operations." In *Understanding Victory and Defeat in Contemporary War,* edited by Jan Angstrom and Isabelle Duyvesteyn, 46–76. New York: Routledge, 2007.

Jones, P. M. *Reform and Revolution in France: The Politics of Transition, 1774–1791.* Cambridge: Cambridge University Press, 1995.

Kacowicz, Arie Marcelo. *Peaceful Territorial Change.* Columbia: University of South Carolina Press, 1994.

Kann, Robert A. *A History of the Habsburg Empire, 1526–1918.* Berkeley: University of California Press, 1974.

Kennedy, Paul. *The Rise and Fall of the Great Powers: Economic Change and Military Conflict from 1500 to 2000.* New York: Random House, 1987.

Kerstetter, Todd M. *God's Country, Uncle Sam's Land: Faith and Conflict in the American West.* Urbana: University of Illinois Press, 2008.

Kincaid, John. "Extinguishing the Twin Relics of Barbaric Multiculturalism—Slavery and Polygamy—from American Federalism." *Publius* 33, no. 1 (Winter 2003): 75–92.

King, Gary. "Event Count Models for International Relations: Generalizations and Applications." *International Studies Quarterly* 33, no. 2 (1989): 123–147.

King, Gary, Michael Tomz, and Jason Wittenberg. "Making the Most of Statistical Analyses: Improving Interpretation and Presentation." *American Journal of Political Science* 44, no. 2 (2000): 347–361.

King, Gary, and Langche Zeng. "Logistic Regression in Rare Events Data." *Political Analysis* 9, no. 2 (Spring 2001): 137–163.

Kinney, Douglas. *National Interest/National Honor: The Diplomacy of the Falklands Crisis.* New York: Praeger, 1989.

Kirshner, Jonathan. *Appeasing Bankers: Financial Caution on the Road to War.* Princeton: Princeton University Press, 2007.

Kisangani, Emizet F., and Jeffrey Pickering. "Diverting with Benevolent Military Force: Reducing Risks and Rising Above Strategic Behavior." *International Studies Quarterly* 51, no. 2 (June 2007): 277–299.

———. "The Dividends of Diversion: Mature Democracies' Proclivity to Use Diversionary Force and the Rewards They Reap from It." *British Journal of Political Science* 39, no. 3 (July 2009): 483–515.

———. "International Military Intervention, 1989–2005." Inter-University Consortium for Political and Social Research. Data Collection No. 21282. Ann Arbor: Inter-University Consortium for Political and Social Research, 2008.

Klarén, Peter F. *Peru: Society and Nationhood in the Andes*. Oxford: Oxford University Press, 2000.

Klein, James, Gary Goertz, and Paul F. Diehl. "The New Rivalry Dataset: Procedures and Patterns." *Journal of Peace Research* 43, no. 3 (May 2006): 331–348.

Klein, Philip S. *President James Buchanan: A Biography*. University Park: Pennsylvania State University Press, 1962.

Knowlton, Brian. "Character Rating Sinks, Raising Questions About Ability to Lead Nation: 'I Misled People; I Deeply Regret That.'" *New York Times*, August 19, 1998.

Kugler, Jacek, and Marina Arbetman. "Relative Political Capacity: Political Extraction and Political Reach." In *Political Capacity and Economic Behavior*, edited by Marina Arbetman and Jacek Kugler, 11–45. Boulder: Westview, 1997.

Ladd, Jonathan McDonald. "Predispositions and Public Support for the President During the War on Terrorism." *Public Opinion Quarterly* 71, no. 4 (Winter 2007): 511–538.

Lai, Brian, and Dan Reiter. "Rally 'Round the Union Jack? Public Opinion and the Use of Force in the United Kingdom, 1948–2001." *International Studies Quarterly* 49, no. 2 (June 2005): 255–272.

Lamar, Howard Roberts. *The Far Southwest, 1846–1912: A Territorial History*. New Haven: Yale University Press, 1966.

Lamborn, Alan C. *The Price of Power: Risk and Foreign Policy in Britain, France, and Germany*. Boston: Unwin Hyman, 1991.

"Latest Intelligence by Telegraph to the New-York Daily Times." *New York Daily Times*, June 9, 1857.

Laven, David. *Venice and Venetia Under the Habsburgs, 1815–1835*. Oxford: Oxford University Press, 2002.

Leeds, Brett Ashley, and David Davis. "Domestic Political Vulnerability and International Disputes." *Journal of Conflict Resolution* 41, no. 6 (December 1997): 814–834.

Lebow, Richard Ned. *Between Peace and War: The Nature of International Crisis*. Baltimore: Johns Hopkins University Press, 1981.

———. "Miscalculation in the South Atlantic: the Origins of the Falklands War." In *Psychology & Deterrence*, edited by Robert Jervis, Richard Ned Lebow, and Janice Gross Stein, 89–124. Baltimore: Johns Hopkins University Press, 1985.

Levy, Jack S. "The Diversionary Theory of War: A Critique." In *A Handbook of War Studies*, edited by Manus I. Midlarsky, 259–288. Ann Arbor: University of Michigan Press, 1989.

Levy, Jack S., and Lily I. Vakili. "Diversionary Action by Authoritarian Regimes: Argentina in the Falklands/Malvinas Case." In *The Internationalization of Communal Strife*, edited by Manus I. Midlarsky, 118–146. New York: Routledge, 1992.

Lewis, Paul H. *Guerrillas and Generals: The "Dirty War" in Argentina*. Westport: Praeger, 2002.

Lian, Bradley, and John R. Oneal. "Presidents, the Use of Military Force, and Public Opinion." *Journal of Conflict Resolution* 37, no. 2 (June 1993): 277–300.

Lieven, Dominic. *Empire: The Russian Empire and Its Rivals*. New Haven: Yale University Press, 2002.

Long, J. Scott, and Jeremy Freese. *Regression Models for Categorical Dependent Variables Using Stata*. 2nd ed. College Station: Stata Press, 2006.

Macartney, C. A. *The Habsburg Empire, 1790–1918*. London: Weidenfeld and Nicolson, 1968.

MacDougall, Walter A. *Throes of Democracy: The American Civil War Era, 1829–1877*. New York: HarperCollins, 2008.

MacKinnon, William P. "Albert Gallatin Browne Jr.: Brief Life of an Early War Correspondent: 1832–1891." *Harvard Magazine* 111 (November/December 2008): 48–49.

———. "125 Years of Conspiracy Theories: Origins of the Utah Expedition of 1857–58." *Utah Historical Quarterly* 52, no. 3 (Summer 1984): 212–230.

———, ed. *At Sword's Point, Part I: A Documentary History of the Utah War to 1858*. Norman: Arthur H. Clark, 2008.

Makin, Guillermo A. "Argentine Approaches to the Falklands/Malvinas: Was the Resort to Violence Foreseeable?" *International Affairs* 59, no. 3 (Summer 1982): 391–403.

Mann, Stefanie. *Peru's Relations with Pacific Asia: Democracy and Foreign Policy Under Alan García, Alberto Fujimori, and Alejandro Toledo*. Berlin: Lit Verlag, 2006.

Mansfield, Edward D., and Jack Snyder. "Democratic Transitions, Institutional Strength, and War." *International Organization* 56, no. 2 (Spring 2002): 297–337.

———. "Democratization and the Danger of War." *International Security* 20, no. 1 (Summer 1995): 5–38.

———. *Electing to Fight: Why Emerging Democracies Go to War*. Cambridge: MIT Press, 2005.

Mares, David R. "Deterrence Bargaining in the Ecuador–Peru Enduring Rivalry: Designing Strategies Around Military Weakness." *Security Studies* 6, no. 2 (Winter 1996/1997): 91–123.

———. *Violent Peace: Militarized Interstate Bargaining in Latin America*. New York: Columbia University Press, 2001.

Marra, Robin F., Charles W. Ostrom Jr., and Dennis M. Simon. "Foreign Policy and Presidential Popularity: Creating Windows of Opportunity in the Perpetual Election." *Journal of Conflict Resolution* 34, no. 4 (December 1990): 588–623.

Marshall, Monty G., and Keith Jaggers. *Polity IV Project: Political Regime Characteristics and Transitions, 1800–2002*. College Park: Center for International Development and Conflict Management, University of Maryland, 2002.

Mason, T. David. *Caught in the Crossfire: Revolution, Repression, and the Rational Peasant*. Lanham: Rowman & Littlefield, 2004.

Mason, T. David, and Dale A. Krane. "The Political Economy of Death Squads: Toward a Theory of the Impact of State-Sanctioned Terror." *International Studies Quarterly* 33, no. 2 (June 1989): 175–198.

Masterson, Daniel M. *Militarism and Politics in Latin America: Peru from Sánchez Cerro to Sendero Luminoso*. Westport: Greenwood, 1991.

Mauceri, Philip. "Military Politics and Counter-Insurgency in Peru." *Journal of Interamerican Studies and World Affairs* 33, no. 4 (Winter 1991): 83–109.

———. *State Under Siege: Development and Policy Making in Peru*. Boulder: Westview, 1996.

Mayer, Arno J. *Dynamics of Counterrevolution in Europe, 1870–1956: An Analytic Framework*. New York: Harper & Row, 1971.

McCaffrey, James M. *The Army in Transformation, 1790–1860*. Westport: Greenwood, 2006.

McClintock, Cynthia. "The Decimation of Peru's Sendero Luminoso." In *Comparative Peace Processes in Latin America*, edited by Cynthia J. Arnson, 223–249. Stanford: Stanford University Press, 1999.

McClintock, Cynthia, and Fabián Vallas. *The United States and Peru: Cooperation at a Cost*. London: Routledge, 2003.

McClintock, Russell. *Lincoln and the Decision for War: The Northern Response to Secession*. Chapel Hill: University of North Carolina Press, 2008.

McGinnis, Michael D. "Policy Substitutability in Complex Humanitarian Emergencies: A Model of Individual Choice and International Response." *Journal of Conflict Resolution* 44, no. 1 (February 2000): 62–89.

McGuire, James W. "Interim Government and Democratic Consolidation: Argentina in Comparative Perspective." In *Between States: Interim Governments and Democratic Transitions*, edited by Yossi Shain and Juan J. Linz, 179–210. Cambridge: Cambridge University Press, 1995.

———. *Peronism Without Perón: Unions, Parties, and Democracy in Argentina*. Stanford: Stanford University Press, 1999.

McPherson, James M. *Battle Cry of Freedom: The Civil War Era*. Oxford: Oxford University Press, 1988.

Meernik, James. "Domestic Politics and the Political Use of Military Force by the United States." *Political Research Quarterly* 54, no. 4 (December 2001): 889–904.

Meernik, James, and Peter Waterman. "The Myth of the Diversionary Use of Force by American Presidents." *Political Research Quarterly* 49, no. 3 (September 1996): 573–590.

Meerse, David E. "James Buchanan, the Patronage and the Northern Democratic Party, 1857–1858." Ph.D. diss., University of Illinois, 1969.

Menzel, Sewall H. *Fire in the Andes: U.S. Foreign Policy and Cocaine Politics in Bolivia and Peru.* Lanham: University Press of America, 1996.

Miller, Ross A. "Domestic Structures and the Diversionary Use of Force." *American Journal of Political Science* 39, no. 3 (August 1995): 760–785.

———. "Regime Type, Strategic Interaction, and the Diversionary Use of Force." *Journal of Conflict Resolution* 43, no. 3 (June 1999): 388–402.

Milton, George Fort. *Eve of Conflict: Stephen A. Douglas and the Needless War.* Boston: Houghton Mifflin, 1934.

Mintz, Alex. "How Do Leaders Make Decisions? A Poliheuristic Perspective." *Journal of Conflict Resolution* 48, no. 1 (February 2004): 3–13.

Mitchell, Sara McLaughlin, and Brandon C. Prins. "Rivalry and Diversionary Uses of Force." *Journal of Conflict Resolution* 48, no. 6 (December 2004): 937–961.

Monaghan, Jay. *Diplomat in Carpet Slippers: Abraham Lincoln Deals with Foreign Affairs.* Indianapolis: Bobbs-Merrill, 1945.

Moore, Will H. "The Repression of Dissent: A Substitution Model of Government Coercion." *Journal of Conflict Resolution* 44, no. 1 (February 2000): 107–127.

Moores, Charles W., ed. *Lincoln: Addresses and Letters.* New York: American Book Company, 1914.

Moorman, Donald R., and Gene A. Sessions. *Camp Floyd and the Mormons: The Utah War.* Salt Lake City: University of Utah Press, 1992.

Morgan, T. Clifton, and Christopher J. Anderson. "Domestic Support and Diversionary External Conflict in Great Britain, 1950–1992." *Journal of Politics* 61, no. 3 (August 1999): 799–814.

Morgan, T. Clifton, and Kenneth N. Bickers. "Domestic Discontent and the External Use of Force." *Journal of Conflict Resolution* 36, no. 1 (March 1992): 25–52.

Morgan, T. Clifton, and Glenn Palmer. "A Model of Foreign Policy Substitutability: Selecting the Right Tools for the Job(s)." *Journal of Conflict Resolution* 44, no. 1 (February 2000): 11–32.

Moro, Rubén O. *The History of the South Atlantic Conflict: The War for the Malvinas.* New York: Praeger, 1989.

Most, Benjamin A., and Randolph M. Siverson. "Substituting Arms and Alliances, 1870–1914: An Exploration in Comparative Foreign Policy." In *New Directions in the Study of Foreign Policy,* edited by Charles F. Hermann, Charles W. Kegley Jr., and James N. Rosenau, 131–160. Boston: Allen and Unwin, 1987.

Most, Benjamin A., and Harvey Starr. *Inquiry, Logic, and International Politics.* Columbia: University of South Carolina Press, 1989.

———. "International Relations Theory, Foreign Policy Substitutability, and 'Nice' Laws." *World Politics* 36, no. 3 (April 1984): 383–406.

Mousnier, Roland E. *The Organs of State and Society.* Vol. 2 of *The Institutions of France Under the Absolute Monarchy, 1598–1789.* Translated by Arthur Goldhammer. Chicago: University of Chicago Press, 1984.

Mueller, John E. *War, Presidents and Public Opinion.* New York: Wiley, 1973.

Muller, Edward N., and Erich Weede. "Cross-National Variation in Political Violence: A Rational Action Approach." *Journal of Conflict Resolution* 34, no. 4 (December 1990): 624–651.

Munck, Gerardo Luis. *Authoritarianism and Democratization: Soldiers and Workers in Argentina, 1976–1983*. University Park: Pennsylvania State University Press, 1998.

Murad, Anatol. *Franz Joseph I of Austria and His Empire*. New York: Twayne, 1968.

Murguizur, Juan Carlos. "The South Atlantic Conflict: An Argentinian Point of View." *International Defense Review* 16, no. 2 (1983): 135–140.

Murphy, Orville T. *The Diplomatic Retreat of France and Public Opinion on the Eve of the French Revolution, 1783–1789*. Washington, DC: Catholic University of America Press, 1998.

Nagourney, Adam, and Michael R. Kagay. "High Marks Given to the President But Not the Man." *New York Times*, August 22, 1998.

Neff, Andrew L. *History of Utah, 1847 to 1869*. Salt Lake City: Deseret News Press, 1940.

Nevins, Allan. *A House Dividing, 1852–1857*. Vol. 2 of *Ordeal of the Union*. New York: Charles Scribner's Sons, 1947.

———. *Douglas, Buchanan, and Party Chaos, 1857–1859*. Vol. 1 of *The Emergence of Lincoln*. New York: Charles Scribner's Sons, 1950.

Nichols, Roy Franklin. *The Disruption of American Democracy*. New York: Collier, 1962.

Norberg, Kathryn. "The French Fiscal Crisis of 1788 and the Financial Origins of the Revolution of 1789." In *Fiscal Crises, Liberty, and Representative Government 1450–1789*, edited by Philip T. Hoffman and Kathryn Norberg, 253–298. Stanford: Stanford University Press, 1994.

Norpoth, Helmut. *Confidence Regained: Economics, Mrs. Thatcher, and the British Voter*. Ann Arbor: University of Michigan Press, 1992.

Nott, John. *Here Today, Gone Tomorrow: Recollections of an Errant Politician*. London: Politico's, 2002.

Obando, Enrique. "Civil–Military Relations in Peru, 1980–1996: How to Control and Coopt the Military (and the Consequences of Doing So)." In *Shining and Other Paths: War and Society in Peru, 1980–1995*, edited by Steve J. Stern, 385–410. Durham: Duke University Press, 1998.

Oneal, John R., and Anna Lillian Bryan. "The Rally 'Round the Flag Effect in U.S. Foreign Policy Crises, 1950–1985." *Political Behavior* 17, no. 4 (December 1995): 379–401.

Oneal, John R., and Jaroslav Tir. "Does the Diversionary Use of Force Threaten the Democratic Peace? Assessing the Effect of Economic Growth on Interstate Conflict, 1921–2001." *International Studies Quarterly* 50, no. 4 (December 2006): 755–779.

Opp, Karl-Dieter, and Wolfgang Roehl. "Repression, Micromobilization, and Political Protest." *Social Forces* 69, no. 2 (December 1990): 521–547.

Organski, A. F. K., and Jacek Kugler. *The War Ledger*. Chicago: University of Chicago Press, 1980.

Ostrom, Charles W., Jr., and Dennis M. Simon. "Promise and Performance: A Dynamic Model of Presidential Popularity." *American Political Science Review* 79, no. 2 (June 1985): 334–358.

Palmer, Alan. *Twilight of the Habsburgs: The Life and Times of Emperor Francis Joseph.* New York: Grove, 1994.

Palmer, David Scott. "The Changing Political Economy of Peru Under Military and Civilian Rule." *Inter-American Economic Affairs* 37, no. 4 (Spring 1984): 37–62.

Palmer, Glenn, and Archana Bhandari. "The Investigation of Substitutability in Foreign Policy." *Journal of Conflict Resolution* 44, no. 1 (February 2000): 3–10.

Palmer, Glenn, and T. Clifton Morgan. *A Theory of Foreign Policy.* Princeton: Princeton University Press, 2006.

Palmer, R. R. *The Challenge.* Vol. 1 of *The Age of the Democratic Revolution: A Political History of Europe and America, 1760–1800.* Princeton: Princeton University Press, 1959.

Parish, Peter J. *The North and the Nation in the Era of the Civil War.* Edited by Adam I. P. Smith and Susan-Mary Grant. New York: Fordham University Press, 2003.

Paterson, Thomas G., and William J. Brophy. "October Missiles and November Elections: The Cuban Missile Crisis and American Politics, 1962." *Journal of American History* 73, no. 1 (June 1986): 87–119.

Paul, T. V. *Asymmetric Conflicts: War Initiation by Weaker Powers.* Cambridge: Cambridge University Press, 1994.

Pearson, Frederic S., and Robert A. Baumann. "International Military Intervention, 1946–1988." Inter-University Consortium for Political and Social Research. Data Collection No. 6035. Ann Arbor: University of Michigan, 1993.

Peralta-Ramos, Mónica. *The Political-Economy of Argentina: Power and Class Since 1930.* Boulder: Westview, 1992.

Pickering, Jeffrey. "War-Weariness and Cumulative Effects: Victors, Vanquished, and Subsequent Interstate Intervention." *Journal of Peace Research* 39, no. 3 (May 2002): 313–337.

Pickering, Jeffrey, and Emizet F. Kisangani, "Democracy and Diversionary Military Intervention: Reassessing Regime Type and the Diversionary Hypothesis." *International Studies Quarterly* 49, no. 1 (March 2005): 23–43.

———. "Diversionary Despots? Comparing Autocracies' Propensities to Use and to Benefit from Military Force." *American Journal of Political Science* 54, no. 2 (April 2010): 477–493.

Pion-Berlin, David. "The Fall of Military Rule in Argentina: 1976–1983." *Journal of Interamerican Studies and World Affairs* 27, no. 2 (Summer 1985): 55–76.

———. *Through Corridors of Power: Institutions and Civil–Military Relations in Argentina.* University Park: Pennsylvania State University Press, 1997.

Poll, Richard D. "The Mormon Question Enters National Politics, 1850–1856." *Utah Historical Quarterly* 25 (April 1957): 117–131.

Poll, Richard D., and Ralph W. Hansen. "'Buchanan's Blunder': The Utah War, 1857–1858." *Military Affairs* 25, no. 3 (Autumn 1961): 121–131.

Poll, Richard D., and William P. MacKinnon. "Causes of the Utah War Reconsidered." *Journal of Mormon History* 20, no. 2 (Fall 1994): 16–44.

Poole, Deborah, and Gerardo Rénique. *Peru: Time of Fear.* London: Latin American Bureau, 1992.

Potter, David M. *The Impending Crisis, 1848–1961.* New York: Harper & Row, 1976.

"The President and Mormons." *New York Daily Times,* June 4, 1857.

"President Galtieri Gives Inaugural Speech." *Buenos Aires Domestic Service,* December 24, 1981.

Price, Munro. "Politics: Louis XVI." In *Old Regime France, 1648–1788,* edited by William Doyle, 223–248. Oxford: Oxford University Press, 2001.

———. *The Road from Versailles: Louis XVI, Marie Antoinette, and the Fall of the French Monarchy.* New York: St. Martin's, 2002.

Price, Roger. "'The Holy Struggle Against Anarchy': The Development of Counterrevolution in 1848." In *Europe in 1848: Revolution and Reform,* edited by Dieter Dowe, Heinz-Gerhard Haupt, Dieter Langewiesche, and Jonathan Sperber. Translated by David Higgins. 25–58. New York: Berghahn, 2001.

Prucha, Francis Paul. *The Great Father: The United States Government and the American Indians.* Lincoln: University of Nebraska Press, 1984.

Purdum, Todd S. "Threats and Responses: The Administration; Bush Officials Say the Time Has Come for Action on Iraq." *New York Times,* September 9, 2002.

———. "U.S. Fury on 2 Continents: Congress; Critics of Clinton Support Attacks." *New York Times,* August 21, 1998.

Radosh, Ronald. *Prophets on the Right: Profiles of Conservative Critics of American Globalism.* New York: Simon & Schuster, 1975.

Ransom, Roger L. *Conflict and Compromise: The Political Economy of Slavery, Emancipation, and the American Civil War.* New York: Cambridge University Press, 1989.

Rapport, Mike. *1848: Year of Revolution.* New York: Basic, 2009.

Rasler, Karen. "Concessions, Repression, and Political Protest in the Iranian Revolution." *American Sociological Review* 61, no. 1 (February 1996): 132–152.

Rawley, James A. *Race & Politics: "Bleeding Kansas" and the Coming of the Civil War.* Lincoln: University of Nebraska Press, 1979.

Redlich, Joseph. *Emperor Francis Joseph of Austria: A Biography.* London: Macmillan, 1929.

Regan, Patrick M. *Civil Wars and Foreign Powers: Outside Intervention in Intrastate Conflict.* Ann Arbor: University of Michigan Press, 2000.

———. "Substituting Policies During U.S. Interventions in Internal Conflicts: A Little of This, a Little of That." *Journal of Conflict Resolution* 44, no. 1 (February 2000): 90–106.

———. "Third Party Interventions and the Duration of Intrastate Conflicts." *Journal of Conflict Resolution* 46, no. 1 (February 2002): 55–73.

Regan, Patrick M., and Daniel Norton. "Greed, Grievance, and Mobilization in Civil Wars." *Journal of Conflict Resolution* 49, no. 3 (June 2005): 319–336.

Reitan, Earl Aaron. *The Thatcher Revolution: Margaret Thatcher, John Major, Tony Blair, and the Transformation of Modern Britain, 1979–2001.* Lanham: Rowman & Littlefield, 2003.

Robben, Antonius C. G. M. *Political Violence and Trauma in Argentina.* Philadelphia: University of Pennsylvania Press, 2005.

Roberts, Ian W. *Nicolas I and the Russian Intervention in Hungary.* New York: St. Martin's, 1991.

Roberts, J. M. *The French Revolution.* Oxford: Oxford University Press, 1978.

Roberts, Kenneth, and Mark Peceny. "Human Rights and United States Policy Toward Peru." In *The Peruvian Labyrinth: Polity, Society, Economy,* edited by Maxwell A. Cameron and Philip Mauceri, 192–222. College Park: Pennsylvania State University Press, 1997.

Roberts, Steven V. "Move in Congress: House Panel, 32–2, Votes to Apply Law Limiting Right to Wage War." *New York Times,* October 28, 1983.

Rochlin, James F. *Vanguard Revolutionaries in Latin America: Peru, Colombia, Mexico.* Boulder: Lynne Rienner, 2003.

Rock, David. *Authoritarian Argentina: The Nationalist Movement, Its History and Its Impact.* Berkeley: University of California Press, 1993.

Rock, Kenneth W. "Felix Schwarzenberg, Military Diplomat." *Austrian History Yearbook* 11 (1975): 85–100.

———. "Reply." *Austrian History Yearbook* 11 (1975): 106–109.

———. "Schwarzenberg Versus Nicholas I, Round One: The Negotiation of the Habsburg–Romanov Alliance Against Hungary in 1849." *Austrian History Yearbook* 6 (1970): 109–141.

Roett, Riordan. "Peru: The Message from García." *Foreign Affairs* 64, no. 2 (Winter 1985): 274–286.

Romero, Luis Alberto. *A History of Argentina in the Twentieth Century.* University Park: Pennsylvania State University Press, 2002.

Rose, Gideon. "Neoclassical Realism and Theories of Foreign Policy." *World Politics* 51, no. 1 (October 1998): 144–172.

Rosecrance, Richard N. *Action and Reaction in World Politics: International Systems in Perspective.* Boston: Little, Brown, 1963.

Rotberg, Robert I., and Theodore K. Rabb. *The Origin and Prevention of Major Wars.* Cambridge: Cambridge University Press, 1988.

Rothenberg, Gunther E. *The Army of Francis Joseph.* West Lafayette: Purdue University Press, 1976.

Rouco, J. Iglesias. "The Foreign Offensive." *La Prensa,* January 24, 1982.

Rozin, Paul, and Edward B. Royzman. "Negativity Bias, Negativity Dominance, and Contagion." *Personality and Social Psychology Review* 5, no. 4 (November 2001): 296–320.

Rudolph, James D. *Peru: The Evolution of a Crisis.* New York: Praeger, 1992.

Rummel, Rudolph J. "Dimensions of Conflict Behavior Within and Between Nations." *Yearbook of the Society for General Systems* 8 (1963): 1–50.

Russett, Bruce M. "Economic Decline, Electoral Pressure, and the Initiation of Interstate Conflict." In *Prisoners of War? Nation States in the Modern Era,* edited by Charles S. Gochman and Alan Ned Sabrosky, 123–140. Lexington: Lexington Books, 1990.

Russett, Bruce M., Harvey Starr, and David Kinsella. *World Politics: Menu for Choice.* 9th ed. Boston: Wadsworth, 2010.

Saba, Raúl P. *Political Development and Democracy in Peru: Continuity in Change and Crisis.* Boulder: Westview, 1987.

Sargent, Thomas J., and François R. Velde. "Macroeconomic Features of the French Revolution." *Journal of Political Economy* 103, no. 3 (June 1995): 474–518.

Schumacher, Edward. "Argentina Sped Past the Point of No Return." *New York Times,* April 11, 1982.

———. "Minister Acts Strongly on Argentine Economy." *New York Times,* February 16, 1982.

Schwarzenberg, Adolf. *Prince Felix zu Schwarzenberg: Prime Minister of Austria, 1848–1852.* New York: Columbia University Press, 1946.

Scott, Clifford L. *Search for Sanctuary: Brigham Young and the White Mountain Expedition.* Salt Lake City: University of Utah Press, 1984.

Scott, Samuel F. *The Response of the Royal Army to the French Revolution: The Role and Development of the Line Army, 1787–93.* Oxford: Clarendon, 1978.

Shakespeare, William. *Henry IV, Part 2.* Edited by Barbara A. Mowat and Paul Werstine. New York: Washington Square, 1999.

Sheahan, John. *Searching for a Better Society: The Peruvian Economy from 1950.* University Park: Pennsylvania State University Press, 1999.

Sheehan, James J. *German History, 1770–1866.* Oxford: Oxford University Press, 1993.

Shenton, James P. *Robert John Walker: A Politician from Jackson to Lincoln.* New York: Columbia University Press, 1961.

Simon, Marc V., and Harvey Starr. "Extraction, Allocation, and the Rise and Decline of States: A Simulation Analysis of Two-Level Security Management." *Journal of Conflict Resolution* 40, no. 2 (June 1996): 272–297.

———. "A Two-Level Analysis of War and Revolution: A Dynamic Simulation of Response to Threat." In *Decisionmaking on War and Peace: The Cognitive–Rational Debate,* edited by Nehemia Geva and Alex Mintz, 131–162. Boulder: Lynne Rienner, 1997.

———. "Two-Level Security Management and the Prospects for New Democracies: A Simulation Analysis." *International Studies Quarterly* 44, no. 3 (September 2000): 391–422.

Singer, J. David, Stuart Bremer, and John Stuckey. "Capability Distribution, Uncertainty, and Major Power War, 1820–1965." In *Peace, War, and Numbers,* edited by Bruce M. Russett, 19–48. Beverly Hills: Sage, 1972.

Singh, Sonali, and Christopher R. Way. "The Correlates of Nuclear Proliferation: A Quantitative Test." *Journal of Conflict Resolution* 48, no. 6 (December 2004): 859–885.

Siverson, Randolph M., and Harvey Starr. *The Diffusion of War: A Study of Opportunity and Willingness.* Ann Arbor: University of Michigan Press, 1991.

———. "Opportunity, Willingness, and the Diffusion of War." *American Political Science Review* 84, no. 1 (March 1990): 47–67.

Sked, Alan. *The Decline and Fall of the Habsburg Empire, 1815–1918.* 2nd ed. London: Longman, 2001.

Skocpol, Theda. "Bringing the State Back In: Strategies of Analysis in Current Research." In *Bringing the State Back In,* edited by Peter B. Evens, Dietrich Rueschemeyer, and Theda Skocpol, 3–38. Cambridge: Cambridge University Press, 1985.

———. *States and Social Revolutions: A Comparative Analysis of France, Russia, and China.* Cambridge: Cambridge University Press, 1979.

Smith, Alastair. "Diversionary Foreign Policy in Democratic Systems." *International Studies Quarterly* 40, no. 1 (March 1996): 133–153.

Smith, Elbert B. *The Presidency of James Buchanan.* Lawrence: University of Kansas Press, 1975.

Smith, William C. *Authoritarianism and the Crisis of the Argentine Political Economy.* Stanford: Stanford University Press, 1989.

———. "Reflections on the Political Economy of Authoritarian Rule and Capitalist Reorganization in Contemporary Argentina." In *Generals in Retreat: The Crisis of Military Rule in Latin America,* edited by Philip O'Brien and Paul Cammack, 37–88. Manchester: Manchester University Press, 1985.

Snyder, Jack. *The Ideology of the Offensive: Military Decision Making and the Disasters of 1914.* Ithaca: Cornell University Press, 1984.

Sprecher, Christopher, and Karl DeRouen Jr. "Israeli Military Actions and Internalization–Externalization Processes." *Journal of Conflict Resolution* 46, no. 2 (April 2002): 244–259.

Stahl, Lesley. *Reporting Live.* New York: Simon & Schuster, 1999.

Stampp, Kenneth M. *America in 1857: A Nation on the Brink.* Oxford: Oxford University Press, 1990.

St. John, Ronald Bruce. *The Foreign Policy of Peru.* Boulder: Lynne Rienner, 1992.

Starr, Harvey. "Revolution and War: Rethinking the Linkage Between Internal and External Conflict." *Political Research Quarterly* 47, no. 2 (June 1994): 481–507.

———. "Substitutability in Foreign Policy: Theoretically Central, Empirically Elusive." *Journal of Conflict Resolution* 44, no. 1 (February 2000): 128–138.

Stein, Arthur A. *The Nation at War.* Baltimore: Johns Hopkins University Press, 1980.

Stewart, Nora Kinzer. *South Atlantic Conflict of 1982: A Case Study in Military Cohesion.* Alexandria: U.S. Army Research Institute for the Behavioral and Social Sciences, 1988.

Stiles, William H. *Austria in 1848–49: Being a History of the Late Political Movements in Vienna, Milan, Venice, and Prague.* Vol. 2. Reprint, New York: Arno, 1971 (1852).

Stone, Bailey. *The Genesis of the French Revolution: A Global–Historical Interpretation.* Cambridge: Cambridge University Press, 1994.

———. *Reinterpreting the French Revolution: A Global–Historical Interpretation.* Cambridge: Cambridge University Press, 2002.

"Stroke of Genius or Fatal Gamble." *Latin America Weekly Report,* April 9, 1982.

Tanter, Raymond. "Dimensions of Conflict Behavior Within and Between Nations, 1958–1960." *Journal of Conflict Resolution* 10, no. 1 (March 1966): 41–64.

Tarar, Ahmer. "Diversionary Incentives and the Bargaining Approach to War." *International Studies Quarterly* 50, no. 1 (March 2006): 169–188.

Tate, Michael L. *The Frontier Army in the Settlement of the West.* Norman: University of Oklahoma Press, 1999.

Taylor, Charles Lewis, and David A. Jodice. *World Handbook of Political and Social Indicators III: 1948–1982.* 2nd ed. Ann Arbor: Inter-University Consortium for Political and Social Research, 1986.

Taylor, Diana. *Disappearing Acts: Spectacles of Gender and Nationalism in Argentina's "Dirty War."* Durham: Duke University Press, 1997.

Terrill, Robert E. "James Buchanan: Romancing the Union." In *Before the Rhetorical Presidency,* edited by Martin J. Medhurst, 166–193. College Station: Texas A&M University Press, 2008.

Thornton, Richard C. *The Falklands Sting: Reagan, Thatcher, and Argentina's Bomb.* Washington, DC: Brassey's, 1998.

Thyne, Clayton L. "ABC's, 123's, and the Golden Rule: The Pacifying Effect of Education on Civil War, 1980–1999." *International Studies Quarterly* 50, no. 4 (December 2006): 733–754.

Tierney, Dominic. "Prisoner Dilemmas: The American Obsession with POWs and Hostages." *Orbis* 54, no. 1 (Winter 2010): 130–145.

Tir, Jaroslav. "Territorial Diversion: Diversionary Theory of War and Territorial Conflict." *Journal of Politics* 72, no. 2 (April 2010): 413–425.

Tomz, Michael, Jason Wittenberg, and Gary King. *CLARIFY: Software for Interpreting and Presenting Statistical Results.* Version 2.1. Cambridge: Harvard University, 2003. Available from http://gking.harvard.edu.

Torre, Juan Carlos, and Liliana de Riz. "Argentina Since 1946." In *Argentina Since Independence,* edited by Leslie Bethell, 243–364. Cambridge: Cambridge University Press, 1993.

Tyler, Lyon Gardiner. *The Letters and Times of the Tylers.* Vol. 2. Reprint, New York: Da Capo, 1970 (c. 1884–1886).

"US and Bolivian Troops Hold Joint Exercises." *Christian Science Monitor,* May 13, 1987.

U.S. War Department. *Annual Report of the Secretary of War.* Vol. 2, Part IV. Washington, DC: U.S. Government Printing Office, 1858.

Vacs, Aldo C. "Authoritarian Breakdown and Redemocratization in Argentina." In *Authoritarians and Democrats: Regime Transition in Latin America,* edited by James M. Malloy and Mitchell A. Seligson, 15–42. Pittsburgh: University of Pittsburgh Press, 1987.

Van der Kiste, John. *Emperor Francis Joseph: Life, Death and the Fall of the Habsburg Empire.* Phoenix Mill: Sutton, 2005.

Varon, Elizabeth R. *Disunion! The Coming of the American Civil War, 1789–1859.* Chapel Hill: University of North Carolina Press, 2008.

Veigel, Klaus Friedrich. *Dictatorship, Democracy, and Globalization: Argentina and the Cost of Paralysis, 1973–2001*. University Park: Pennsylvania State University Press, 2009.

Vovelle, Michel. *The Fall of the French Monarchy, 1787–1792*. Translated by Susan Burke. Cambridge: Cambridge University Press, 1984.

Wallis, John Joseph. "American Government Finance in the Long Run: 1790 to 1990." *Journal of Economic Perspectives* 14, no. 1 (Winter 2000): 61–82.

———. "The National Era." In *Government and the American Economy: A New History*, edited by Price V. Fishback, Robert Higgs, Gary D. Libecap, John Joseph Wallis, Stanley L. Engerman, Jeffrey Rogers Hummel, Sumner J. La Croix, Robert A. Margo, Robert A. McGuire, Richard Sylla, Lee J. Alston, Joseph P. Ferrie, Mark Guglielmo, E. C. Pasour Jr., Randal R. Rucker, and Werner Troesken, 148–187. Chicago: University of Chicago Press, 2007.

Walt, Stephen. *Revolution and War*. Ithaca: Cornell University Press, 1996.

Watts, Dale E. "How Bloody Was Bleeding Kansas? Political Killings in Kansas Territory, 1854–1861." *Kansas History* 18, no. 2 (Summer 1995): 116–129.

Wawro, Geoffrey. "The Habsburg Flucht nach vorne in 1866: Domestic Political Origins of the Austro–Prussian War." *International History Review* 17, no. 2 (May 1995): 221–248.

Weber, Caroline. *Queen of Fashion: What Marie Antoinette Wore to the Revolution*. New York: Macmillan, 2006.

Welch, David A. *Justice and the Genesis of War*. New York: Cambridge University Press, 1995.

White, Eugene Nelson. "The French Revolution and the Politics of Government Finance, 1770–1815." *Journal of Economic History* 55, no. 2 (June 1995): 227–255.

Whiteman, Jeremy J. *Reform, Revolution and French Global Policy, 1787–1791*. Burlington: Ashgate, 2002.

Wilkenfeld, Jonathan. "Models for the Analysis of Foreign Conflict Behavior of States." In *Peace, War, and Numbers*, edited by Bruce M. Russett, 275–298. Beverly Hills: Sage, 1972.

Williams, David A. "President Buchanan Receives a Proposal for an Anti-Mormon Crusade, 1857." *Brigham Young University Studies* 14, no. 1 (Autumn 1973): 103–105.

Wilson, Mark R. *The Business of Civil War: Military Mobilization and the State, 1861–1865*. Baltimore: Johns Hopkins University Press, 2006.

Wise, Carol. "State Policy and Social Conflict in Peru." In *The Peruvian Labyrinth: Polity, Society, Economy*, edited by Maxwell A. Cameron and Philip Mauceri, 70–103. University Park: Pennsylvania State University Press, 1997.

World Bank. *Argentina: Economic Memorandum*, Vol. 1. Washington, DC: World Bank, 1985.

Wright, Quincy. *A Study of War*. Chicago: University of Chicago Press, 1964.

Wynia, Gary W. *Argentina: Illusions and Realities*. 2nd ed. New York: Holmes and Meier, 1992.

Zakaria, Fareed. *From Wealth to Power: The Unusual Origins of America's World Role.* Princeton: Princeton University Press, 1998.

Zakheim, Dov S. "The South Atlantic Conflict: Strategic, Military, and Technological Lessons." In *The Falklands War: Lessons for Strategy, Diplomacy, and International Law,* edited by Alberto R. Coll and Anthony C. Arend, 159–188. Boston: Allen & Unwin, 1985.

Zanjani, Sally. *Devils Will Reign: How Nevada Began.* Reno: University of Nevada Press, 2006.

Zelizer, Julian E. *The Presidency of George W. Bush: A First Historical Assessment.* Princeton: Princeton University Press, 2010.

Zelner, Bennet A. "Using Simulation to Interpret Results from Logit, Probit, and Other Nonlinear Models." *Strategic Management Journal* 30, no. 12 (December 2009): 1335–1348.

Zinnes, Dinna A., and Jonathan Wilkenfeld. "An Analysis of Foreign Conflict Behavior of Nations." In *Comparative Foreign Policy: Theoretical Essays,* edited by W. F. Hanrieder, 167–213. New York: David McKay, 1971.

Index

Italic page numbers indicate material in tables or figures.

The authorized representative in the EU for product safety and compliance is:
Mare Nostrum Group
B.V Doelen 72
4831 GR Breda
The Netherlands

www.ingramcontent.com/pod-product-compliance
Lightning Source LLC
Chambersburg PA
CBHW030349270326
41926CB00009B/1022